On the Safe Edge

ON THE SAFE EDGE

A MANUAL FOR SM PLAY

Trevor Jacques

with

Dr. Dale
Michael Hamilton
Sniffer

WholeSM Publishing
Toronto

First edition, first printing, August, 1993

This book is printed on recycled, acid-free paper.

 The paper used in this book meets the minimum requirements of the American National Standards Institute for Information Services—Permanence of Paper for Printed Library Materials, ANSI Z39.48-1984.

WholeSM Publishing Corporation

 P.O. Box 75075-880,
20 Bloor Street East,
Toronto,
Ontario. M4W 3T3.
CANADA.

SAN: S1196111

Canadian Cataloguing in Publication Data

Jacques, Trevor, 1956—

   On the Safe Edge: A Manual for SM Play

Includes bibliographical references and index.
ISBN   1-895857-07-4 (leather bound) —
ISBN   1-895857-06-6 (bound) —
ISBN   1-895857-05-8 (pbk.)

   1. Sadomasochism. I. Dale, Dr. II. Hamilton, Michael III. Sniffer IV. Title.

HQ79.J33 1993   306.77'5   C93-090090-1

Typeset in Toronto, Ontario. Printed in Ann Arbor, Michigan.

TO
THOSE WHO HAVE TAUGHT US SO MUCH
&
THOSE WHO HAVE YET TO LEARN

"Thank goodness we're all different," said Alice.

ACKNOWLEDGEMENTS

We would like to take some time and space to thank those people who donated their time and energies, knowingly or unknowingly, to helping with this book.

The review team: Ms. Victoria Baker, Ms. K. T. Chase; Ms. Kay Hallanger; Ms. Sue Johanson; Ms. Karen Kircher; Ms. Rachel Melzak; Ms. Raven Rowanchilde; Ms. Susie Shepherd; Mr. Guy Baldwin; Mr. Race Bannon; Mr. Robert Brown; Dr. Tony DeBlase; Mr. David Rhodes; Mr. Robert Schneider; Mr. David Stein, Mr. David Taber; and Mr. Richard Walker.

Those at the AIDS Committee of Toronto: Mr. Ed Jackson; Mr. John Maxwell; Mr. Glen Pelshea; and Mr. John Russell.

We'd also like to thank the contributors to The Merck Manual for producing such complete descriptions of drugs and diseases. These were used extensively as source material for the appropriate sections.

And all those who gave us ideas during the last we-don't-know-how-many years.

CREDITS

We would thank the following for their permission to use and/or adapt texts from their publications.

Those who let us pinch some of their writings: The Chicago Hellfire Club; Mr. Guy Baldwin, M.S.; Dr. Tony DeBlase; Mr. Richard Hunter; Mr. David Stein; and Mr. Jim Stewart.

We have used many sources during the production of this book, some of which were unidentifiable. Consequently, there may be ideas and small pieces of text in this book that we have unwittingly plagiarized. We apologize for not being able to identify you and hope that you understand that we only included them because we felt it was worth doing so.

GMSMA, New York, New York for the page numbering.

SM Gays, London for the contact advertisement abbreviations.

FOREWORD

A few years ago at Chicago Hellfire Club's Inferno a group of friends from Toronto asked me to join them, Race Bannon, Guy Baldwin, and a few others to discuss a project they had in mind. They had received funding from the AIDS Committee of Toronto to organize and conduct a series of safe sex seminars for leather men and women, and to prepare a study guide to go with the course. The annotated outline they circulated at that meeting looked wonderful, challenging, and (I thought to myself) overly ambitious. Later as the manuscript developed I was impressed by the organization, the writing, and the basic good sense of the book. I read it closely, provided numerous comments on content and style, and encouraged them to make it available to a wider audience than the leather men and women of Toronto.

The authors (the FourSM) have definitely achieved their ambitious goal. As I review the most recent working draft, I am again impressed with its organization, and I am struck by the ease with which it can be used as a reference volume. The very long and well divided table of contents, together with the numerous headlines, make it very easy to look up just the subject you want to read about. I am not saying that the book should not be read from cover to cover, it should; but once that is done, it will not be put on the shelf and forgotten but will frequently be pulled out to check on a fact, a thought, or a technique.

As little as twenty years ago, there were only three sources of SM information. The first, and still most important, was networking with other SM people. Second, if you happened to live in or near New York city, were the programs offered by the Eulenspiegel Society, which had been founded in 1971. And third, was Larry Townsend's *The Leatherman's Handbook* which had been published in 1972; a shockingly honest and explicit book, for its time, on the real world of SM sex.

Things improved slowly. In 1974, the Society of Janus was founded in the San Francisco area and began giving public programs. In 1978, Samois was founded for SM women in San Francisco and Inferno started including lectures and demonstrations in its programs. In 1979, I started publishing *DungeonMaster*. In 1981, GMSMA started holding public meetings in New York city. They were the first to hold SM how-to lectures and demos that were truly open to anyone, of the correct gender, who walked through the door. Later in 1981, Samois published *Coming to Power* and SM Gays organized in London, with GMSMA as the model. In 1982, VASM was organized in Vancouver, and Dreizehn in Boston. Avatar in Los Angeles followed in 1983. All three of these had how-to presentations as the primary program.

In the ten years since 1983, the pace of SM education has increased even more. SigMa, the Outcasts, PEP, and many more program oriented groups have formed in towns and cities across North America. In 1986, the National Leather Association was founded, held the first Living in Leather conference, and began facilitating the development of chapters. In 1987, the National Leather-SM conference was held in conjunction with the March on Washington. The Sandmutopia Guardian and Checkmate began publication.

Now we have a national conference each year, numerous annual regional conferences and regular monthly program meetings in cities across the continent, three SM how-to periodicals, and five how-to books that have just been, or are about to be, published. This is the only one of these five books that I have, to date, examined closely. It is the only one of the five created by committee. This is usually *not* a compliment, but in this case it is. The team of authors has brought the work a variety of backgrounds and points of view that has facilitated the broad coverage of the field. As a former college professor, text book author, and frequent SM teacher, I can only say to the FourSM, "Well done! I look forward to using your text to teach a course."

Anthony F. DeBlase
San Francisco, February, 1993

PREFACE

This book is the first of a series that we intend to publish to provide information about safe practices in SM play to both experienced practitioners of SM and to those just starting to explore their interests in SM. We initially conceived the project as a means to promulgate information that would promote safe, sane, and consensual practices in all those who felt the desire to engage in SM play. We sought a forum for the dissemination of this information, and, initially, we anticipated offering private seminars and demonstrations to small groups of interested people. As discussions continued, we realized that we wanted to include all of the sexual groups in our target audience, i.e. to our initial target group, homosexual men, but also to homosexual women and to heterosexual and bisexual men and women. The result, is a series of seminars and books that is truly pan-sexual in nature.

One of the results of this decision was that we made many friendships with homosexual and heterosexual men and women. It seems that the SM community, as nebulous as it may be, is a place where men and women, heterosexual and homosexual alike, are prepared to accept each other for what they are. This was a very refreshing experience, given some of the prejudices we had all experienced in other areas. We hope that this unity will, ultimately, extend to all sectors of our heterosexual and homosexual communities, so that one day there will be no distinctions made between the sexual groups.

Before any of the book was published, we consulted with as

many experts from all the subgroups in the field as possible. Women were consulted for the female issues, likewise for the men.

Phrasing of the text has caused a few minor problems. Each of the subgroups has, to some extent, its own vocabulary. We have endeavoured to use the most generic language possible in all cases. This has occasionally led to the use of somewhat clinical language, but it seems to be the only fair way to deal with the differences without offending anyone. We hope that you understand our predicament and that you can tolerate the resultant vocabulary. Where a particular subgroup is targeted in the text, we have deferred to the vocabulary of that subgroup if generic vocabulary would not suffice.

Also, since it takes two to tango, we have not made any distinction between the Top and the Bottom as far as the contribution each makes to the relationship (or play), the players are equal but different. Therefore, we have capitalized both the words "Top" and "Bottom" to demonstrate that both players are equal, but different.

We come from very different backgrounds. One is a physician with great experience in the SM field, another is a dentist who is beginning to explore his SM tendencies. Both of these could best be described as mature individuals. The remaining two are younger men with considerable SM experience, one a restaurant manager and one a physicist/engineer. Also, we all have interests in different fields of SM play. The variety of backgrounds has led to some lively discussions about the contents of the seminar and book series. It has also allowed for full and reasoned discussion of the topics from many points of view. We believe that this range of experience, talents, and skills has contributed greatly to the balanced nature of the book.

We could not have produced all this without "a little help from our friends." We owe a great debt of gratitude to all those from whom we have solicited help and information. They are too numerous to name here; you know who you are. Thank you.

We will, however, single out the following for their help and encouragement at the outset of the project. Without it and their continuing support, we would not have had the stamina to complete the œuvre. They are Ms. Kay Hallanger, Mr. Guy Baldwin, Mr. Race Bannon, Dr. Tony DeBlase, and Mr. Glen Pelshea.

Trevor Jacques, Dr. Dale,
Michael Hamilton, and Sniffer
(collectively, the FourSM)
Toronto, August, 1993

Contents

Figures

Tables

Warning—Disclaimer

This book is designed to give information in regard to the subject matter covered. It is sold under the understanding that the publisher and authors are not engaged in rendering professional services. If legal or other expert assistance is required, the services of a competent professional should be sought.

It is not the purpose of this manual to reprint all the information that is otherwise available to the authors and/or publisher, but to complement and extend other texts. You are urged to read all the available material, learn as much as possible about SM play and sadomasochism, and to tailor the resultant information to your own needs.

Everyone assumes risks, be they associated with crossing the road or parachuting. SM play has the potential to provide greater risks than, say, crossing the road, but less, perhaps, than a Himalayan climb. Anyone who engages in SM play must inform themselves and assess the risks involved before proceeding.

Every effort has been made to make this book as complete and accurate as possible. However, there **may be mistakes** both typographical and of content. Therefore, this text should be used only as a general guide to the basics of SM play and not as the ultimate source of information on the subject. Furthermore, this text only contains information on SM play up to the time of printing.

The purpose of this book is to educate. The authors and WholeSM Publishing shall have neither liability nor responsibility to any person or entity with respect to loss or damage caused, or alleged to be caused, directly or indirectly, by the information contained in this book.

If you do not wish to be bound by the above, you may return this book to the publisher for a full refund.

INTRODUCTION

This book is intended for those people who have an interest in sadomasochism (SM) as part of play (sexual or otherwise) but were afraid to ask. It has come about for the same reasons condoms are advocated for sex: we know that some of you are going to do it, and we want to ensure that there is a source of information that will help you do it as safely as possible. We hope to provide an introduction to the variety and potential depth of SM play to those just beginning to explore this area of their sexuality, and also to provide a reference guide to the basics for those who are sure of their interest.

For novices, we realize that exploration of SM play is like a "coming out." We hope to remove some of the myths, mystery, and resultant fear associated with the subject. For the experienced, we think that there is information here you can use to improve your play.

Please note that, rather than "SM sex," we have used the term "SM play." We realize that SM does not *necessarily* involve sex. Equally, we know that some SM practitioners feel that what they do is very serious and they do not regard it as play; play to them describes frivolous activities. We have decided to use "play" throughout the book, mainly because of the pleasure we have derived from the activities. This is not meant to demean the activities in any way (otherwise we wouldn't have written the book...).

The book covers the full gamut of SM play at the "101" level. It is intended to provide you with a guide to the basics of SM play. As will become clear as you read the book, the responsibility for safe SM play lies with *you*. No-one else will be there to help you. You must ensure that neither you nor your partner is put in any unsafe position. We cannot stress this enough.

Background

At the time the authors started to think of the SM 101 seminar, there was no single source of basic information for those interested in SM play. We felt that such a source was well overdue and that we had access to the information needed to put it together.

This book started life as a small text to accompany an SM 101 seminar for homosexual men. We felt that it was too limiting, and perhaps unfair, to restrict the intended audience to homosexual men. We intended to share the wealth of knowledge to which we had access. It quickly seemed necessary to share it with all those who are interested. Equally quickly, it became apparent that even the most basic instruction included an enormous breadth of information.

We felt that the essentials could not all be crammed into a single seminar without leaving out or merely skimming some of the issues. So, the best approach was to touch on the most important subjects during the seminar, so that the audience was aware of the issues, and then cover the details far more thoroughly in an accompanying, basic text: this book. It would cover all aspects of SM play and coming out into SM. The issues had to be covered to an extent that would ensure that the audience would walk away with enough of a grounding in SM to play responsibly. This meant giving our audience a means to recognize a lack of knowledge on their part and providing them with an avenue to the required information.

From the start, we knew that the seminar and book would be the first in a series; they would handle the fundamentals. The future seminars and accompanying books would build upon these, and give more detail on specific subjects, such as whipping, toys, bondage, etc..

Given the potential for problems with this form of play, we felt that to fully appreciate the content of the more detailed seminars, it was important that any audience attending them be well acquainted with the basics of SM play. To that end, we strongly recommend both attending a basic seminar and reading this book before "graduating" to the more esoteric subjects; a "walk before you run" approach.

We also felt that our seminar should provide experienced players with information they may not have encountered. This meant that our research and review had to be thorough. We believe that we've succeeded. We feel that we have collected enough information in the following pages to give anyone interested in pursuing SM an appreciation of the risks and responsibilities involved in safe, sane, and consensual play, but we don't profess to have *all* the answers.

We hope to provide SM players with the basic information they need to play safely, and we would appreciate your comments, both complimentary and critical, sent to us care of the publisher.

Objectives

We intend this book to help people explore safer enjoyment of SM play, and to dispel the myths that surround the subject. We feel that the it offers education about pleasure rather than titillation.

We wish to help those interested in SM play enjoy their activities in a manner that is as safe as possible. Without going into a long discussion about them, we feel that you may find the following, somewhat loose, descriptions useful as you read this book.

Promotion of Safe, Sane, & Consensual Play

You will notice that, where responsibilities are concerned, in this book we have made no division between the Top and the Bottom. Unless specifically required, we will not. The Top for the purposes of this book is the one who "does things" to the Bottom. Likewise, the Bottom is the recipient of the Top's attention and ministrations.

Safe	All players have taken the necessary precautions to prevent psychological and physical damage to themselves, including the transmission of disease.
Sane	All players are in full possession of their mental faculties and are fully aware of the risks involved in the play they intend.
Consensual	All players fully understand the potential risks of their intended play and have consented to the activities. This consent can be withdrawn or modified by any player at any time.

Without the consent of all parties to sane practices, safe play cannot be achieved. The contents of this book should provide you with a further guide to what counts as sane. You should consent to any practices before engaging in them. This is for both your safety and that of your partner(s).

Safety, sanity, and consent are the responsibility of all parties at all times.

Scope

This book attempts to cover all aspects of basic SM play. It addresses the psychological, corporeal, and material aspects of safety in SM play. Details of methods or types of play are not covered here; these are covered by other seminars and books in the series that will deal with those more specific topics.

Intended Audience

This book is intended for all novice and experienced players.

We recognize the temptation to delve straight in, but we also know that many of the subtleties of the text will be lost on the novice reader if a "101" or other basic SM seminar has not been taken before reading this book. For this reason, we very strongly encourage you to have attended an introductory seminar before proceeding further into the text.

If there are no seminars being given close to you, then we'd suggest that you read the book from front to back, rather than peeking ahead. That way you'll get the most out of it.

Authors

We come from many walks of life: a physician, an engineer, a dentist, and a restaurant manager. We all contibute actively to the SM community, sometimes on radio and television. Three of us are members of one of North America's premier SM organizations. We believe that our diversity of experience both with respect to SM play and outside the SM world has allowed for a well balanced view of the topic.

We can all be reached through the publisher.

WHAT IS SM?

That's a very good question. We can't answer it, either. We *can* tell you a few things that SM is not. And we can give you more than a few good pointers as to what SM might be. The problem is that, like people, SM comes in many shapes and sizes.

The words sadism and masochism are derived from the names of two European noblemen, the Marquis de Sade, (1740–1814), and Austrian novelist Count Leopold von Sacher-Masoch (1836–1895). de Sade wrote *Justine, Juliette* and *The 120 Days of Sodom*, and von Sacher-Masoch wrote *Venus in Furs*. Both men wrote about (and are reputed to have performed) acts that included erotic pain, domination, and submission.

In the late nineteenth century, the two words were joined to form *sadomasochism* by Richard von Krafft-Ebing, as a means to categorize behaviour of this type. This constructed word has continued into modern usage. Unfortunately, its meaning is often confused with the meaning of the word *algolagnia*, which means the infliction or receipt of pain for sexual pleasure. Sadomasochism (often written SM, S&M, or S/M), as currently used by safe, sane, and consensual players, does not necessarily involve physical pain; it could be just domination and submission. We've found that the common thread running through all SM activities is control.

The clinical definitions of sexual sadism, sexual masochism, and mental disorder are given by the American Psychiatric Association

(APA) in its *Diagnostic and Statistical Manual of Mental Disorders, Third Edition–Revised* (DSM-III-R) as follows:

Sexual Masochism   The essential feature of this disorder is the recurrent, intense, sexual urges and sexually arousing fantasies, of at least six months' duration, involving the act (real, not simulated) of being humiliated, beaten, bound, or otherwise made to suffer. The person has acted on these urges, or is markedly distressed by them.

Sexual Sadism   The essential feature of this disorder is the recurrent, intense, sexual urges and sexually arousing fantasies, of at least six months' duration, involving acts (real, not simulated) in which the psychological or physical suffering (including humiliation) of the victim is sexually exciting. The person has acted on these urges, or is markedly distressed by them.

Mental Disorder   is conceptualized as a clinically significant behavioural or psychological syndrome or pattern that occurs in a person and that is associated with present distress (a painful symptom) or disability (impairment in one or more important areas of functioning) or with significantly increased risk of suffering death, pain, disability, or an important loss of freedom. In addition, this syndrome or pattern must not be merely an expectable response to a particular event, e.g., the death of a loved on. Whatever its original cause, it must be currently considered a manifestation of a behavioural, psychological, or biological dysfunction in the person. Neither deviant behaviour, e.g. political, religious, or sexual, nor conflicts that are primarily between the individual and society are mental disorders unless the deviance or conflict is a symptom of a dysfunction in the person, as described above. ...A common misconception is that a classification of mental disorders classifies people, when actually what are being classified are disorders that people have ...Another misconception is that all people described as having the same mental disorder are alike in all important ways.

There are some interesting points to note here. Those of us who play in a safe, sane, and consensual manner are not distressed by our fantasies and play, but rather enjoy what takes place. At the time of printing this book, DSM-III-R is being updated and an attempt is being made to have the American Psychiatric Association change the words "or is markedly distressed by them" at the end of the sadism and masochism definitions to "and is markedly distressed by them." This would mean that, if one read *only* the definition(s) of sadism and/or masochism, safe, sane, and consensual players would not be diagnosed as having a mental disorder.

According to the clinical definitions, safe, sane, and consensual SM players do not have a mental disorder. That's refreshing to know, isn't it? Try convincing your neighbours, however.... Neither partner is presently distressed (more likely refreshed) by his/her activities; no areas of functioning, significant or otherwise, are impaired; and their is no significantly increased risk of death, pain, disability, or a loss of freedom. (Any argument about increased risk of death or pain during play should be weighed against the additional risks undertaken when one takes up activities such as mountain climbing, scuba diving, car racing, etc.. People who enjoy these sports are not considered mentally disordered. Any argument about a significant loss of freedom should note that, in safe, sane, and consensual play, any party to the scene can stop it at any moment.) We may be deviant (read kinky), but we are not dysfunctional.

There is much debate in and out of the SM and psychiatric fields about whether safe, sane, and consensual SM play is real or simulated. Some argue that, because no long term or more than trifling damage occurs (nor is any intended in safe play), the play is a simulation of reality. Others argue that a bullwhip is pretty darn real.

Given the debate, it seems that some better definitions are probably in order. A the end of this section, we'll give you a few ideas of what we think SM might be to its practitioners.

A few extra points from DSM-III-R should also be noted. World-wide, there are people who like to perform types of autoeroticism (sex play on your own) which very often include forms of breath control (hypoxyphilia). Data from the U.S., Canada, the U.K., and Australia indicate that about 1 to 2 people per million die each year from hypoxyphilia. This is not as high as one might expect, given the high risks involved. There are no data in DSM-III-R about the relative percentages of the sexes who have the clinical disorder of sexual sadism and masochism, although the *Merck Manual, Sixteenth Edition* notes that they are much more common in men than women.

For the purposes of this book, we have shortened sadomasochism to SM because it is the term most often used by those who enjoy this form of play. Also, one often hears people linking the word sadomasochism to the idea that "those" people inflict pain or injury on others without their consent. As you will see throughout this book, this is not what we're about, so a term different from sadomasochism is appropriate.

For many people, SM is represented by bikes, whips, leather, etc., and in the homosexual male SM world "leather" has often become synonymous with "SM." This is a little unfortunate, because there are those into leather without the slightest interest in SM, and many are into SM without any interest in leather fetishism. The words in some cases have become so entrenched in current vocabulary that some men, both outside and inside the SM world, have trouble envisioning a distinction between leather and SM. Outside the homosexual male world, the images and associated vocabulary seem to be even less well defined.

The mental leaps required to move from images of leather-clad bikers to police motorcyclists to uniforms of all sorts are not great, but there are many who enjoy uniforms who do not consider themselves into SM. Yet most people into SM would consider uniforms as SM (possibly because of a perceived domination by, or of, the uniform wearer). Likewise, one of the reasons that this book was entitled "SM Play" rather than "SM Sex" was because SM does not *necessarily* include sex.

Where does this lead us? SM can probably be considered to exist in the mind of the person watching or participating. If the person likes the idea of SM, any activity may be included in his/her definition of SM, even if it's only scratching or biting during play; on the other hand, if he/she doesn't like the idea of SM, the activity is not SM in their view, even if it includes spanking, bondage, bootlicking, etc.. Some people like to be the slave/boy/girl/son/daughter/whatever to be submissive to another's will; pain is not part of the turn on for them. Others like both pain and domination/submission, but the extent of pain and domination/submission is highly variable. Still others want no domination/submission at all in their play; enduring pain in and of itself is a sign of power and strength on their part, they want to prove how much they can take. So, if you like to be whipped bloody but can't take having a tit pinched or if you like cock and ball torture but hate spanking, your SM is no more nor less real than anyone else's because of these preferences.

Imagine two Top/Bottom couples coming into a restaurant. In the first couple, the Top gives the menu to the Bottom and has the Bottom do the ordering. Meanwhile, at the next table, the Top orders off the menu and the Bottom will eat what is ordered, no questions asked. Which is "right?" Is there a "right" way? We believe that they are both right. They are both doing what works for them, within their relationship, for that stage of their relationship. Who are we to question what they enjoy?

Now that we've said that pain is not *necessarily* part of SM, we'd like to discuss it a bit, anyway. Pain is the body's first line of defence for staying alive. Pain simply tells us that something potentially damaging is happening. A lot of SM play involves hurt and pain. Whipping a back hurts, electricity can hurt, and so can bondage. But there is a very big difference between the pain you intend to inflict, or have inflicted, and unintentional pain.

If someone is standing on a cold or jagged rock, it's possible that this will be all that he/she can think of. Someone with a back that looks like hamburger, and able to enjoy that level of whipping, could forget it all if he/she stubs a toe at the wrong moment, thereby screaming in pain. This unintentional, as opposed to non-consensual, pain will completely draw attention away from the intentional pain.

Be very careful to use pain to your mutual advantage; either the intentional pain that is the purpose of the scene, or the unintentional pain that is an indication that you should slow down or stop to investigate the cause before continuing. *Unintentional pain is a warning.*

The important distinction here is between hurt and injury. As can be seen from the two preceding paragraphs, *hurt* and *pain* can be what turns us on and carry no negative connotations in the context that this book is written. The book is about how to avoid unwanted *injury*.

Depending on whether they are into the SM, and which aspects of it they like if they are, people are likely to have their own concept of SM. Below, you'll find not so much a list, but a series of thoughts on what SM might be. If you see a pattern that suits you in what follows, then that may be your particular form of SM. There appears to be no right or wrong SM, only the one that gives you pleasure. As you go through what follows, you will realize that, because people are so different, SM cannot be easily and neatly wrapped into a single, one sentence definition.

Before we go into what SM can be to people who enjoy it, we feel it is important to dispel the main misconceptions, stereotypes, and prejudices about SM, by stating what properly practised SM is *not*. As you make your way through this book, you'll realize how unlike the myths and stereotypes proper SM play really is. Many of the phrases below come from the late Don Meisen.

SM is *not* only about pain.	SM is *not* abuse.	SM is *not* without love.

SM is *not* demeaning to women or men.

We're sure we won't be able to cover everything, but we hope that what follows will give you some idea of the possibilities. The statements below are not given in any particular order:

SM is about communication.	SM is about parity.	SM is about ritual.

SM is playing cops and robbers, and the contented excitement of the victim – all tied up and the centre of attention.

SM is when the belt hits – first it hurts, then it glows… just the way we like it.

SM is trying to piss when in bondage, while your mistress holds your cock and makes comments.

SM is about negotiation.	SM is about rôles.	SM is about a journey.

SM is the dentist from out of town who you keep in chains all weekend, while your friends come over to play with her in every possible way.

SM is wondering what the other executives would say (or think) if they knew about the welts and sticky panties under your Oh-so-conservative suit.

SM is about how those tit clamps hurt just right; about the pain when the clamps bite a bit more; and how the tits adjust to that, too.

SM is the Sunday brunch at a gay SM bar, even though you're a straight couple; and knowing that the leathermen and leatherwomen there know that you're into it, too.

SM is screaming "That's ONE, Madam! Thank you, Madam!" at the top of your lungs.

SM is the thrill you get when the man at the party asks you to try on handcuffs, "...just to see how it feels."

SM is dragging yourself to the gym, even though you desperately don't want to go.

SM is your Top making you wear a steel cockring to set off the airport metal detectors.

SM is about the Top's needs.	SM is about fantasy.	SM is about the Bottom's needs.

SM is putting your boyfriend into a French maid outfit to serve lunch to you and your women's lib girlfriends.

SM is your lifelong gratitude to the person who helped you come out. (Homosexual men and women, only, need apply.... Ed.)

SM is your lifelong gratitude to the person who helped you come out into SM. (This one's for all you kinky people.... Ed.)

SM is your slave holding up her hair, without being told, so that you can put a collar around her neck.

SM is Errol Flynn tied up by pirates.	SM is about humiliation.

SM is hearing people who know nothing about SM say how bad it is, and you want to giggle because they're so serious.

SM is the quiet typist by day, dominatrix by night.

SM is about controlling.	SM is about being controlled.

SM is about sleeping with both your hands and feet bound, and the dreams that you have....

SM is your new slave blindfolded, masturbating, and telling you his secret fantasies while you watch and listen to every wonderful word.

SM is the humiliation of discovering that your new slave knows far more about SM than you, ...and has far more experience.

SM is about sweating, wondering whether you're going to pass out, and finally relaxing into it all.

SM is wishing you could afford two of everything in the leather store.

SM is wishing that you could afford just *one* of most things in the leather store.

SM is the anniversary of the date your lover had a gold ring put through your labia (no anæsthethic); then she holds you and says you're hers forever; and you'd do *anything* for her.

SM is about submission.   SM is about domination.

SM is identifying that veteran, gay Bottom on the bus; short haircut, polished boots, tattered jeans, fraying leather jacket, and a heavy chain and padlock about his neck – quiet, upright, proud, centred, and content..

SM is about the   SM is about the
exchange of power.   exchange of trust.

SM is about the tiny pair of gold handcuffs on your Chanel dress when you go to the opera.

SM is trying to explain the massive frame and eyebolts to your little, old landlady.

SM is knowing that the first person to bottle the smell of new leather will die rich.

SM is the uniform you wear on Saturday nights.

SM is about giving pain.   SM is about receiving pain.

SM is being taken downstairs and noticing that it's been sound-proofed.

SM is the perfume of sweaty leather.

SM is a highly styled and carefully managed vulnerability for all participants.

SM is screaming "That's ONE, Sir! Thank you, Sir!" at the top of your voice.

SM is finding the perfect pair of boots.

SM is how hot her ass feels as you caress the welts.

SM is putting up with a picky, uncertain novice who doesn't know what he wants or how to express it; but, when he manages, he takes your breath away with the totality of his submission.

SM is hurting the one you love, just right.

COMING OUT INTO SM

Remember those swashbuckling pirate movies of your youth? The ones that had the hero (or villain, for that matter) bound, spread-eagled, to the rigging, being whipped to within an inch of his life. At the time, it didn't seem like a very wholesome way to take a tropical cruise. But it was mystifyingly exciting. We always liked to see the hero win in the end; but the images of those bodies being abused (some tanned and/or muscular; others helpless and desperately in need of being saved) would stay with us for a long time.

Fast forward to your first sexual awareness. Those teen years when you went through the motions of being a good boy or girl, dating as you were supposed to, but sneaking into the drugstore to find magazines with pictures of men and women that seemed to mean a lot more than just a nice set of muscles. At the time, some of us were inexplicably, drawn towards bikers on their Harleys. Was it the bikes? Was it the leather? Or just the idea of being down and dirty?

Others among us liked ritual and ceremony. Perhaps we never even associated them with something a bit …no, a lot deeper.

The evolution from admiring and getting that unexplained feeling from the sights in films or magazines to actually touching those bodies takes many years for some of us. Others are fortunate enough to pass through the phase in a matter of weeks or months. It takes one through quite a bit of mental trauma. "Should I, shouldn't I? I want to so much.…"

Some people had intense feelings of shame and guilt that they had a form of unnatural perversion. This led some of them to bury their SM feelings, and hide the ones they did acknowledge. There was a kind of puritan feeling that we should not enjoy ourselves too much, particularly with such "perverted" activities. At this stage of our coming out into SM, we were not yet sufficiently confident of our sexuality. It is a stage similar to that of homosexual men and women who know their sexual orientation, but are not yet ready to accept it fully; not yet ready to equate "kinky" with a healthy sex life.

The descriptions above and below summarize the experiences of a typical gay man into SM and leather, as described by David Stein in *Leatherfolk* (adapted with permission). Lesbians and bisexual and heterosexual men and women who like SM were also out there looking for that special something; and having many similar feelings.

In society at large, there is a great deal of pressure to conform, or at least to be seen to conform. Often, this causes those coming out into SM to hide their sexuality, which further damages their self-confidence and self-esteem. Our city of Toronto has been rated by at least one UNESCO survey to be the most culturally diverse city in the world. We speak over 140 languages here. Yet it is outwardly a very conservative city, and is only slowly accepting all aspects of its diversity. For example, it took more than eight weeks of wrangling with editors for one reporter to get a positive piece about SM into one of the three major newspapers.

The pressure to conform leads some people to our local institute for psychiatry, in the search for a "cure." For many of the applicants, the physicians find that, in the same way that those who want to be "cured" of homosexuality, there is really no illness, only a harmless, healthy deviation from the norm.

The phrase "coming out" is used by homosexual women and men to describe the process of accepting their homosexuality. The process of accepting that one enjoys SM follows similar patterns of fear, guilt, experimentation, and acceptance, so we use "coming out" to describe acceptance of SM feelings. Also, please note that leather does not *necessarily* mean SM, nor does SM *necessarily* mean leather. There is, however, a significant overlap.

Some homosexual men and women "came out" during the golden years of gay history, the early seventies, after Stonewall and before AIDS. It was an era of free sex and abandon for the homosexually active. Anything that could be done, was done. (A decade earlier, a similar liberation occurred for the heterosexual community.) In those days, when men went to gay bars and discos, they always went dressed in the hot look of the day: plaid shirt (or no shirt), or perhaps construction boots and hard hat. They were all construction workers (clones, as they were known). The New York pop group The Village People reflected the homosexual culture of the day. All of its members represented popular fantasy images that could be seen any night in the bars. All the fantasies could be put together without too great an expense.

In the heterosexual community, fantasies tended to be generally less well explored or expressed. (Maybe because the heterosexual men and women had not gone through a "coming out" process, thereby forced to face some very uncomfortable realities about their sexuality.) There were not many places where sexual fantasies could be freely engaged in. Images of the fantasies could readily be seen in movies, skin magazines, and even on the street. They were, however, still compelling.

Back then, fantasy played a large rôle in our lives. But there was something missing from the reality. That is, until we walked into a real leather or SM bar. Totally intimidated and very frightened, we summoned up the courage to fake a stumble into some hot number so that we could run our hands over one part or another of that body. We earned ourselves a scowl, thought we'd be punched or thrown out of the bar, and left. Never quite the same, we wanted to be one of those people, to fit easily and seamlessly into such an establishment.

This is when we started our "fashion awareness" phase. It was easy to become a leatherwoman or leatherman. All we had to do was buy a leather vest, maybe a pair of chaps, and act cocky. We knew we'd fit in.

And fit in we did. Many in the bars were in "leather," too; others were in lace or latex; still others in little more than chains. We would go out to the bars, get well turned on by each other, and then go home to have what has since become known as "vanilla sex." This was just what we had been doing during all those years of boredom and frustration.

But something was still missing, despite the kinky clothing. We didn't fail to notice that, although porn was hot, it was always better when someone was in bondage or being controlled in some other fashion.

If anything was going to happen, it looked like we'd have to hang around in the "serious" leather bars. Those ones that we had been so scared to go into a while back. The people there seemed to take their leather much more seriously than the leather-clad "disco queens" (to use a gay phrase). There were few leather bars, even in a big town. Finding them was perhaps easier in the homosexual community; at least they advertised themselves. Once in the bar, we could easily have been the ones who coined the phrase: S and M means Stand and Model. We were terrified of rejection and/or ridicule.

We started to go to leather oriented competitions, such as the International Mr. or Ms. Leather, or leather conventions such as Living In Leather. At these events, we had wonderful, if sexless, times surrounded by some of the hottest leather people we'd ever seen. It was Stand and Model all over again. We were so afraid of being brutalized or injured if we met someone who might really give us what we *thought* we wanted.

The trouble was that we still didn't know what we really liked or disliked. Lots was going on, but you still had to be invited to the party.

As is the case in other parts of our lives, the invitations seemed to go first to the young, the beautiful, and the reckless. You couldn't talk your way in, because bar etiquette (at the time) required that you should not ask naïve questions. To do so was to admit your inexperience. This, it seemed, was a sure way to ensure that you did not get the experience you sought. So, if you didn't know the score already, you'd better be prepared to fake it, or you'd never get a chance to play.

That's 15, Sir!
Thank you, Sir!

Where were our rôle models and mentors to assure us that SM was OK, to show us that it could be done safely, positively, and not self-destructively? There we were, leathermen and women, full of inner inhibitions and turmoil.

Until, that is, we met our first warm, gentle, and skilled player. He or she was willing to share knowledge unconditionally, to take us gently as far as we could towards where we wanted to go. After playing once or more with this mentor, and possibly with others, we knew that a new world of eroticism, sensuality, sexuality, and fantasy had opened up for us. We would never look back.

The above could be the story of many a homosexual man into SM. The feelings experienced during the coming out process are shared by most people, but the actual process of coming out is different for lesbians and heterosexual men and women. The homosexual male community is based upon its sexuality, and, therefore, its expression tends to be more obvious in their clubs and bars.

For women, particularly homosexual women and those who are Bottoms, the potential for and reality of abuse looms large during the coming out process. And from two directions. There is the abuse itself and the prejudice of others who feel that any woman as a Bottom is being abused and/or violated, whether or not she enjoyed the play. During their coming out into SM, many women try to convince their partners to experiment by taking the rôle of the Top (with varying degrees of success and safety). Many of those women found that all they got was abuse or a disinterested beating. It is rare to find anyone who understands the emotional content of SM, or those feelings and yearnings that were described above.

Generally, heterosexual bars are not based specifically around their clients' sexuality. This means that finding partners in bars is nigh impossible. Feelers have to be put out until the right people (or perhaps the right sex toy stores) are found. These lead to other people and information about SM, and reassurance that SM can be practised safely and with due consideration for all parties involved.

At the beginning of our "coming out" into the SM world, we all wondered if we'd be able to experience those exceptional times that would encourage us to continue our exploration of SM, or whether we'd be put off by the whole experience. At some point, we all get at least a taste of how much pleasure we can derive from SM. Besides, that compulsion to look at fantasy in movies, that compulsion that first drove us into the bars where we could express our SM tendencies, would likely have continued to drive us until we did experience what we were searching for.

The search will be much easier if you have some play that works so well during your "coming out" into SM that you continue the search for what you want. Having the courage to ask someone, or being lucky enough to find a mentor will ensure that you finally get there.

Come with me.
I will take you places you have never been before.
I will show you things you have never seen before.
I will teach you things you have never known before.

Having tasted the glass of wine, we wanted the whole bottle.... We knew that this was what we wanted, but it raised a lot of questions:

- What rôle do I play? Top or Bottom? How do I use it to have a fantastic time? Can I be Top one night and Bottom the next?

- What techniques do I use to ensure that the play is safe? What do I avoid?

- What are the other fetishes and activities that might turn me on, but that I've never even dreamed of?

- How do I find and use, and safely at that, all that fascinating equipment I've seen in catalogues?

- Is it OK to be into bondage, but not pain? Can I like mild pain but not heavy pain?

- Is it OK to be turned on by electricity but not by flogging?

- If I just want a little tit play and a bit of spanking, will I be thought too much of a novice?

- Etc., etc., etc.....

During the process of coming out, the feelings of being alone, of being the only one with a need for this alternate sexuality, were abating. We still had to be careful with our friends who were not into the SM world, however. We "knew" that if we opened up to them about our desires, that they wouldn't understand. So we had to deal with the feelings of being ashamed of our fantasies and pleasures.

If one were to define a novice as someone whose SM life consisted largely of fantasy or who is still feeling some form of guilt about SM, then, at this point, we were novices. More and more, though, we met people who were into the same things as us; many even more so. We saw what great people they were in their own right, outside the arena of SM play. This gave us confidence that, not only were we not alone, but also that it was OK for us to come out into SM.

That's 17, Sir!
Thank you, Sir!

Why

As you've seen from the above generalization of the process of coming out into SM, we do it because somehow there is something inside us that drives us to it. Some want to know what it is that causes this desire. The authors have been happy to accept that the feelings and drive are there, part of the way we were made, much the way that homosexual men and women accept that this was the way they were made. It would seem that homosexual men and women know why they are *that* way no more than heterosexual men and women know why they are *their* way. Consequently, we feel no compulsion to explore our SM sexuality. We simply accept and enjoy it. Provided no-one gets hurt (beyond what they'd like, of course), we see no problems, in fact, we see only benefits in coming out into SM.

The benefits can include the feeling of relief that we are not the only ones into this form of play and the sense of release achieved during the play itself. The pleasure of dressing in sensual clothing that stimulates us in any number of ways. The pleasure of, once again, regaining childlike playfulness as an adult. The satisfaction of being tied up, or tying up. Experiencing things we know few people have had the privilege to see or in which they've been able to take part.

How

There are many local SM organizations that have sprung up in the last ten to fifteen years. They are dotted all over North America and Europe. They meet regularly, exchange information, and many have play parties. There are now enough that national organizations have formed. Some of these put on large conferences so that we can meet with others who enjoy SM. They come from so many places that you might even think that travel was a prerequisite for SM play....

Every year, the National Leather Association in the U.S. holds an event called Living In Leather. People come from all over the world to be there. They can make new friends, exchange information, and learn from the many seminars given by experts in the field. This is a resource that you can and should use as you explore your SM sexuality, if only because it will make things much easier for you.

This book came about from our recognition that the safety information and techniques we had learned should be shared with novices, and with experienced players who may not have experience in some areas of SM play. We knew that it can be difficult to accept and then to investigate one's SM feelings. By putting on the seminars and writing the book to accompany them, we hoped to show novices that they are not alone and that there are groups able and willing to help.

At some point, as you come out into SM, you're going to have to bite the bullet and go up to someone to chat. It's the same as in the world of non-SM play and relationships. In the SM world, though, the main difference is what you're after and how you're dressed when you go after it. Some ladies wear Laura Ashley clothes. Some wear biker's leathers. Some gentlemen wear preppie ties. Some are body builders. (Any combination of these could be into SM, maybe not.) Maybe the outer presentation is part of the game, and there is a different "drag" underneath; say, leathers under the Laura Ashley or lace under the leathers (this applies to both men and women). What's your bag?

There is another aspect to coming out into SM. It is the process of coming out to other people. As coming out does for homosexual men and women, SM follows a pattern of knowing about one's SM tendencies oneself and then admitting to them; telling friends and others who are into SM; and telling friends and others who are not into SM, including genetic family if you want to. If done openly and honestly, telling people about one's SM play can help healthy relationships with these people.

Like those who are homosexual (who often want friends and relatives to know that they are homosexual), SM players often feel the urge to tell the people close to us about the pleasure we derive from SM. If you feel the need or desire to tell someone, it's best not to avoid the issue, otherwise it may just gnaw at you from the inside.

One of the authors remembers the thoughts he had when determining whether to tell his parents that he was homosexual. The family had always been close, but he had not had the confidence to tell them. When he did tell his parents, it was because he figured that not telling them was a lie of omission, and he would not stand for lying to his parents. He used the same logic for telling friends and relatives about the wonderful pleasures he derives from SM.

Before telling his parents, he knew he had to be properly prepared to discuss any questions they might have. This meant getting his own house in order to be prepared for any questions they might ask. Why did he think he enjoyed SM? Was he really injuring himself and/or others? Etc., etc..

Even if you don't yet feel the need to tell someone, it is a good idea to prepare for when someone unexpectedly asks *you*. You'll be ready to answer clearly, openly, and honestly. There are many things to address as you prepare to tell others. We'll address some we've addressed ourselves and some others written about by Guy Baldwin.

Why do *you* enjoy SM? Sit down one day over a coffee or something and write a list of the pleasures you have had from it. What do you enjoy doing or having done to you? Is there any pattern to your play? It might be the clothes, the toys, the people, or the places. Setting it down will help to clarify your thoughts. As you do so, other thoughts will emerge. Use them all to find the answers, if you can. One of the authors can pinpoint no event or other reason in his past that he could claim "caused" him to like SM. On the other hand, since he knows he likes SM, he just looked for the kinds of play that turn him on and made a note of them.

If the situation is that you know that you want to tell someone else, ask yourself why. Is it a question of honestly to someone? Do you want it to shock someone? Maybe, there's another reason. You should be convinced that you're doing it for the right reasons, otherwise it may not come off as well as you want.

Often, the best time to tell someone is when you're both relaxed, like when you're doing the dishes after a meal, or off to do some shop-ping As many homosexual men and women have discovered, there are some people for whom the time will never be easy. If you've chosen a relaxed moment, it will be much easier to "bite the bullet."

If the day comes that they ask *you*, ask yourself quickly why they would want to know. Is it genuine interest, fear, or do they have some malicious intent? Usually, if someone asks you, he/she is ready to hear at least some form of "Yes." After all, there had to be some suspicions to prompt the question. If you suspect that the he/she is up to no good by asking you, ask why he/she would want to know. Anyone with any bad intentions will probably go on the defensive very quickly. A genuine questioner will simply give you the reason.

When you answer, be sure that your responses are appropriate. Some people can only take so much. Give out the information a little at a time, checking that it answers the question fully. How does your questioner react? If you force the issue, you will give more than was asked, possibly against the person's wishes. SM play should be consensual, even with those not into the scene.

By checking, you will know when the answers have reached the threshold of what the person is ready to hear on this occasion. You may be asked or you may want to fill in more details at a later date, after your questioner has had some time to digest what you have just said. Your mother may want to hear less than your neighbour's punk, teenage daughter (who you always suspected of having an interest in SM). Or it may be the other way around: one of the authors never ceases to get direct questions about SM from his mother.

When we started to put our SM seminars together, we knew that we had to inform all those who attended of the SM credo: Safe, Sane, and Consensual. It is a good idea to ensure that one of the first things that you tell someone about why you like SM is that this is the *only* way you will play. This not only helps to put, say, your sister's mind at rest, but it is important to make sure that as many people as possible are aware that we are not dangerous people, simply kinky ones having good, clean, dirty fun.

When you answer questions, be sure that you present yourself as the same person your questioner has always known, rather than some "other" side of yourself that has hitherto been unknown to your questioner. This will help ensure that he/she is put at ease, that the conversation flows freely, and that your questioner will accept your answers with the truth that they contain. If you don't know the person before you have to answer questions, just be open, frank, and clear. Any half truths or avoidance of issues at this point will only serve to reïnforce any thoughts your questioner may have had that you were hiding something.

Eventually, you're likely to get a question that you can't answer. Don't try to answer it with anything other than an "I don't know." If you try to reply about a subject about which you don't know that much, you're likely to misinform your questioner. This could do more harm than good. Tell the person that, since you don't know the answer, you'll try to find out. You don't have to make any promises to reply that you might not be able to keep.

We have heard many analogies made for why we like SM and what we do. The two that we like the best are the buffet table and the musician. Guy Baldwin has described a buffet table where there are many dishes, and, depending on how we feel at the time of the "meal," we will put various things on our plate. Add a little control or domination/submission and you have an SM meal: a little rope, a little tit clamp, a bit of suspension, and perhaps a whipping for dessert. What are your tastes today? Maybe some electricity and sensory deprivation for tomorrow's meal?

SM scenes have often been compared to a musician playing an instrument. The musician (the Top) tries to the best of his/her abilities to exact the most exquisite music from the instrument (the Bottom). The abilities, training, preparation, and experience of the musician are as important as those of the instrument. Together, there is the potential for a concert as great as any given by Rubenstein playing a Steinway, or Pagannini playing a Stradivarius.

Openness, knowledge, and confidence in yourself, coupled with a little bit of preparation, will show through any discussions you have with those you'd like to tell, or who have asked you for information about SM play. They will also make the process a lot easier.

You will help to dispel some, of not most, of the myths and misconceptions about SM You'll also be able to show how much fun can be had by being kinky, and by consenting to that kinkiness safely and sanely. Kinky, yes; menacing, no.

Social

There are many ways to find people into SM. The following are the main ones, but you will certainly find others, such as a chance meeting in the shopping mall, on the street or maybe the local charity/church hall/community centre.

Local, Regional, & National SM Organizations

These come in various forms: local ones designed specifically for a particular community (be it for homosexual men, dominant women and submissive men, etc.) and pan-sexual and national ones. The latter cover similar communities and are sometimes divided into local chapters. The North American national organizations will be able to tell you if a local chapter exists near you, and how to contact it. You may even want to form one. SM magazines bought in your local leather or sex store, often have listings of SM organizations. The gay and lesbian directories usually list the national organizations.

Try looking up your local magazines. Very often the local arts paper will have some information in this vein. If you're heterosexual, remember that the homosexual population seems to have its act together a bit better in the larger cities and will usually have a local publication with ads for local bars or stores that could help you. Also, your local leather and sex toy shops will have a lead to the organization that you're looking for. Don't worry about being intimidated, just ask. No-one will bite your head off. Sometimes a friend, or a friend of a friend, can lead you to the organization. Maybe you have a few ideas already.

Bars

Bars come in at least two forms that we know of here in Toronto. Maybe where you are they are like this, too. We have the usual leather bars for homosexual SM men. These are often frequented by homosexual SM women, too.

We also have a "Fetish Night" once or twice a month, sometimes in homosexual bars, sometimes in heterosexual ones. This is for both heterosexual, homosexual, and bisexual women and men. Everyone dresses up in the manner that they like, provided that it is kinky (otherwise you don't get into the bar that night). There are usually one or two mild whippings being done, more for humiliation purposes than to hurt, but it does allow anyone interested to get a look. If you wore "normal" street clothes there, you'd look out of place. One thing we've noticed about this event is that it brings together absolutely *everyone*. There are no animosities or fears about an unknown part of the community. Everyone is accepted for what they are or project to the other attendees. Consequently, it's one of the most relaxed places in the city to go to experience a bit of SM or other kinkiness. Everyone talks with everyone else.

The authors have been in many conversations about what one talks about in a leather bar. Well, it turns out, you can talk about just about anything. Jokingly, this has many times been expressed as "quiche and crochet" or "opera and cookery." The consensus seems to be that the intimidating image of the leather and other aspects of an SM bar are about as far removed from reality as could be. You'll find that you can talk with just about anyone in the bar. The first time we all went into such a bar, it scared the you-know-what out of us. We had conjured up an image of intimidation before we got there, so we got just what we expected. If you go there expecting to meet fine people, you'll find them. Just inside the leather.

Our experience is that the majority of those who play in SM are very creative and imaginative people. They love to talk about just about anything. Some of them can even conduct learned conversations on nuclear physics, if you want. In an SM bar, you're unlikely to find too many people who have only about two brain cells. But they are there, so be prepared for them.

Networking

Amongst your friends, you may have one or two who you know to be into SM or at least to have dabbled in it. Seek them out. Talk with them. Do they know someone who knows someone, who knows..., etc.? You'd be amazed what, or who, comes out of the woodwork. The girl or boy next door may just be the one who surprises you the most and the best.

You may find the mentor we all hope for. Someone who will draw you out of your shell, to enjoy those things you want so much. As you explore the SM world and meet more people, the circle of friends you have in it will expand more and more rapidly. These are birds of *your* feather, and you'll start feeling at home. It will be easier to introduce yourself to the people who used to intimidate you. You'll have learned what little new vocabulary is needed to move in these circles, and you may realize suddenly that you've become one of the people you initially thought were so unapproachable.

Get involved in the local community. This could be by helping out a health organization. A hepatitis or AIDS organization, perhaps. You would learn a lot, be able to help others, and perhaps meet new and interesting people you'd never have met otherwise. Who knows, even "Meals on Wheels" could be the avenue that leads to someone.

As you try these avenues, remember that there are many clues that might tip you off to someone who is into SM. Just as homosexual men and women have had to show indications of their leanings to those who might show an interest, many of those into SM leave little clues. These could include, but certainly not be limited to, the type of earring, keys, bandannas, collars, tie pins, cufflinks, brooches, boot chains, etc.. The sign/clue could indicate only that a person is into SM, that the person is into a particular activity, and/or whether the person is Top, Bottom, or both. Beware that any of the clues could be worn by those not into SM, so tread carefully, at first....

If you are already experienced, we urge you to give as much information and confidence as you can to those you know to be just coming out into SM. Remember what it was like when you first experienced leather and SM? Wouldn't it have been great if someone had taken you by the hand (or whatever) and in a very unthreatening way guided you to where you were comfortable with your "new" self? We would have all been very glad of it. It unnecessarily took up so much of our time and effort to come out into SM. People shouldn't have to go through that. It's one of the reasons we wrote this.

Phone Lines

'Phone lines come in at least two flavours. One is the community help lines, often staffed by volunteers. Regrettably, they tend to be found mainly in the larger cities, not out in the countryside, but they can be called from anywhere. Also, they do not always have someone plugged into the SM network, so you may have to encourage them to do some digging If you feel that you need the anonymity of one of these lines to ask questions, use them. They're there for *you*. They're there to deal with your fears, questions about safety, etc..

The other kind of 'phone line is the sex talk lines. These may help you get your jollies, but they may end up being unsatisfying (and expensive) because, ultimately, you really want to be doing what you've been talking about (unless you get off on just talking about it…). Much of the involvement or use of 'phone lines is to do with the fantasy, not the reality of SM. Perhaps finding a mentor or partner in one of the ways mentioned above may be a lot better for you.

Publications

Particularly for those who get a thrill by playing with someone unknown (a potentially dangerous practice), responding to ads in the local press may be a good way to meet people. The classified ads are usually full of personal ads and business personals. The national SM press always has a goodly selection of ads placed by those into SM, as does the non-SM press. Please see the section on Further Reading & Viewing for a discussion of the various publications available.

Classified ads may be the most important way people meet each other for SM play. If you have attended an SM class in your area (they are given in most large metropolitan areas by many and diverse groups), using ads may be of little use to you. The vast majority, however, will find that ads are the only means available. Those who attend SM classes have often gone beyond basic coming out into SM, and plugging into their local SM network. Their atten-

That's 25, Sir!
Thank you, Sir!

dance provides a great way for novices to network and to find out their own interests by discussing them with other people. If you feel that ads are the only means available to you, by all means use them.

For your own sake and that of others, please be honest in your ads. If either the advertiser or the respondent is not fully honest, you're both going to be disappointed. If you're forty-five, slightly over-weight, and something of a novice, make sure that is clear, rather than portraying yourself as a Greek god. Also, don't expect to meet your knight in shining armour (or whomever) on the first try.

There are ways to help screen out weirdos who advertise or respond to ads. You may want to set up dinner or another meeting before you play, to establish a good feeling about the person Alternatively, you might try to find out discreetly whether you have mutual acquaintances; you could then check a few of these references. Perhaps the person regularly goes to a particular watering hole; you could check with people there, too. If you use your imagination and instincts, you should be able to detect the weird ones.

Computer Bulletin Boards

There are many of these available to homosexual men, but fewer for the rest of us. One advantage of the boards is that they can be called from anywhere, but that may mean they're expensive. Many of the boards are listed in SM publications such as the Sandmutopia Guardian, The Leather Journal, and Dungeon Master Occasionally, they publish articles about the boards. Like all bulletin boards, some have been around for a while, while others don't last.

Professional Dominants, Etc.

Of particular importance to heterosexual men and women is the use of professional dominants. For many, if not most, submissive hetero-sexual men (a *very* large percentage of the SM population), this is the first and only SM experience they can get. So much so that in the het-erosexual community this is as an important an avenue as leather bars are to homosexual men.

THE MIND

Your greatest sex organ is your brain.

In it, the mind has lots of wonderful ideas; some of which we can act on, others we can't. The ideas for play begin with the mind, although they do not necessarily end there. "Wouldn't it be fun to try this...or that?" This or that may be to go bungee jumping, cook a wedding cake, write about medieval history, or tickle someone mercilessly with a feather. Let your imagination work on the ideas, and your brain on how to do it. Knowing what you want, accepting what you want, is just the beginning.

Below we discuss some of the ways that the power of the mind can be used to enhance play, and prevent accidents.

Fantasy & Reality

Fantasies and ideas for play rely on our continued imagination and creativity. Some of them "require some assembly," but the mind is the place where the whole thing starts. An idea or fantasy is created in the brain. Do not deceive yourself, fantasies are real. They exist in your brain, so they're just as real as a table. Taking the fantasy and making it a real event is no more than representing the reality (fantasy) in a different manner and enjoying yourself while you're at it. (We will continue to refer to the reality in the mind as fantasy for the sake of convenience.)

The mind is an expert at ideas; it can create them, improve them, and destroy them. These things can happen at any time; before, during, and after play. Play itself requires that both partners be aware of what is happening. Hence, reality plays a great part in the appreciation and enjoyment of a scene. (For the rest of the book, we will often refer to the realization of a fantasy as a "scene.")

An appreciation of fantasy and reality is necessary to maintain one's trust in the scene itself, let alone one's partner. Later we discuss some potential areas of fantasy: how to deal with trying to do something that is not part of everyday life within the confines of the real world. Very few fantasies can be had perfectly. This, however, doesn't mean that we can't have fun....

Fantasy

What have you always fantasized about? What would you like to have someone do to you? or do to someone? Be outrageous; what did you want to do but never thought possible? Perhaps you always wanted to be a star quarterback or a ballerina. Did the mere thought of it turn you on like crazy? Is it time to try to make it a reality?

You will start to see from the examples given throughout the book that SM is as much about control as about stimulation (including body stress up to and including pain). There are those who want to control, and those who would like to lose it or give it up to someone else. Physical pain is irrelevant to some forms of SM; the pleasure/pain is in the mind.

Do not, however, discount the potential for psychological damage; some scenes involving only the mind can be as damaging, if not more so, than those involving mainly the body. You wouldn't want to spoil that fount of wonderful ideas.

Before you go out and get wild, let's consider some of the more common fantasies. Later, we'll get into how they can be carried out safely.

With Whom Do We Want To Play?

Skin magazines and other adult press exist to fulfil the sexual desires of the public in one way or another. Like the oldest profession, they have been around for a long time and will continue to be for some time to come. Whether those publications are to a person's taste or are within the bounds of local, current moral boundaries is not for discussion in this book. They exist and depict a large variety of play, be it inclusive of the sexual act or otherwise. From the readily available *Playboy* to the more esoteric and bizarre, they exist to serve a market. There's no profit for the publisher in something no-one will buy. Many of us have, in our youth or later, seen or bought such publications. Why did we buy them? Because the contents or perceived contents excited us, or, at the very least, gave us some ideas for play. Or just because we wanted the answer to the question "What *do* the kinky folk do?"

Again, the mind is the root of our desire to buy these publications. The variety is massive. From ginseng to genitalia, from leathers to feathers, from muscles to monasteries, from.... That's quite a mouthful, but it serves to illustrate that the choices for play are great. We've all seen or heard or fantasized about some of them to some extent at some time.

Within the SM publications, we see such things as Master/Mistress/Slave, Master/Mistress/Dog, Daddy//Boy/Girl, Police/Innocent/Guilty, French maids, Jocks, Bikers, Body Builders, Scouts/Guides, Masters/Mistresses, Transvestites, etc.. Did we miss your favourite fantasy? Remember that these are only a few of the more common ones. Who or which rôle did you last fantasize about? If you've done something about it, we hope it was fun; if not, in your position, we'd be working at it....

Many people feel that to act upon such ideas or fantasies is not right. If no-one is hurt, we feel that consenting adults have far more to gain than to lose by playing along with their ideas. If you'd like to play "patient" to a "nurse" for a bit of fun, go do it. Maybe you could call your wife and tell her that when you come home you want her naked on the bed, and the whole feather collection laid out on the dresser for you. This can also be a form of SM.

What Forms Could Play Take?

Now that you've decided with whom you're going to play (or who you're going to become) for the evening, weekend, month, etc., what are you actually going to do? Again, there are many ways to play. Some have more relevance to particular rôles than others, but a suitably imaginative couple (or single person) can always find a way to introduce just about anything into their particular fantasy. Below we've listed just a few of the things you can do. These are some of the common ones, but then you've probably already thought of some variations....

Touch:	When someone is unable to move, just touching them can be a wonderful means of control. You could use your fingers, feet, arms, legs, feathers, brushes, cloth, leaves, toothpicks, drumsticks, etc., etc..
Hair Removal:	Shaving by razor or credit card (the latter gives the feeling of a shave on short body hair without removing hair. This is a form of control of the mind in play); depilatory (cold waxing);
Bondage:	Simple restraints like handcuffs or ropes, bandages, Saran wrap, duct tape, medieval iron hardware, etc.;
Authority:	Control of what the Bottom is allowed to do. For example, boot licking, when he/she can piss, when he/she can climax, humiliation, etc..
Whips:	Short, long, and anything in between.
Electricity:	AC/DC (*never* above the waist), Violet Wands (anywhere but the face);

Got any other ideas? We know there are a lot more floating around.

Where Do We Like To Play?

Where is all this "kinkiness" to happen? Again, it may depend on the rôles you want to play. A touching scene in a "dungeon" may be just as erotic as a biker scene on a "beach." The quotes are there because these places are probably going to have to be in your mind as part of the scene. It is extremely inconsiderate to involve beach-goers in your sexual predilections, or the police for that matter (and if that's your bag, you're just going to have to do that in private, too). You would be doing it without their consent. It requires only a small amount of imagination to make a bedroom into a public washroom for the sake of your scene.

Maybe your scene involves doing that "something" in a forest. At least that can be arranged if you can get access to some private woods.

Don't let the desire for a real location interfere with where your fantasy takes place. It's possible to play without a playroom or dungeon and have fulfilling play. Use what comes to hand, and use your greatest sexual organ to fill in the rest. Blindfolding or hooding a person will allow them to place themselves anywhere they want, if they let their mind do that part of the play. Your bedroom has lots of possibilities if you let your imagination run riot. That way, you don't have to buy an old château in France to play "in a dungeon."

When Would We Like We Play?

Some people like to play in broad daylight, others in the depths of the night. A surprise can always be fun. Some people would just love to get unexpectedly "arrested" and have a cop dominate them for a while. The pretext of the "arrest" may not be relevant to the scene, but the "arrest" could be sufficient reason for the "cop" (your partner) to take you home and do those wonderful things you both talked about last year. A "quickie" while the dinner guests are downstairs has been had by more people than you could shake a dildo at. It may just be the thrill of being caught....

Alternatively, you may go willingly at any time. Even by prior arrangement. If you know something's going to happen at a particular time, both as a Bottom and as a Top, the anticipation of the event can build up to significant levels and make the play that much more intense and/or enjoyable. Often, the longer it takes to get to the time, the more the anticipation. The "appointed hour" could be midnight. How are you going to feel as the clock strikes out twelve?

(There is one potential problem with scheduling play in advance: one/both/all of you may not be in the mood, you may not be healthy, etc.. Our moods can change from hour to hour, let alone day to day or week to week. It may not always be advisable to go ahead with a pre-planned scene just because the appointed hour has arrived.) You decide when is best.

How Do We Play?

The means by which one comes to the end can be quite interesting, too. A ticklish person tied down to a bed unable to do a thing about having feet, sides, and even having one's lips tickled may be having as much fun as a slave being tortured "viciously." To many, a feather can be just as vicious as a whip.

If a Bottom is used to a Top being very rough, the semblance of being tender could keep the Bottom in a state of delicious anticipation. This is because there would always be the potential that something else is just around the corner, even if it isn't.

Some people enjoy the flagrant display of domination or submission. There are bars where you can go wearing a slave collar. The collar is, after all, only another piece of clothing. The feeling that it imparts to the wearer in public may be how the Bottom gets a kick out of the scene. (We'd recommend, however,, sticking to the bars where it's quite the norm.)

Why Do We Do It?

Aye. Here's the rub….

Why do we do all the above? Simple: *Because it turns us on.* What's the point in wasting effort being ashamed about what you are or what you enjoy? Life's too short.

Done in the right place, at the right time, nobody is offended or injured. If you indulge your fantasies safely and with due regard for others, you'll serve your physical, emotional, and intellectual needs.

We started this section by noting that all of SM play stems from the mind. Well, the mind likes it when the body gets excited. Or is it the other way around? No matter. As we've mentioned, your brain will remain your greatest sexual organ. Use it, explore it, and enjoy it.

Reality

We have covered the fantasy aspects of SM play, but there comes a time when reality has to rear its head. It's one thing to play with wild abandon on an almost inaccessible beach at three in the morning, it's quite another to do the same on the bus to Boondock, Iowa at three in the afternoon. Some things can be done; others, patently, cannot.

Some fantasies are unsafe and/or insane and/or non-consensual. These should not be brought to reality. The brain, however, can play out many of those fantasies safely: in the written word, in drawings, even as the imagination during play that "fills in" those unsafe parts of the fantasy. So you can have your fantasy and "experience" it. To an extent, it's just an attitude of mind

What are the main parts of the real world that can play a part in modifying a fantasy that you're about to enact? They fall into the basic categories below.

Safety

So, you've had a fantasy to be hanged? Realizing that fantasy is not a practical proposition. It would be so dangerous to try that you probably shouldn't even consider it. You like the idea of seeing someone with massive electrodes across the chest? Fine, but you'd interfere with the electrical rhythm of the heart and probably cause a heart attack. A dead person is not much fun to play with next time.

These are extreme examples, but the message cannot be made strong enough. There are some things that cannot be done because they're simply not safe. Use your imagination to make it look like you're doing your fantasy without actually putting yourself (yourselves) at risk. Would you like to suspend your partner from the rafters? Then remember to check that you have installed a quick release mechanism such as panic snaps, and that the hooks in the rafter(s) and the chain or rope are *both* strong enough, not only to take the weight of your partner but *also* the added pull when your partner struggles. This added weight could be a few times their actual weight!

Physical safety is only one aspect of safety, emotional safety is just as important. Psychological scars can take a lot longer to heal than a broken leg.

Everything we do involves a level of risk; from getting out of bed to stunt riding a motorcycle to breathing. It is up to us to decide the level of risk we are prepared to accept. That decision could be influenced as much by feeling as by an awareness of our skills. Therefore, what one of us considers safe another may not. Also, don't forget that consent should be informed; that is, we cannot accept a level of risk if we don't comprehend the risk itself. (We hope that's why you're reading this book.)

Safety in as many forms as we could think of is the reason we wrote this book. Please read as much about the safety of an SM activity as possible before you engage in it. While the authors have tried to cover as much as possible, other books may have even more information about the activity you intend.

Respect & Consideration for Others

Let's say you're very good friends with the two blue-rinse ladies in your apartment building. Are you going to let them catch you in the elevator wearing chrome-plated spikes on your codpiece pants, a chest harness, and tit clamps with a heavy weight on the chain between them when they thought of you as a quiet, civilized yuppie? We thought not.... Even if they *did* get a kick out of it. Like our note a few sections ago about sexual predilections at the beach, to wear all this SM paraphernalia would involve others in your fantasy without their consent. You don't pry into their sexual habits, why thrust yours into their faces?

We all maintain some form of image of ourselves. That image may be one that is ever present, or it may differ depending on the occasion or people present. Many of those into SM have no wish to thrust their sexuality onto their family, so they present themselves at home as the family has always known them. This is merely a mark of respect and consideration for them.

One of the authors is an engineer, a typical "guppie." He wears chic suits for his business days, and preppie clothes at most other times. He windsurfs only when there is a storm warning, he goes to the ballet, and has restored veteran cars. Another part of him likes to wear as much leather as possible and to be something of an exhibitionist about it. On visiting an SM bar for a soda after getting very dehydrated windsurfing, and wearing his skin-tight, black neoprene drysuit, he was informed that "rubber night" was next Saturday. His windsurfing maniac persona had been mistaken for a fetish. In such a bar, this was acceptable because no-one would be offended and the author knew it. Had it been a fetish, it could have been carried off elsewhere, because it is not usually associated with a sexual fantasy. (To an extent, there is a fine line to be drawn in this argument: if we take consideration and respect for others too far, we might run the risk of creating yet another closet to hide in.)

Please, however, don't think anyone in church will accept your tit clamps at Sunday services or that you can whip someone on the steps to your courts of law.

Consideration is given, and respect is earned.

Other Implications of Reality

You Can't Always Have All You Want

So you want to tie Grandma to the oak tree and have your way with her? You'd be disowned when they found out, and probably put away for more than a little while, either to a funny farm or the local prison. As mentioned above, there are definite limits to what you can do to realize some of the more esoteric fantasies. This means that you'll just have to accept that if your fantasy is one that would break the law or be too risky to be safe, you won't be able to do it. You may be able to *simulate* it elsewhere, however.... The latter merely involves using the mind to filter out some of the actual location of the play so that the fantasy can take shape; the fantasy setting and its details are completed in and by the mind.

Neither you nor the law is perfect. And the only way around some fantasies is to ensure that they never happen. You can enjoy thinking about them, but that's going to be the extent of it. It may be that both you and your partner want to do it, but both of you would rather that the Bottom was still in good health to play again. So find a creative way to get around the problem. You can probably think of many ways to restrain someone, so you probably can find many ways to simulate a flogging in the middle of St. Peter's Square, Rome....

Fantasy May be More Than Reality Can Handle

You've been having fun having your genitals tortured for the last hour. (It's possible.) Then the form or level of the pain changes, and now it really hurts in a very uncomfortable way, that's no fun at all. The Top may not be aware that this form of pain is one that you really don't like. Your fantasy has just been destroyed and your level of excitement is dropping like a stone. In some play, most people have a threshold below which the play is fun, if painful, and above which the pain takes away from the scene completely because it hurts too much. This level is generally different for different people, but thresholds seem to exist for everyone. Some stimulations turn us on, some don't.

The implication is that, to continue to have fun, it is important for the Bottom to signal to the Top that the play has gone too far. It is equally important for the Top to try to recognize this development before it happens and to instantly respond to the Bottom's signal that the limit has been reached. The Top is also responsible for calling a limit that is dangerous when the Bottom is still eager for more, i.e. when enough is too much. These are realities to be faced and respected if you're to have fun playing and want to play with each other again.

Also, don't underestimate the residual effect of a bad experience. An accident during a scene can leave lasting signs. A broken arm may fix fairly quickly. It won't help the relationship with your partner, though. Accidental castration or pregnancy have more lasting and far more significant effects that are not only physical. A complete breakdown during an interrogation scene may cause nightmares in the Bottom for years to come.

Ensure that no scene comes even close to leaving a bad taste in your mouth, let alone a scar on your or your partner's body or psyche.

Punishment

Many people are excited by punishment, be it in films, books, or porn, or by being part of it. If punishment is brought into a relationship and it is allowed out of the playroom, there is a great potential for psychological damage. Usually, it is the result of fantasy and play being confused in some way with reality.

A masochistic Bottom may want punishment, and the pretext for the punishment may be a mistake or transgression. If the pretext for the punishment happens outside of the playroom, it may lead to the Bottom having to do wrong in order to initiate play. The converse is also true; in order to avoid play, the Bottom may have to be perfectly good; and, if the Top wants to play, he/she may have to make up a false pretext for punishment.

Under these circumstances, the Bottom can lose self-esteem and self-respect. If this is allowed to continue, it may lead the Bottom into a depression. Anyone in a depression could not be described as the life and soul of a party. The reasons for the loss of self-esteem and self-respect are tied to rewarding failure or wrong-doing with sexual play. This is a very strong inducement for the Bottom to continue to fail or to do wrong.

Ultimately, this leads to confusion in the Bottom's mind. If the Top makes a mistake and is not punished, the confusion will be even greater. Often, Bottoms who need a pretext for punishment were trained during childhood that punishment requires a transgression. Since they enjoy pain and/or punishment, they also feel the need to do wrong in order to have a pretext for play. To have "good" they must be "bad." Another source of confusion for the Bottom is to receive punishment or pain on one occasion for a transgression and on another as an "I love you." In time, this would confuse anyone .

The confusion will not bode well for your mental health, if you're the Bottom. Anyone who cannot enjoy pain, in and of itself, without setting up a pretext for punishment can end up on this downward slope. You wouldn't be much fun for yourself or others.

Studies have shown repeatedly that corporal punishment does *not* work. Children in school, rather than being caned, are now supported in a way that can correct the offending behaviour. A Top can help to break the cycle of "transgression for pleasure" by using the same support methods used for children. If the child/Bottom is really bad, then tell him/her why, and withdraw the source of pleasure. It is a very effective method of teaching proper behaviour.

The best way to deal with punishment as part of SM is to reserve it for play time, i.e. for a well behaved Bottom. That way, the mental health of the Bottom will not be endangered. You will have kept your punishment play safe and sane, and you'll both feel good about it.

Reality Can Mean Facing Truths About Oneself

Suppose that you're playing in a fantasy scene where you've decided that you're off to the bar with your partner in a collar. The rules were that your partner would stay one pace behind you and always below you. This gets your partner really turned on, despite the fact that you're usually the Bottom. There's no disgrace. It's just something new to explore. Remember how you felt the first time you admitted that you enjoyed SM? and how you think about it now? (If you're new to SM, don't worry. Reread the section on Coming Out Into SM.)

It's all about accepting the way we are, rather than the way we'd like to be or have others perceive us. It's a hurdle much like the one that homosexual men and women have to overcome in accepting, rather than just admitting to, their sexuality. It's no big deal after you're over the hurdle, but before then it's a mile high wall. In the words of a popular song: Relax.

So, you're kinky. "Thank goodness we're all different," said Alice.

Creativity

Creativity is required to start and maintain a scene. We'd like to think that, other than for information on safety, one of the reasons you're reading this is to get some new ideas for play. Besides, variety is the spice of life....

Yet again, we come back to the mind. Without it, none of those silly, kinky, fun, outrageous ideas would be formulated. It is important to use the objects available. (You'd be quite surprised to find out what you can do with a toothpick.) Creativity for play will come in every category of who, how, when, and where mentioned above. It's one thing to play in the bedroom, but have you considered playing on the dining room table? When used properly, a one-inch piece of coarse string can be devilishly fun.

One of the first places to go when trying to find new toys to play with is the local hardware store. There is a name for the contents of a hardware store when they're used in play: "pervertibles." In the store, you'll find chains, Saran Wrap, rope, brushes of all kinds, gloves of different textures, lumber, etc.. Take the time to investigate your store. We'll bet that you're taken aback by what your mind does, now that it's looking at things differently.

Then take a look inside a kitchen store….

Next time you go for a walk in the woods, notice the many different textures available, courtesy of Mother Nature. The location can be pretty fun, too (think of it as environmentally friendly play). Just because you've decided that you're going to have an interrogation scene doesn't mean that it has to be restricted to a police or prison cell. The French Foreign Legion could be a good setting, as could a physician's examining room.

We encourage you to let your mind create the scenario and then work on how to enact it. And don't let yourselves get caught in a rut. Master/Slave relationships of all levels can be very fun and satisfying to the participants, but there may come a time that you want to change the arrangement. Maybe because it has become a bit stale, or just for the sake of a change.

Creativity lies mainly in experimenting with ideas and "what if"s. So the last idea you had was a dud? Modify it, try another idea, maybe you just weren't in the right mood. Give it a try, chances are you'll have more fun than disappointments.

Rôles

Under normal circumstances a person's mood and personality varies from time to time and situation to situation. The same is true for our SM personality. Guy Baldwin described it as lying somewhere along three scales at any one time. Exactly where on each scale will depend on the person and the circumstances.

Dominant   ⟷   Submissive

Sadistic   ⟷   Masochistic

Aggressive   ⟷   Passive

It is very possible for someone to be a dominant, aggressive masochist. (They're often referred to as "pushy Bottoms.") You might also be a passive, submissive sadist. We're all different and quite unlike the stereotypes that would have us forever pegged completely on the left or right side of these scales. Likewise, you might feel like being a pushy Bottom one day and a passive Top the next.

As you forge a relationship with your partner(s), you may want to take a look at your SM personalities to see how they complement each other. Where there are similarities, rather than complements, you may have to work on how you're going to satisfy those needs for both (all) of you. We've found that one of the great things about this process is that we can learn from and teach one another. There's no better way to learn than from someone you trust and whom you know has the required information. If you want to experiment with submission, but were scared to do so, it would be great to learn from someone who has readily submitted to you. You'd have a mentor for your exploration of your SM personality. Likewise, you could learn particular techniques from one another.

Rôles and rôle playing involve needs and meeting them. To do that, frank discussion between partners is a must. The longer the rôles are kept, the more discussion and honesty needed.

Top or Bottom—Who is Which?

This is where the illusion of reality and the reality of the illusion can become a grey area. The trick to making the scene work is to maintain the illusion during the scene that the Top is in control. We say illusion here because the real control rests with the agreement the Top and Bottom made before the scene began. Within the limits of the agreement, the Top is in control and has a responsibility to stay within those limits. The Top should also to be wary during the scene that this was a reasonable limit for the Bottom.

During the scene, the Bottom can modify the play to some extent within the agreed limits, but not control it. The control rests with the Top. So, while some would argue that the Bottom is in control, because it's the Bottom's limits that must be respected, this really isn't the case. The Bottom agreed to limits, and, within those, the Top is in total control.

Understanding the real dynamics and rôles of a scene will almost certainly help you pull it off successfully.

Acting Out a Rôle For a Scene

Assuming the rôle (deciding that you want to be the rôle for the duration of the scene or longer), as opposed to acting it out for the duration of the scene and for the benefit of your partner, may be the most effective way to ensure that the scene is a success, but reality should never be allowed to retire from the scene. If you don't feel that you can fully assume the rôle, then act it out for the duration of the scene and for your partner's enjoyment. If the scene really is not working for you, and you find that you dislike it, then get out of it, or try to modify it as you go. It's very possible that any scene you agreed to start might have a permutation that you will enjoy. If at first you don't succeed….

Living a Rôle

There are many permutations of rôles in relationships. They may involve when and where, as well as the degree of rôle play. Some want to live as, say, Master/Mistress and Slave or Dog. Whatever the rôle, living it will require a substantial commitment, and it is advisable for the definition of the rôles to allow for the players to exit from them, at least temporarily.

Before you undertake any arrangement whereby you will be living the rôle, make sure that you have talked about it. A lot. The most successful couples living rôles have talked about it thoroughly, over a long period, before committing to this life. If there was little or no frank discussion beforehand, life can be terrible for both players. Your discussions should be held out of rôle.

As with most aspects of SM play, honesty is the essential ingredient to success. Any concealment of facts and/or desires will have to be addressed eventually, so it really is best to get them out before things start. In a way, you will be interviewing each other, maybe even reversing rôles a bit to get the information you need. You could start by using something like the questionnaires at the back of this book to see which issues come out of the answers.

Some Tops take complete control of the Bottom's life, handling money, career, day-to-day activities, etc.. Others hand over these issues to the Bottom. You'll have to find out which arrangement suits you best. Your arrangement may hold for all occasions, except (maybe) when your natural family or work colleagues are close. You will have to talk about how to handle this before you begin your new life.

A person's needs run deep, many of them coming from education and childhood experiences and pastimes. In the long term, you will have to ensure that these needs are met. For almost everybody, it is impractical to be completely under the Top's control. Besides, your Top may feel like a rest now and then. Interests in, say, music or sport may not be the same for Top and Bottom, so you'll have to find a way for both to satisfy these interests, in or out of rôle, separately or together.

It is very easy for a Bottom to convince his/herself that he/she has no needs other than those of the Top. This is unlikely to be the case in fact. In the extreme, it can lead to questions from the Bottom like "Should I wash your car from the front to the back, or back to front, Madam?" Hence, your discussions should include talk of the extent to which the Top will control the activities of the Bottom, and how much judgement the Bottom may be allowed to exercise. Again, these discussions should be held out of rôle.

There is one issue that may not have to come up in the discussions between Top and Bottom but is, nonetheless, the responsibility of the Top in long term rôle play. The Top must make provision for his/her incapacity or .death A dependent Bottom could easily go to pieces if the Top were suddenly not present. After all, the Top is only human. Unless provision is made, it could do lasting psychological damage to the Bottom, and the Bottom may take a long time to trust him/herself to a Top again.

One way for the Top to provide for his/her absence is to ensure that there is a network of friends/Tops able and willing to take over and provide the necessary emotional support if an incident occurs to make the Top absent.

From this quick discussion, we hope that you have some idea of the commitment necessary for living a rôle. It requires talk and care. By talking a lot beforehand, when you're relaxed, you'll leave little to chance.

That's 41, Sir!
Thank you, Sir!

Rôle Reversal

If you're known as a Top, there's no disgrace in being seen as a Bottom. So, if you're inclined to try out being a Bottom for a while, do it. It's what *you* want to do and enjoy that matters. Others can think of you whatever they like. You're having fun playing.

We have known couples who have been in the Master/Slave rôles for years, and then they decided to reverse the rôles and become Boy/Daddy. Their friends took a lot of time to adjust, mainly because they had assigned labels to the pair. Our couple, meanwhile, were having fun, but they did spend a little time wondering what all the fuss amongst their friends was about.... Regrettably, even in the SM community there are those who would assign labels and stereotypes.

Rôle reversal can come in other forms. Consider a homosexual man playing an SM scene with a woman. To quote one of the authors: "Now, *that* would be kinky." He also meant that it might be fun, simply because it was different from anything he's done in the last while. That example is a form of rôle reversal. If it feels good, what's wrong with a man playing with a woman?

You can see how easy it is to have preconceptions of what "should" or "should not" work. There really aren't any hard and fast rules when it comes to rôles. We have to work with ideas and fantasies until they can be used for play. Make up your own fantasies and the rules within them, then enjoy them. Again, it's all in the mind.

Responsibilities & Other Duties

By now, you've probably realized that there's a lot to think about before, during, and after a scene. This section contains a summary of the major things that everyone really wants to know, things that they have to accept and bear in mind to ensure that play can proceed without accident or unwanted trauma.

They're all just common sense, but we're all too apt to forget them in the heat of the moment. Do you have a condom in case your partner doesn't? Did you check that the chains can take the weight? Etc..... Even the experts make mistakes. Your responsibility is to both yourself *and* your partner.

It bears repeating that your greatest sexual organ, the brain, is the one that accepts the responsibility for safety. Please use it wisely.

Consent

We have relationships with everyone we meet. From the few seconds as we buy a newspaper, to the decades we spend with our family and friends. In relationships, we give and receive consent for how close we can get at any moment. The more we know someone, the more intimate we are allowed to become. The ability to give and receive consent develops in our childhood and stays with us until we die or become senile. There are a few exceptions to this generalization: drugs affect our ability to understand any consent we give or receive, and, on a day-to-day basis, we have to assent to the demands of legal authorities. Otherwise, we consent to everything we do.

It is important to understand the nature of *informed* consent. Unless we fully understand something to which we agree, our consent is neither proper nor complete; i.e. we are not qualified to give it. This is always a useful yardstick during negotiation of an SM scene: If you don't understand what you're getting into, don't agree to it.

Consent works much like a traffic light. I has its red, yellow, and green. It is always operating. Your traffic light can be badly affected by mind altering substances (please see the section on Mind Altering Substances for more on this). The operation of the traffic light is fairly simple. As you negotiate a scene, everything is at green and you're excited. It's what you want. Then, at some point during the scene something happens or someone suggests something that you're not sure about. Your light instantly goes to yellow. This is a warning that maybe you should do some more negotiating, or perhaps slow the scene down a bit. If you know that your Top is great with electricity, but he/she gets out a whip as though to use it on you, you may be concerned that your Top has little or no experience in this area. This could be because you didn't discuss it beforehand, or because you know that your Top does not have whip expertise. Don't assume that a Top or Bottom expert in one area will be expert in another.

Whatever the cause for the yellow light, and the reasons behind it, you should slow down or stop the scene to reassess your levels of consent, and do any renegotiating that may be necessary. One or both of you may need to reassure the other that things will be fine. If you want, you can do this while still in your rôles.

In any situation, you earn respect and give consent. Trust develops in a relationship over time, sometimes a long time, and with that trust comes consent. Once the trust is lost, the consent will disappear almost immediately; and trust can be lost in an instant. In most circumstances, trust and consent will go hand in hand, measure for measure.

The consent that players give during a scene allows them to influence a scene, but not necessarily control it. But, once your traffic light has gone to red, you're likely to withdraw your consent completely, thereby ending the scene, or at least suspending it for a while.

We'd recommend not playing with anyone who does not appear to understand the way informed consent works, because he/she may not understand when to stop, either. It is probable that anyone who claims to want to give total submission or domination does not understand how consent works.

More often than not, your gut will tell you when something is not going the way you'd like, and it will turn your light to yellow. Do *not* ignore this feeling, investigate it. If necessary, talk about it with your partner(s). Sometimes you may feel that you have given too much consent, thereby turning your light to yellow. If so, withdraw as much consent as is required to make you feel comfortable again.

Consent is one part of three parts of the SM credo. Without it, SM play could easily cross over into assault. We owe it to ourselves, and others who enjoy SM, to lead by example, and to ensure that our play is beyond reproach.

Responsibilities—Who for Which?

Any activity usually comes with some level of responsibility. Bearing children requires a commitment once they're conceived. Being chairman of the local parent-teacher association requires another form of commitment. Tying someone to a bed requires yet another.

As a parent or a Top, we accept considerable responsibility for the well-being of others. As a Bottom, it is important to ensure that you never put your Top a position where unwanted damage could be done to you.

All too often, the Bottom, particularly a novice, will think that the limit of play is further than his/her real limit. The Top must at all times be aware that this might be the case and govern the scene accordingly. The responsibility for the Bottom during a scene is to ensure that the Top is always treated as such. The Bottom has many means to signal what is desired or required: body language, verbal cues ("Please,..."), the release of a grip, touching, etc..

It may be quite appropriate to one scene to have the Bottom begging for the Top to stop and for the scene to continue, but *only* if this was agreed to beforehand and there is another way to determine that the Bottom's limits have been exceeded. This begging may, under other circumstances, be the point that should never have been reached in the scene.

Negotiation

Everyone goes about negotiating a scene in a different way. There is no right or wrong way. It is not necessary to rattle off all of your aches and pains before starting a scene; but you should make sure that anything that may affect the current scene is well understood by your partner. Different kinds of scenes require varying quantities of information. Ensure that you feel comfortable with what you have told your partner, especially about any physical limits, handicaps, or other potential impediments to the scene *before the scene begins*. Make sure that you discuss what is relevant. For example, food allergies are not important to a whipping only scene, but a seizure disorder, or cardiac or neurology condition would have to be discussed in full.

Be honest. This is difficult for some, especially for Bottoms. If you can't or don't want to do something, say so before the scene gets under way. There's absolutely no need to feel embarrassed about your limits. If you are and you fail to mention them, you may find your Top pushing you beyond them, through no fault of his/her own. If you have hæmorrhoids, you have hæmorrhoids, and that's that. Your Top is unlikely to be clairvoyant....

Let's take a look at some of the things that you should consider each time you negotiate a scene.

From a medical perspective you should consider many things (please see the section on Safety). Medication, and when the medication has to be taken may be relevant. If the scene might continue past the time that the next dose should be taken, will you be in a position to take or administer it? Some medical conditions have a routine or pattern that may be relevant to the play. Check for this before you play. You may want to discuss under which circumstances the medical condition happens. For example, some people get migraines only at a certain time of day, say at night, so you might want to limit your play to the day-time. For others, migraines may be the result of certain type of play. The length of the scene may be relevant. Some people, both Tops and Bottoms, can manage only short scenes, others can go for days. The severity of the scene can come into the negotiations, also. How much can the Bottom, or Top for that matter, take during a scene? There may be limits to the endurance of the Bottom, but the Top may run out of muscle or patience, depending on the scene. More intense scenes will require more preparation and negotiation than lighter ones. Make sure that you're both clear in your minds about who can go where and why.

Environmental conditions such as temperature and altitude can be relevant to the play. If you hail from The Great White North, consider that what you feel as a comfortable temperature in the playroom while naked may be quite insufferable to someone from Florida. This is a sure way to put an end to a good scene. Altitude may affect people with asthma, allergies, or other breathing disorders. The same goes for temperature, it affects how you think, how you feel, and how you're stressed.

Remember that the physical condition of the Top can also be important to a scene. For example, an octogenarian Top will likely not be able to keep up a vigorous whipping the way a twenty-year old could. If a Top has a migraine, it may or may not be important to the way he/she plays.

You may also want to negotiate emotional aspects of your play. There are some things that trigger an emotion that you would rather not let enter a scene, because that emotion may spoil the scene.

Listen for clues from your partner during negotiation.

Deciding what the scene will comprise is a kind of contract. It's simply agreeing to do this or that. If the scene is only a one-night tryst, you're not going to write a 20-page contract. You might want a long one, though, if you're about to enter a one-year Mistress or Master/Slave relationship.

While being too specific about how the scene should proceed (either from the Top *or* the Bottom's point of view) may spoil the spontaneity, it is very important to ensure that what you *don't* want is expressed before it's too late and you're having second thoughts in the middle of the scene. Honesty with yourself and your partner can only make a scene better. Getting your wishes out in the open will go a long way to providing a memorable scene. ...Can we talk?

Who's in Charge?

Ultimately, the limiting factor, other than the safety of the Bottom, is the extent to which the Bottom *consents* to go.

Once the Bottom's consent has been exceeded, at least one person is no longer enjoying the experience. This alone is sufficient reason for the scene to stop immediately or for reaching a new agreement of limits, physical *or* psychological, by mutual consent, so that the scene can continue. No matter how far the Top *wants* to go, the Top cannot and must not go further than the limit consented to by the Bottom. It's also quite possible that the Top may not be able to go that far, if the Bottom didn't fully understand the implications of his/her stated limit(s). The Top has to determine whether this is the case, making the Top's part in the play that much more difficult.

During your negotiation, it might be advisable to allow for a limit that is not too rigidly defined. Otherwise, you could end up in a situation where exploration and expansion of limits cannot happen, nor will you be able to try out something new. If the limit is too broadly defined, the Bottom (or Top) may have to end the scene; if it is too narrowly defined, the players' limits cannot be explored. You should be able to work something out before the scene begins. For example, "Well, I've never tried electricity, and it scares me a bit. Let's try it slowly and, if I really can't bear it, I'll let you know."

You should never let your play get to the point that your Bottom withdraws consent, because you were supposed to be having fun, not providing fodder for the scandal tabloids.

Top & Bottom Should Establish The Scene Beforehand

Suddenly you realize that your back is being flogged hard. It hurts. The whipping you had wanted was of your penis.... Did you tell your Top this beforehand? Too often, the cause of a scene's failure is simply bad communication, or, worse yet, a lack of communication.

Make sure that you both understand what the other wants out of the scene and that you're both prepared to have that kind of scene. This is particularly true when you've only just met your partner. One of you may just want to go further than the other is prepared to.

To establish a scene, you might explore each other's erotic interests while talking in a bar, or discuss the specific scenes and fantasies at home. Experienced Tops sometimes "set up" a scene simply by watching a Bottom's reactions to suggestions, such as "I'd like to watch your back get rosy as I flog it," or by having the Bottom kneel at the Top's feet in the bar. Granted, it is generally an experienced Bottom who can communicate well this way, but it can be done.

By establishing the guidelines and limits of a scene, you protect both participants and increases the chances that you'll play together again. As mentioned above, it's just a matter of respect for your partner. And courtesy, come to think of it.

Bottom Must Signal Problems

Since it is usually the limits of the Bottom that must be respected, the Bottom would be very wise to ensure that the Top is given enough information to determine whether the limits have been reached. Not only can exceeding the limits destroy the scene, it can also do nasty things to friendships. As a Bottom, it is your responsibility to ensure that your Top has enough cues as to whether you want more or less.

Cues to the Top can come by means of body language, verbally, by touch, etc.. Use any means available to you to get the message across. "Ten, Sir! Thank you, Sir!" "Ow!" "Arrgh!" Use a safeword for the scene. (A safeword is a word that you both/all agree upon *before* the scene. The Bottom uses the safeword to have the scene *completely and immediately stopped*.) Use a word like "Uncle" or "Red" for "Stop!" We recommend that you *don't* use the Top's name (because you may forget it in the heat of the moment). A raised finger may suffice. This way, the Top will know to check how you are feeling, and how you'd like the scene to proceed. Even if that means you want it to stop.

We have witnessed a growing movement that advocates the use of "Safeword" as the safeword for a scene. We like it because it is easy to remember and very difficult to confuse with anything else a Bottom may say during a scene. You may want to adopt it as your safeword, too.

If you don't tell your Top to take it easy, don't conclude that you can pass on the blame for the scene going further than you wanted or could take.

Bottom Must Signal Wishes To Go Further

By the same token, the Bottom should make it clear to the Top that the scene can go further than was originally intended. But don't forget that this could be further than the Top may be willing to go.

Top Must Recognize Problems

As a Top, you may be asked to put the Bottom into a situation where communication is difficult. Equally, it may be easy to communicate, but the Bottom may be inexperienced and loathe to call an end to the scene for fear of being perceived as "not heavy enough." Your responsibility as Top is to be constantly on the alert for any forms of signal from the Bottom that the pace or severity of the scene should be changed, or that the Bottom is in real, as opposed to "rôle," trouble. Very often, the Bottom may not be in a position to do it.

A novice Top or Bottom will likely encounter much talk of negotiations and safewords, but there appears to be a diminishing attention to the responsibility of Tops to "read" their Bottoms. As a result, newer Tops often turn over all responsibility for a scene to the Bottom, in the form of having the Bottom communicate problems. This is an abdication of responsibility. In an ideal situation, a good Top should *never* have to hear a safeword. He/she should be able to "read" the Bottom – be it in the form of body language, vocalizations, the look in the Bottom's eyes, etc. – and *know* the state of the Bottom. This is a skill that it is the Top's responsibility to develop It is the most important skill a Top can have.

As a Top, take your responsibilities seriously. You both want to have fun, not end up in the Emergency Department of your local hospital.

Trust

Trust is an important ingredient in creating a scene that works, but maintaining one foot on the ground is far more important, because it may save your life. Properly conceived and engaged, SM play is safe; but rashness, mind-altering substances (including alcohol), and other irresponsibilities could do more than just spoil a scene.

Can you really trust a Top you've only just met? What could the Top do to you that you'd hate or may harm you? Can you look your Top in the eye, before the scene, as you agree to its limits? One way to ensure that you have confidence in the answers to the first two questions is to try the third. Anyone whose eyes evade your direct questioning is probably not to be trusted. Your partner's eyes and body language will generally reveal far more than the words you hear. Combine the eyes and body language with the words, and you have a reasonable way to decide whether to trust your partner. It's by no means foolproof, though; there are expert liars out there.

Trust can also come into play during the scene itself. If, as a Bottom, you've agreed on the basic parameters for a scene, it is your responsibility to trust the Top to remain within those guidelines. While keeping a foot on the ground to ensure that nothing untoward happens, you must also allow the Top the freedom to develop the scene.

The credit card shave is a good example. If the Bottom has agreed to having all leg hair removed, the Top may also decide to play a "mind fuck" on the Bottom. Applying shaving cream to the Bottom's chest as well and then taking it off the chest with a credit card will feel very much like a real chest shave. The Bottom has to trust the Top to stay within the guidelines of shaving the legs, despite apparently also having a chest shave. The Bottom may want to keep all his chest hair, and has to tread a fine line between trusting the Top to stay within the guide-lines (even though it *feels* otherwise) and calling an end to the scene because he is sure the chest hair is being removed.

The Top has to trust that the Bottom has honestly and fully expressed his/her wishes for the scene. Otherwise, the Top will never know when to stop or if the Bottom can take more.

This can all appear to get a bit complicated. The implication is that complete honesty on the part of everyone concerned is the best, if not the only way to play at SM.

Check Toys are Safe Beforehand

To have the slave you've been working on suddenly fall, because you didn't check that the supports in the ceiling were strong enough to hold the weight, is more than a little disconcerting. Did you put something underneath to ensure that, should this happen, he/she would not fall far? It is essential, as both Top and Bottom, you try to think of as many of the things that could go wrong before play begins; a form of "expecting the unexpected." (Were *you* a good Boy/Girl Scout?) At least, you should be sure that some provision has been made to rapidly release the Bottom from any restraint. A sudden cramp, an equipment failure, or your mother walking through the front door are all situations that might demand a quick release.

Are the toys clean and, if necessary, sterile? (For definitions of clean and sterile, please refer to the section on Hygiene) Did you, yourself, check how they were cleaned? Did you check that the supports and chains or other suspension equipment are strong enough to take the kind of play you intend? If you're using a toy in a manner that was not intended, can it take the abuse? (For instance, a Melamine spatula may produce the effect you're after, but what if it snapped? It could easily put a nasty gouge in the recipient's skin.)

Was the type of knot you used one that can be easily undone? Again, if it wasn't meant to come undone because it was supporting something or someone, was the correct knot used?

If you have someone in chains, there should be a pair or bolt or chain cutters within easy reach. You'll also need ambulance scissors close at hand to cut clothing, rope, leather, etc. should an emergency arise.

Please see the section on Safety for a more thorough look at safety of toys and the playroom. It's one thing to be carried away by the moment, but don't let that risk your health or that of your partner. Question as often as you feel you need. Anyone responsible will respect you for your caution and thought for safety.

Check First Aid Beforehand

As for the toys, so for First aid. Do you have alcohol, peroxide, Betadine, etc. in the playroom? Bandages? Band-Aids? Paper towels? Do you know how and when to use these things? If you're playing outside (or inside), do you have a blanket nearby to ensure that exposure is not a problem? There are many first aid kits available that are sold as a complete kit for very reasonable prices. They are very cheap insurance. If you're really conscientious, a course in CPR (Cardio-Pulmonary Resuscitation) is cheap insurance, too. You cannot be *too* concerned with your or your partner's health. (Please see the sections on First Aid & Equipment for more information.)

Panic

As opposed to simple, anticipated fear and trepidation that a Bottom may feel during a scene, real panic can be the cause severe damage to both the Bottom *and* the Top. Panic can happen for both physiologic and psychologic reasons. Usually, it will be from psychologic stress. A Bottom may suddenly get to a point that causes a form of terror in his/her mind, maybe because the trust that had been placed in the Top is no longer sufficient to override any concerns about physical or mental safety.

Panic will cause a fight or flight reaction that comes directly from the autonomic nervous system. Because it is such a basic, instinctive reaction, it is very powerful; both in its effects on the body and the mind. A panic attack may last only a few minutes, but it can last up to an hour or two. The person experiences a sense of terror that arises for no apparent reason, and a kind of dread of a nameless, imminent catastrophe, preventing rational thought. The person may thrash about wildly and utter many loud threatening comments. At the same time the heart rate rises considerably, as does the breathing rate. Sweating, nausea, and occasionally diarrhœa can also occur (the latter is where the phrase "shitting your pants" comes from). The person may feel a sense of hunger for air and this will probably lead to hyperventilation. The excess of air in the body caused this way may then lead to forms of muscular stiffness and pins and needles around the mouth and fingers. These symptoms help to convince the person that they're about to lose consciousness or die. To the Top, many of the symptoms will look like a heart attack, save perhaps the verbal abuse from the Bottom. To the Bottom, this panic attack is all going to be very, very real and extremely urgent. The older a person is, the less likely the chance that they will have a panic attack.

If a Top takes restraints off a Bottom as the panic begins, there is a good chance that the Bottom (still in the panic attack) will attempt to physically attack the Top, since the Top is ostensibly the cause of the terror in the mind of the Bottom. The threats from the Bottom are not empty.... This means that the best thing for a Top to do is to stop the scene and, leaving the restraints on for the moment, quietly calm and reassure the Bottom that no harm will come. This may take a little while, but eventually the Bottom will come out of the attack, the body will stop thrashing about and the voice will calm. Only at this point, when the Top is sure that the Bottom is calm, should the Bottom be released. There are two reasons for this: the Top could be injured, thereby minimizing the Bottom's chances of release; and the Bottom could be injured as a limb came free, by attempting to harm the Top and in fact doing damage to him/herself.

Hyperventilation

Hyperventilation causes loss of carbon dioxide (CO_2) which, in turn, causes a constriction of the blood vessels to the brain. As a result of hyperventilation, people complain of anxiety (which may have been the cause in the case of panic), fear of heart problems, and are often completely unaware of their hyperventilation. When the person is aware of the breathing problems, the most usual complaint is of inability to "catch my breath" or to "get enough air," despite the unobstructed overbreathing that is happening.

Generally, treatment is by reassurance until they calm down. Rebreathing carbon dioxide from a *paper* bag may occasionally be helpful (note that plastic bags may cause accidental suffocation and should therefore *never* be used for this). Once the Bottom is calm, he/she should be gently released and comforted. As you release the Bottom, be aware that he/she may have expended a great deal of energy during the panic attack and now be somewhat weak.

Anticipating Panic

What can you do to avoid panic? Other than ensure that you know where a paper bag is, probably not much before the event. When a panic attack has begun, both parties should try to remain as calm as possible (this is unlikely to be an option for the Bottom). If the Bottom senses panic approaching, he/she should *immediately* inform the Top that something is happening. (Before you started the scene you should have established a means to do this.) The Top may be able to see the attack coming by a change in the reactions of the Bottom, and slow down or stop the scene. It may be possible to avert the attack if it's caught early enough. If not, pretty much everything is going to be up to the Top. He/she must remain calm, determine where the means to release the Bottom can be found, and reassure the Bottom. Do *not* leave the Bottom alone at this point; what the Bottom needs most of all is comforting out of his/her state of terror.

Potential Causes of Panic

Scene Becomes Too Extreme as a Whole

It's possible that, although the scene is within the agreed parameters, aspects of it become difficult for either Top or Bottom (or even both) to accept. Both of you have the right to stop the scene at any time. This is a time to exercise that right. Discuss what was too difficult *after* you have completely halted the scene. It may have been something minor or major, but discussion will help ensure that the conditions that caused stopping the scene do not recur. It could simply have just been that things were going too fast. Well, next time go slower. We've found that the longer scenes, when everything can be ramped up and down properly, can be the best.

If your partner stops a scene, remember that it is his/her right, and don't allow yourself to feel bad about it. Even though you were having fun, your partner was not. You can both use this incident to learn more about each other. It's not a time for confrontation.

Concern Over Physical Well-being

If you've noticed that your Bottom is having either physical or mental problems with the progression of the scene, change the pace, discuss potential problems, do whatever it takes to allay your concerns. If it means stopping the scene, do so. Both players should be happy to continue. As a Bottom, you need to be aware of the ability of your Top to continue. Again, communicate your concerns to your Top until you're sure that the scene can continue.

Top Too Much for Bottom & Vice Versa

If a player gets "carried away," it is very important that the other exercises the right to stop the scene. Chances are that one of you is experiencing unintentional physical or mental pain. If the scene doesn't work for you, it should be modified or stopped. You should not be in an unwanted situation, nor should you allow it.

No Reaction from Bottom

The Bottom may show no reaction to what the Top is doing. Before you continue, ensure that this is a normal or desired reaction of the Bottom. A Bottom in bondage may have become unable to communicate. A good Top will ensure that not only is communication possible but also that any lack of perceived reaction is not a sign of problems.

Spirituality & Ritual

Spirituality means different things to different people. Nietzche said: "Our certain duty is to develop ourselves, to expand ourselves wholly in all our potentialities. It is to succeed in becoming fully what we feel ourselves to be. What we want is to become ourselves. Nothing that is should be suppressed. Nothing is superfluous." That potential is different for everyone, as is the way to attain it. Many have found that their route to wholeness includes pain.

Ecstatic rites involving pain are found in most cultures. In Africa, we find scarification at puberty, and rites of passage involving pain at or before marriage and other rituals. In Australia and New Guinea, circumcision and subincision form part of some rites. In India, sadhus suspend themselves by flesh hooks in the body, as do some of the North American tribes (e.g. the now illegal Oh-Kee-Pa ritual). In Java and other parts of Asia, there are many examples of piercing. And then there's Christianity.... The Christians seem to have cornered the market in self-flagellation, for which they devised many instruments. They also brought methods of torture to a fine art. Yet another way to integrate ritual and SM is ecstatic shamanism (a term coined by Fakir Musafar to describe the rôle of a facilitator, i.e. having experience leads to the ability to guide the experience of another).

These days, there appear to be three main reasons that people turn to SM spirituality. First: many people feel forms of alienation; from society, and from themselves. No one likes to feel cut off from his/her society, nor do most people like to feel that their head is wholly separate from their body. For these people, there is a void, and, for some, SM spirituality helps build the bridge across it.

Many of those who feel a void also find that everyday thinking results in a heavy, low state of being that involves thoughts of the past and future, but very little of the present, of simply *being*. Between these two states one can consider another state, of *doing*, but not yet simply being. The gap for these people lies between the weight of being a thinking entity to the lightness of one who simply *is*.

Second: Some feel disenchanted with organized religion. They disagree with the formalism and dogma associated with such structured worship and codified Gods and/or spirituality. They want to experience their God first-hand, by whichever route they feel is needed for communion with that God and/or the inner self. Alternatives to organized religion are becoming more common. If organized religion doesn't work, many are quite willing to try alternative paths to worship and internal spirituality, such as rituals of their own devising.

Often, ritual will involve the use of candles, percussive instruments (e.g., drums and sticks), and a goal or purpose for the ritual itself, to set the atmosphere. It can be regarded as high drama for those whose lives feel hard and dull, possibly lacking in eroticism. It can evoke very powerful moods, emotions, and motivations. For these people, ritual can provide empirical evidence of the sublime, in the way that others might go into rapture over a ballet or an opera.

There are three basic phases of ritual. Before the ritual, a person may feel that daily life is mundane and that there is something else to life:

the sacred and the profane. These two are alternate sides of the same coin, in that they are, literally, extraordinary: unlike the daily grind. In times past, spirituality and eroticism were inextricably linked (e.g., the Beltane fires in England), but today they appear to be separated. Many would like to bring them together again. The second phase of ritual is during the ritual itself. It is a liminal period, where a state of limbo and/or confusion may occur, and it might extend beyond the ritual. (If the ritual is an SM scene, it is important for the Top to ensure that there is clear communication with the Bottom at this point.) The final phase of ritual is a new state of being or awareness, where people describe a feeling of being connected to something beyond themselves; of some thing or some thought that can improve them and their lives; and of having learnt something more about themselves. It could be described as a new form of reality for that person.

The third reason for turning to SM spirituality is that, in the search for meaning in their life, some find that actual experience is more important to them than any form of rote or dogma. This could include forms of physical and/or mental testing, and ritual.

There is often an overlap between the three reasons for the search for spirituality. In the modern, western world, there are very few physical rites of passage that are also spiritual. Certainly, there are currently few organized, religious means to put a person into an state of altered consciousness.

There are many paths to SM spirituality. Sex and tantra (the use of sex, other forms of eroticism, and sometimes breath control to alter consciousness), scourging and/or flagellation, and blood control can be used alone or in combination to good effect. Blood control can include "body play" (another term coined by Fakir Musafar) with constriction, cutting, piercing, and/or puncturing the skin. Other paths include changing the body state, such as with breath control (controlling the intake and pace of intake oneself or by another), and chanting and singing. If carefully managed, masks, hoods, and gags can all be used in this context, and can lead to very powerful feelings and states. Dancing and drumming can also induce altered states, particularly if used with forms of breath control. Likewise, meditation and trance can alter states, but many people find it difficult to set aside the time. A trance state can be attained through dancing and drumming, and flagellation and blood control, and these may be an easier way than chanting "ah-oom" for hours at a time. (We know of some people who can reach trance states just by doing housework, so not everyone needs SM or religion to get there.) Exhaustion has been used as a path to spirituality, but it also takes time to get there this way. (It could also be very dangerous in an SM context, due to one's diminished concentration when in this state.)

The ceremonial sacraments can be used to attain an altered state. We are careful here to separate the term recreational drugs from drug initiation. Using the sacraments during ritual initiation is an advanced practice. It does not work well with *any* form of SM practice, because the person using the drug cannot properly assess the risks involved. Also, the "set" and "setting" (Timothy Leary's terms for the state of mind of the person using the drug and the environment in which the drug is taken, respectively) can drastically alter the effects of most drugs. This is particularly true for psychedelic drugs. If you involve a mind trip with the drug, you might end up with semi-permanent or permanent psychological damage. Please inform yourself well before you decide to use any ceremonial sacrament/drug. (The section on Mind Altering Substances has some more details on drugs and their use.)

Many use rites of passage and body play to attain their altered states. These can include contortion (gymnastics, yoga exercises, enlargements of piercings, stretching parts of the body like the labia, lips, or ears, cupping (suction cups on the back), high heel shoes, and foot binding); constriction (mummification, compression, ligatures, belts, tight clothes, body presses, and other forms of bondage); deprivation (food and/or senses, attention control, restriction of movement, isolation boxes, bondage suits, bags, multiple layers of clothing (this can be dangerous because you're playing with the homeostasis of the whole body), and sound and light deprivation); encumberment (the use of heavy objects like anklets, leg irons, etc. to restrict the person's movement); heat (sun tanning, electricity, baths, sweat lodges, branding, burning, etc.); penetration/invasion (flagellation, puncturing, piercing, spikes and skewers, tattoos, beds of nails, and ball dancing); suspension (by the ankles, wrists, etc., or by flesh hooks); and forms of sensory overload (light, sound, and mind fucks, all of which can cause the mind to shut off).

That's quite a list, particularly since they could all be mixed in varying quantities. Both those who enjoy SM and those who practice alternate spiritualities are likely to recognize or to have practised many of them. This easily accounts for much of the crossover from SM to spirituality and *vice versa*.

These activities can lead to ecstasy, which has been described by Terence McKenna as "a complex emotion containing elements of joy, fear, terror, triumph, surrender and empathy." Broadly, the states of ecstasy occur at the lowest level in the body (sensation), and proceed through the heart (catharsis), to the head (insight), where the greatest rewards tend to be found. Descriptions of physical ecstasy include self reward and feelings of extreme vitality and well-being. Catharsis from SM can cause forms of release and purification, and communion with one's partner or one's self. Many describe the rewards from insight as a powerful increase in knowledge and self knowledge, creativity, understanding, and further, intellectual communion.

The ecstatic states can provide positive loss of inhibition (also called boundary ecstasy), i.e. loss of personal limitations, fears, sorrows, desires, and attachments); loss of senses of time or place; loss of structured thoughts in the forms of words and images; and, ultimately, loss of the controlled self (also known as ego dissolution). There is a sense that all forms of boundaries are dissolving. At this point, the connection between the Top and Bottom is probably at its peak. These states can also lead to feelings of continuousness, such as unity, eternity, and heaven; communion with a higher power, with one's self, and possibly, with other worlds and times; catharsis is a release into pure feeling, often in the guise of salvation and freedom; and also joyous satisfaction. Other rewards include insight, in the form of knowledge and creative inspiration; feelings of death and resultant rebirth; an intense physical well-being; and a courage borne of an increased self-esteem.

There are quasi-physical experiences associated with ecstasy from SM play and spirituality. They have been described as a high; senses of light and dark; feeling changes of energy that make a person feel as though he/she is taking up the whole room, or has withdrawn inward with a sense of inner peace and calm; sensations of flowing; and "electric" feelings of tingling and being on fire.

With these rewards from SM activities during spiritual expression, it is no surprise that there are many who have crossed from SM play to spirituality and *vice versa*. As the last decade has progressed, we have seen more people integrating one expression into the other. Perhaps this is because they now feel freer to do so, in the same way that the rigour of the SM old guard is being replaced by a newer, more relaxed climate in the SM community, where people feel much freer to admit to being "switches."

That's 58, Madam!
Thank you, Madam!

THE BODY

Anatomy

In this section, we'd like to give you some idea of what lies beneath the skin and other coverings that the body may have at the time of play. We do not, however, intend to turn you into anatomists. We will look at the general construction of the human body, discuss plumbing apparatus, and the differences between men and women; then we'll go into an appreciation of the erogenous zones. Finally we'll consider the use of materials in the various aspects of play.

Suppose that you have had a good night (or day) of play and are feeling generally satisfied. As you ruminate over the activities, you suddenly discover at least one body part left over.... Where did you go wrong (assuming that it was not intentional)? To ensure that limbs don't go missing and that other injuries don't take place, some basic anatomy is essential before you start to participate in any vigorous activities.

One can appreciate the basic construction of the body from the illustrations, drawn from life (and death), by Andreas Vesalius in the 16th. century. Vesalius examined the human body (see Figures 4–1 and 4–2) to determine its construction and created a series of wood-cuts that, by stripping away the muscles and internal organs layer by layer, show the whole body.

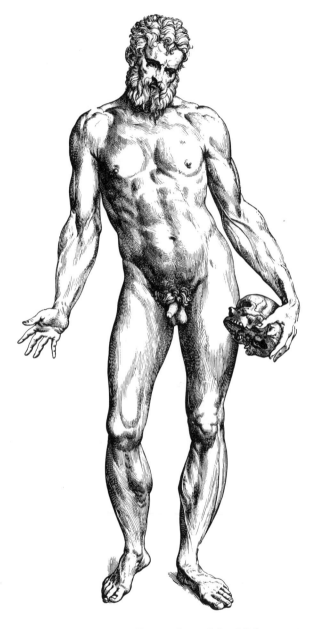

Figure 4–1.   Illustration of the Male

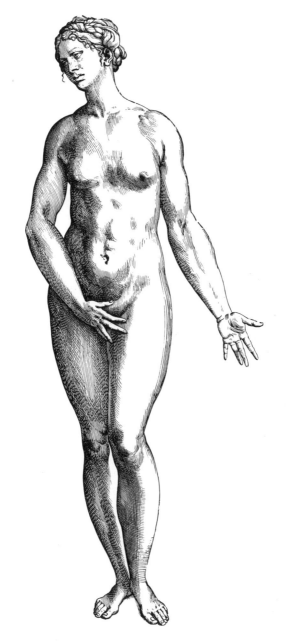

Figure 4–2.   Illustration of the Female

That's 61, Sir!
Thank you, Sir!

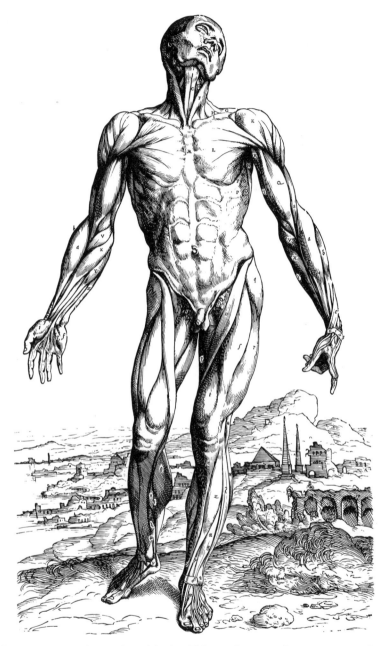

Figure 4–3.   The Body with the Skin and Fatty Tissue Removed

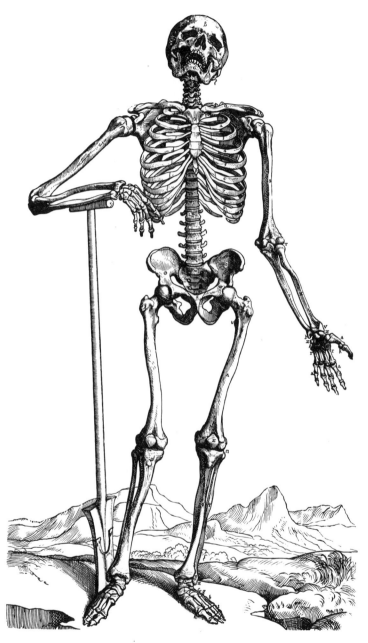

Figure 4–4. **The Skeleton from the Front**

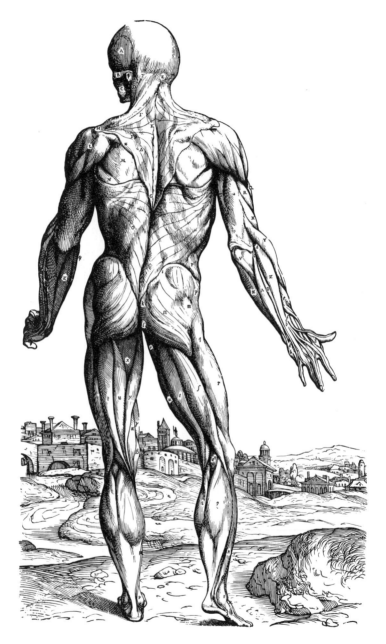

Figure 4–5. **The Body with the Skin and Fatty Tissue Removed**
(Rear View)

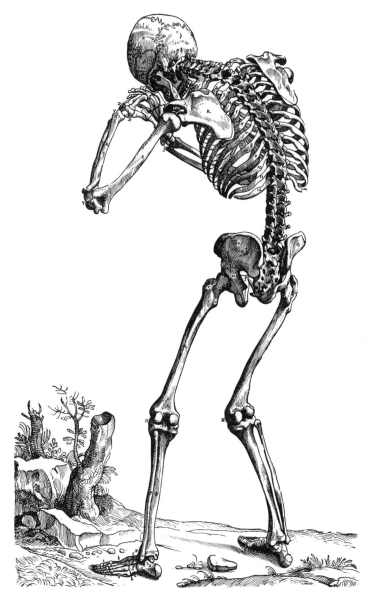

Figure 4–6.   The Skeleton (Rear View)

That's 65, Sir!
Thank you, Sir!

As a rough guide, the bones and muscles encompass and give some protection to the internal organs; the limbs are used for locomotion; and the head is for whatever thinking may go on....

The thorax is the region enclosed by the rib cage (see Figure 4–4). The thoracic organs are also protected by the shoulder blades (see Figures 4–6), by the spinal column, which is fairly strong, and by the overlying muscle, which tends to be fairly heavy and thick (see Figures 4–3 and 4–5). The thoracic organs include the lungs, the aorta (which is the major blood vessel leading from the heart), and the heart itself. The kidneys and the spleen are partially protected by the ribs but are below the diaphragm. The liver (see B in Figure 4–7) runs from about the nipple line to the rib margin on the right of the chest.

At the front of the body, the musculature, which in some people is quite heavy across the front of the chest, does afford quite a lot of protection. The breastbone is fairly solid, and the front of the rib cage affords good protection, but it opens as an inverted "V," exposing the soft parts of the belly (see Figure 4–3).

At the back , the important organs are the kidneys. Figure 4–7 shows the lower ribs broken and pulled back to reveal the middle and rear inside of the torso. As shown by T and V in the figure, about half of each kidney is above and half is below the bottom of the rib cage, so the bottom parts of the kidneys are not well protected. They are, therefore, vulnerable to injury from any blunt or penetrating force. The kidneys are also vulnerable because they are tightly attached to the back body wall. Blows in this area are transmitted *directly* to them.

The heart (see F in Figure 4–7) and lungs are completely encased within the bony thorax and, therefore, have added protection. The lungs rise to the top of the rib cage. The heart's right edge is just behind the breastbone and the left edge swings off in a shoe shaped area in the left of the rib cage. The point of the heart in the normal adult is just under the left nipple. The heart is protected by both muscle and bone, but it can be jolted (this is something that should be borne in mind during play).

The spleen (O in Figure 4–7) is an organ that can be readily ruptured. It is located on the left, between the lower three ribs, and so it is protected by bone all the way around. If a person has a viral infection of the spleen, such as "mono" (i.e. Mononucleosis), the enlarged spleen will descend below the ribcage and become exposed in the soft part

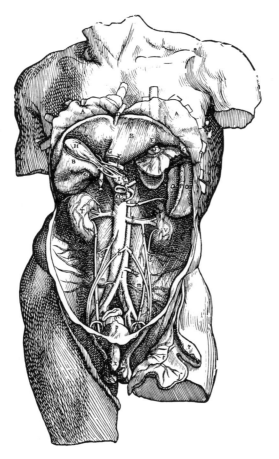

Figure 4–7. Dissection of the Torso, All Intestine and Partial
Stomach Removed

of the belly, thereby becoming vulnerable. So, if you whip with a
wrap-around whip, be careful to protect that area, because you may
be cutting into or bruising the soft tissue at the front of the body.

The abdomen (shown well in Figure 4–3) has a bit more, but not
much more, muscular protection than the back and encases organs
that move more easily over each other and that are suspended from
ligaments. They are not tightly attached to the abdominal wall,
which is why punches to the abdomen are safer than kidney blows
(unless, of course, there is an abdominal problem like an enlarged
appendix). The aorta, which is beside and in front of the vertebral

column (as shown in Figure 4–7), is usually well protected, unless there is a severe pulling force (not expected in, say, a flogging).

The brain has a thin bony covering, the skull; but the sense organs, such as the eyes and ears, are *very* vulnerable. Below, we'll look at some of the aspects of our activities and how they might affect the body.

Differences Between The Sexes

As far as SM play is concerned, there are not many areas in which the sexes differ. Women tend to have somewhat more fatty tissue (therefore they will bruise more easily), on average they have a little less muscle, their breasts need to be treated with more care than a man's, and the vagina is a great breeding ground for infections (but then, so is under the foreskin). In the experience of the authors and many players with whom we have talked, women (both heterosexual and homosexual) tend to be somewhat more aggressive at the physical and psychological levels than men.

Erogenous Zones

Any area of the body may be erogenous, but the tits, genitals, and the nine openings of the body tend to be more so, possibly because they tend to have more nerves around them. That is really all there is to say about erogenous zones. Everybody has them and everybody's are different. Finding them is the fun part....

Percussion

Implements used for percussion play can be broken down into their characteristics and the way they are used. No matter what is used or how it is used, it is important to avoid the joints and the eyes. (The joints are readily apparent in figures 4–4 and 4–6.) For more about types of percussion implements, and the resultant effects, please see the section on Whips, Paddles, Rods, & Other Percussive Toys.

Paddles

These can bruise deeply and transmit the forces of the blow well into the body. The only areas that would be appropriate to paddle would be the heavily muscled ones. The ass is a wonderful area for paddling. It is well protected by muscle and the pelvic bone. The only organ of any consequence in this area is the rectum, which is well protected by the layers of muscle.

Rods And/Or Canes

For rod work, the ass is a safe target. For light rod work, the musculature of the upper back is also a safe area. If the back is very heavily muscled (it will always be less so in the female) one can use rods with reasonable force (provided that this doesn't reach the bone-breaking level). The heavy mask of muscle in the trapezius, the rhomboid, and the latissimus muscles (N, M, and Δ in figure 4–5) is sufficient protection for the organs under this area of the body.

In terms of the limbs, the muscles at the back, front, and inside of the thigh are fairly heavy in the well developed individual. In those that are not well developed, there may be a lot of fat. Fat can be damaged by this form of activity. The cells can be ruptured, and there can be a lot of bleeding deep inside. Therefore, a note of caution is warranted here for the heavy fatty areas of the limbs, although this area is generally satisfactory for rod and paddle work. The buttocks are fine for rod work. Men can have the pectoral muscles worked on with rods but it is inadvisable to attempt this form of play with women.

Whips & Floggers

These have a short, sharp focus of energy on the skin, which may break the skin and cause deep bruising, depending on the nature of the whip, the force, and the technique used. Consequently, they should only be applied to the heavily muscled areas of the back and the ass. The areas to avoid are those in the lower back because of the distance that the kidneys extend below the rib cage. This implies that heavy tactile activity below the shoulder blades puts you at great risk of damaging the kidneys. As can be seen in Figure 4–6, the shoulder blades do not come down as far as one might expect. A leather weight-lifting belt does a fairly good job of protecting the kidneys.

As for rods and canes, when whipping women, avoid the breasts for all but the lightest surface work.

If the legs are not fatty, the areas between the joints, i.e. the thighs, the back of the thighs, and the calves are good areas for whipping provided that care is taken to be gentler to the smaller muscles. Make sure that the knees, behind the knees, the ankles, and the feet are properly protected from the whip.

Bondage

The important thing about bondage is that, depending on where the bonds are tied, how they're tied, and where the knots are placed, pressure is placed on the tissues underneath. You must avoid places where nerves or blood vessels are close enough to the surface of the body to be exposed to this sort of pressure.

One of the common areas for bondage is the wrist. The radial nerve, which ends here, runs down the thumb side of the forearm to supply the thumb (see Figure 4–8). If the bondage, such as rope or a metal restraint, is too tight around the wrist, within about twenty minutes the result will be a numb thumb. If the pressure has been applied for a few minutes, the numb thumb may last from a few days to a week, because the nerve has only been bruised, not permanently damaged, but the potential for permanent damage exists. If you do leave the bondage on and damage occurs, the numbness will *not* go away. When playing, remember to check periodically that there is sensation in the thumb; if not, loosen the restraint. Knots put extra pressure where they meet the skin, so they should not be put over the thumb side of the wrist. The front of the wrist (the less hairy side) contains a mass of tendons, one nerve in the centre, and arteries. Given the structures at the front of the wrist, it is a reasonable place to apply *some* pressure, but you should take care when putting bondage here.

The palm side of the hands is purely tendinous, and has no major nerves or blood vessels of consequence close to the surface.

Another pressure point is the ulnar nerve, which runs along the inner side of the elbow. It is moderately protected, being inside a bony groove of the elbow. It is referred to as the "funny bone." Numbness and weakness of the muscles of the hand will result from pressure to this, inner, aspect of the elbow.

If arms are held above the head, the major nerves and arteries to the arms, which pass deep in the hollow of the armpit, are exposed. If you apply pressure under the armpit, you're likely to cut off circulation and bruise the nerves to the arm. Inexperienced players often try to hang someone up by ropes passed under the arms. This will cut off circulation to the rest of the arms and hands. When you're going to wrap any form of bondage in this area, go around the top of the arm, not under it, where nerves, or blood vessels might be affected.

In the lower leg, there is a superficial nerve that runs around the top

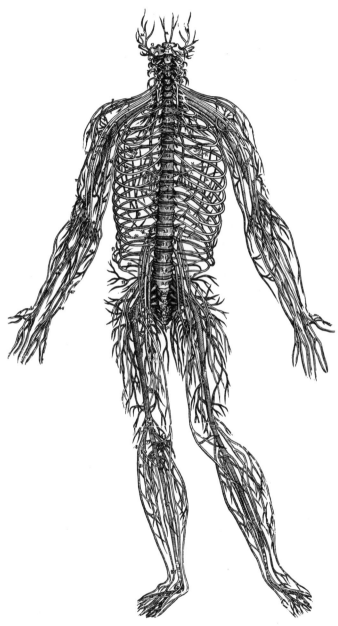

Figure 4–8.   Nervous Systems of the Body

That's 71, Sir!
Thank you, Sir!

of the fibula, the small bone just below the outer side of the knee (see Figures 4–4 and 4–6). If pressure is applied to this area, bruising of the nerve may occur and a "dropped foot" may result. This is because the nerve supplies the muscles of the foot and provides for sensation from the foot. The foot will be unable to be lifted. This condition could last for several weeks. Therefore, you should avoid pressure on the outside of the knee, just below the knee joint.

In the area of the groin, the major artery runs from the aorta to the leg and crosses the groin in the mid-point between the pubis and outer hip bone. The major nerve follows the same path. In the crease of the groin there are major tendons, but you're well away from nerves and blood vessels. This means you can put traction here. It may cause a lot of pain to the tendons, even a tendonitis, but you won't interfere with arteries or nerves in the front of the leg.

As we move around, we're fighting against gravity. When we walk, the leg muscles contract and work like pumps to force the blood through the veins from the lower limbs back to the heart. When we stay in the same standing position for a long period without moving the legs, blood may pool in them. Therefore, less blood returns to the heart, cardiac output falls, and blood pressure drops. As a result, the person may begin to feel light-headed or faint. This happens to some guardsmen on parade. There is a similar hazard when a person is put into vertical mummification. You should stay in contact with the person you're playing with, so that any dizziness or faintness can be dealt with immediately.

When a person is released from a mummification, pooling of blood may have occurred elsewhere in the body. The blood may not have returned to the heart, and, as the pressure of the bindings is released, the person may faint almost immediately. Therefore, it is wise, when finishing a mummification, to have the person horizontal, or at least be prepared to put them horizontal, otherwise the person may faint.

The trachea is a fairly firm structure and, unless you apply moderate to severe pressure, you probably won't reduce the air supply to the lungs. Note that this is true only for wrapping style bondage. If a collar is tugged from the back, that moderate to severe pressure is very easily achieved and the person will choke.

If you put a wrapping around the neck, before air supply restrictions due to impairment at the trachea become a problem, you're likely to run into blood supply problems due to impairment of the two major arteries to the brain. These arteries, the carotid arteries, are at the sides of the neck and have a sensor just below the angle of the jaw. It's called the carotid body. If pressure is applied to the carotid body, it may cause a marked drop in pulse rate to as low as 30 to 40 beats per minute and a marked drop in blood pressure, easily enough to cause a faint. Overall, be very careful when applying any restraints to the neck, particularly in the region of the jaw.

Insertional Activities

In the normal anatomy, behind the pubic bone is the bladder, which, when full, is in danger of being torn or ruptured (see B in Figure 4–9). Note that the bladder in the figure has been brought forward and to the left for clarity). If the bladder is empty, it is unlikely that you'll rupture it. If you're beyond the length of a finger during rectal activity, you're beyond the neck of the bladder and the prostate, up into the pelvic cavity which is much larger (see also Figure 4–4). This area can take larger objects or liquids as long as the rectal tissues will stretch enough to allow the object to reach that far.

Never, *ever*, insert a glass object of any kind up someone's ass, into the vagina, or into the penis. (The same applies to the more brittle plastics.) It might break. No matter how strong the glass, the muscles of the backside and rectum may be stronger. You can't afford that kind of risk under any circumstances.

Likewise, be careful of any metal object not specifically designed to go places few objects have ever gone before. Any sharp edges, even moderately sharp, can do a lot of damage to these sensitive areas; this includes fingernails. Note that chrome-plating has a tendency to flake off, if it is of poor quality or a bit old. (Remember cutting yourself on an old car bumper?) Chromium produces very strong, jagged, and very sharp edges. Also, remember that some people may have bad, allergic reactions to certain kinds of metal, e.g. copper or nickel. Stick to stainless steel or well chrome-plated toys.

The urethra is the passage from the bladder to the outside of the body. In women, it is very short, and straight. Behind the female bladder is the vagina, and deep in the vagina is the cervix, about one finger's length into the vagina. If you go beyond that, you may move the cervix and uterus around. The uterus is deep inside the pelvis.

In the male, the urethra starts at the tip of the penis and runs up to the prostate, where it does a right angled turn into the bladder. Insertional toys must be able to go around this corner without perforating the urethra or prostate. This is an important technique when catheterizing a man. So, if you want to catheterize a man, *learn from a medical practitioner before you start*. Note that catheterizing a man should *never* be painful. If it is, *stop*, and find out what is wrong.

The male rectum is behind the bladder, and below the bladder outlet is the prostate, a walnut sized organ in younger men which enlarges with age. Rectal activity within a finger's length into the rectum may interfere with the prostate and bladder, if the activity is vigorous.

Losing Objects in the Rectum

Anything inserted into the body should have an end large enough to prevent it entering completely into the body, or should have something attached to it so you to pull it back out of the body, should it enter completely. For example, your butt plugs should have a chain built into the plug, so that, if the rubber breaks, you can still pull the plug out of the ass. (This sort of plug seems to be more easily found in Europe than in North America. In North America, plugs tend to simply have large, flat ends.)

You may also be surprised at the size of some objects that have made their way up the ass. Someone who can take a fist to the wrist can take quite a lot of other things, too. Remember, Emergency Departments of hospitals have seen everything. It's one thing to experiment, but things do break and human tissue can tear.

"I'd like to speak in defence of the cucumber!" said the lawyer. He has a good point. There are many things, usually organic, that, if lost in the rectum, may not cause a problem. Softer ones, like hard-boiled eggs, may do little harm, but if a carrot snaps while up there, the edges at the break could easily tear the lining of the rectum.

If you lose something in the ass that will not cause damage by scraping the inner lining of the rectum, such as ass balls or a dildo without a pair of "balls," remember that the ass is designed to eliminate solid or semi-solid objects. In a panic, perhaps caused by losing an object in the ass, the human nervous system tends to shut down peripheral functions, such as bowel movement, causing the sphincter muscles to tighten. To help alleviate this problem, try to reassure the person containing the lost object, thereby switching those functions back on. We know it sounds terribly British, but "administer" a cup or two of tea. Tea stimulates bowel and bladder movement. Time and relaxation usually do the trick. What goes up, normally comes

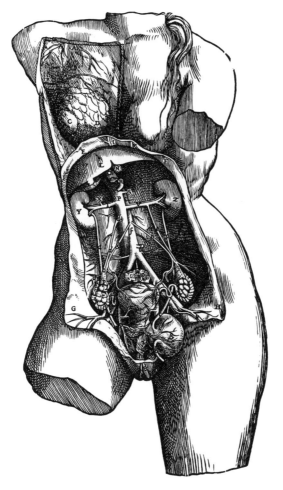

Figure 4–9.   Dissection to Show the Bladder

down. By the way, if it's something heavy like an ass ball that you lose, do not expel it over a toilet bowl. It will probably come out quite fast, and may shatter the bowl. Squatting over a folded towel is a good way. The act of squatting is a more natural position to take a shit, anyway, so it should be a bit easier on the Bottom.

If something breaks while in the ass, we recommend that you leave the task to the Emergency Department of your local hospital. Don't feel embarrassed going there. They've probably seen the same, or more exotic, before. And, yes, they may be chuckling about it for a few days. So what? At least you're in good hands there.

Pulling Objects Out of the Rectum Too Fast

Sometimes, when something put up the ass is pulled out too quickly, part of the rectum is pulled through the anus, i.e. outside the body. This is not too dangerous, but must be dealt with immediately. Very gently, with one clean finger, ease the rectum back into the body. Have the person lying, with legs supported, breathing slowly and deeply, with the mouth open, and the lower jaw relaxed. This helps to relax the sphincter. A little pressure may be required. Just be gentle; this is a very sensitive part of the body. Take care not to let a fingernail cut the rectum as you push it back. If the tissue is swollen, such as with piles, ice may help shrink the swelling. To allow the rectum time to recover, don't have any ass play for several days.

Tit Torture

Tits are wonderful things. They are a very sensitive area, full of nerve endings. They are of similar construction in the male and female, although the distribution of fat in the tit is slightly different in the sexes. In both male and female, there is a duct system and a glandular system behind the tit itself. In the female, the glandular system is much better developed and surrounded by a deeper layer of fat, thereby accounting for women's breasts. In the male the glands are rudimentary and they usually have less fat, although this will vary from person to person. The tit area is extremely sensitive, with many bare nerve endings, making it a wonderfully erogenous play area.

The female breasts should not be flogged at all if they have cysts. They can take a good deal of pressure (as any woman who has had a mammogram can attest), so wrapping them with rope is fairly safe.

We all know that women produce milk in their breasts, but so do some men. This can happen on its own, or as the result of stimulating the tit. This lactation is nothing to worry about. Many men who have had their nipples pierced lactate often after piercing.

Over a period of time and with heavy tit play, it is possible to abrade and break the skin over the nipple. Breaking the skin this way should be treated the same way that any other skin breaking/bleeding, since this is an open path to infection. If you're into pressure in this area, though, remember that it *is* possible to bruise the tits.

Both men and women can successfully have their nipples wrapped with string or dental floss, but be careful to ensure that the wrapping does not last so long that the tissue starts to die from lack of blood.

Cock & Ball Play

The cock and balls also have many nerve endings to provide a variety of sensations. An important thing to remember about the balls particularly is that the suspensory apparatus in the ball sack (scrotum) that keeps the balls at the right height can be stretched with ball stretchers. The suspensory apparatus comprises ligaments and a muscle (the cremasteric muscle). In the younger man, this muscle causes the ball to shoot up into the abdomen when one stokes the inside of the thigh. This is a juvenile reflex reaction that men lose as they grow older. During play when you're stimulating the inside of the thigh, it is possible that you will come across this reaction and see a "migrating" ball... (don't worry, it will come back down).

If one stretches the balls, stretch downwards *slowly*, gradually putting more traction on the balls. This allows the tissues, muscle, and the rest of the suspensory apparatus a chance to stretch. It may be a great sensation to violently grab the balls or put a very heavy weight on them quickly, but you may also damage them. Any of these activities are more fun done slowly and are much safer that way. Where the cock and balls are concerned, "slow and steady wins the race." Also note that the balls can be severely damaged by a kick, knee, or other sharp blow crushing them against the pelvic bone.

The cock is a good subject for play when it's flaccid, but as it hardens, it becomes easier to damage both the shaft and the head. The tissues in the shaft of the cock can be ruptured by piercing the shaft or by hitting an engorged cock too hard. For example, a pouch lined with pin-pricks can be very stimulating to a flaccid cock, but the pressure caused by the cock as it hardens could cause a pin-prick to puncture the skin, and even to rupture tissues inside the shaft.

A flaccid cock can take moderate whipping or slapping around; this is not true for a hard cock. A general rule is that an erect cock is more fragile than a limp one, even though it feels harder.

Electrotorture

Electricity is a subject that both scares and excites people. You cannot use any devices intended for household use. The power of most motors is great enough that severe bruising can be done to the body, should the motion be allowed near the body. Likewise, any electrical connections that could be made to the body may well cause enough of a shock to kill a person. So, stay well away from devices intended to be plugged in the wall outlet.

There *are* electrical devices that can be used for play. They are generally battery operated. (Devices like vibrators, teeth cleaners, and other similar devices are designed to be used in a particular fashion. Do not attempt to use them for activities for which they were not designed.) If you own a device to pass electricity through the body (Relax-A-cisor, TENS unit, etc.), check with someone knowledgeable in the field *before* you use it. Ensure that you understand the electricity being produced. (Alternating Current (AC) is very different from Direct Current (DC). Static electricity devices such as the Violet Wand produce only voltage, i.e. no current.) The electrical devices for use during play few because of the potential danger to the Bottom (and sometimes the Top).

All electrical play must be kept below the waist. This is because the brain and heart rely on very small electrical impulses to function. External electrical stimulation in the area of the brain or heart could disrupt their functions and rhythms, thereby creating havoc, so keep electricity well away from them. The heart can be *stopped* by an electrical current. The brain doesn't take too kindly to electricity either....

The *only* exception to the "below the waist" rule is the static discharge from the Violet Wand, because it produces no current. The Violet Wand produces a series of electrical discharges (similar to when you take off a wool sweater on a dry day). It can be used anywhere on the body *except* the eyes. The tissues of the face are too delicate to have those violent sparks near them. Be careful, also, of any metal piercings of the body. If the spark is left to work on the piercing, it will heat up the metal and burn the wearer. Likewise, do not leave the wand to work on the same area of skin continuously; it will cause a similar heating, sufficient to burn the skin (in effect, branding the person) at the time and cause a localized sunburn later due to the ultra-violet light coming from the sparks.

The sparks produced by the Violet Wand are so highly charged that they also react with oxygen in the air to produce a slightly metallic smell. This is due to the creation of ozone around the spark. It is wise not to breathe too much ozone (which has the ability to kill bugs in the same way that bleach does) because the oxidizing effect can also

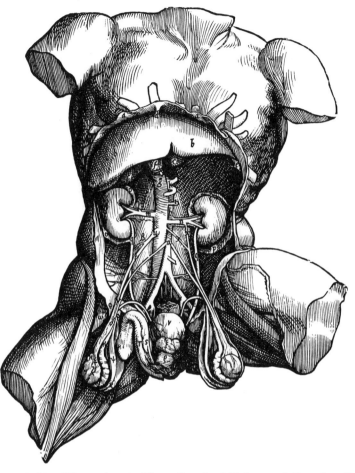

Figure 4–10. Dissection to Show Seminal Veins and Construction of Male Genitals

kill the *good* bugs in your nasal passages and lungs. For normal use of the Violet Wand, limit yourself to 5–10 minutes at a time, so that ozone does not become a problem.

Despite this being the section on the body, we have laboured long here on the safety of the devices themselves. This is because one small error could cause a great deal of damage. If you feel at all interested in this form of play, make sure that you get instruction from a medical practitioner or someone very skilled in electrotorture.

Scat, Watersports, & Raunch

Urine and stool tend to stay on the outside of the body, so there is really no *anatomical* safety consideration, other than where the person wants to have it put, i.e., don't piss in the eyes or mouth. Normal urine is bacterially sterile, unless the bladder, prostate, or urethra are infected (this will feel painful during urination). Shit is full of bacteria, viruses, and possibly parasites, so it is not sterile. Nor is any part of the body that has been in or around the rectum, penis, or vagina. These parts should not handle food nor be put into any bodily orifice during play. So, like your mother told you: wash your hands....

Urine is not necessarily virally sterile. Our research has shown that there are few studies of virus transmission through urine. HIV has been found in small quantities in urine, as has cytomegalovirus. It is likely that stomach acids will kill small quantities of these viruses, but not certain, so you must be prepared to accept the risk involved.

Temporary Piercing

Because the skin is meant as a barrier to most infection, it's fine to do what we do on the surface. The instant we pierce the barrier, the body is open to infection. The underlying tissues are sterile until you break the skin. They should stay sterile, even during play, so you have to pay attention to keeping everything that touches the pierced area absolutely sterile. So, safe piercing guidelines should always be followed by both the Top and the Bottom. (Please see the sections on Cleanliness & Disinfection and Blood Letting Toys.)

If you can pinch it, you can pierce it; *except* for the shaft of the penis and the balls. So, if you can get two fingers around it, you can stick a needle through it. Beginners often start with the loose skin at the front of the penis or the skin of the scrotum, but *not the balls or through the shaft*. The shaft has many nerves and large blood vessels, so don't poke holes in it. Scrotal skin piercings are often bloodless.

It is *extremely* dangerous to pierce the balls. It is a very, very advanced technique, only to be considered by those who have been properly taught. The balls must be *perfectly immobilized*, so that they will not move, no matter what you do. If the juvenile retraction of the ball occurs when the thigh is stroked during a ball piercing, the ball will be torn and greatly damaged. It will be a very unpleasant situation; definitely not the pain that anyone would find pleasurable.

Physiology (Response To Stimuli)

The body reacts to the stimuli its senses receive. This may at first seem obvious, but there are ways of stimulating the body that do not occur in everyday life that can be used to great effect during play. For instance, repeatedly and lightly touching any part of the skin, particularly something like a nipple, can sensitize it so much that the very slightest touch will cause a reaction far in excess of the usual one. Alternatively, you could sensitize the skin around someone's stomach while the person is lying face up, such that the merest touch to the stomach area will cause the person to arch violently off whatever he/she was lying on. The body is not used to this kind of stimulus and eventually it starts to produce endorphins to minimize the reactions to what now appear to be enormous stimuli (see below).

A general rule when playing is to ramp up your play slowly and then to ramp down. This gives the body time to react to what you do. It's like a warm up before you exercise. The body needs to be ready for what you are about to do to it. When you have finished playing, you should ramp down, much like cooling down after a workout.

In the sections on Pain and Play, we describe some of how the body reacts to what you do to it, so that you can use this knowledge to play creatively and safely.

Endorphins (Load & Overload)

Under normal conditions, the body is in a form of dynamic equilibrium. All systems are measuring what needs to be measured and maintaining the proper balance by secretion or inhibition of hormones, fluids, etc.. Even under normal conditions, the body continuously changes the amounts of hormones in the body.

When the body is under significant stress, the pituitary gland and hypothalamus produce hormones not normally needed. We've all experienced the rush of adrenaline that follows the initial shock of being suddenly frightened by something. Our heart beats faster, our breathing changes, and we know that we're better prepared for whatever we may meet. When the body is put under more long term stress, such as a marathon run, or long periods of stimulus (such as pain or the prolonged sensitizing of the skin), natural opioids, called endorphins, are produced. Like the synthetic opium derivatives, the endorphins bind to the opioid receptors throughout the central nervous system to block pain signals before they get to the brain.

Often, in SM play, one of the goals is to stimulate the body sufficiently for it to produce those endorphins, because, like the synthetic drugs, these natural drugs have the ability to make a person feel euphoric. Ask any marathon runner why it's called the "runner's high." The pleasure of the high for both runners and those who enjoy SM play is worth enduring what it took to get there.

Many athletes who push their bodies to their limits experience the endorphin highs, but, if they don't exercise for a week, they will probably experience forms of exercise "withdrawal." This may be explained partly by the simple underuse of a body that is used to being used, but it is likely that part of the reason is because the body has also become used to fairly frequent endorphin release. The symptoms of withdrawal can usually be overcome by exercising again or reducing the amount of exercise to a level that does not cause endorphin release as often or in the same quantities as before.

To our knowledge, it is not possible to overdose on one's own endorphins. By the time you get to that point, you'd probably be well past unconsciousness…. A Top, however, should try to recognize when the Bottom has reached the point of endorphin release, because the Bottom may not be in a state to realize that the pain now being easily endured may too much for his/her body. This is the point at which the Top should start to wind down the scene.

Pain

The body reacts to stimuli in as many ways as there are stimuli, and different people react differently to the same stimulus. For example, some people love to be tickled, other hate it; some like to be whipped, others don't. There are several levels of stimulus to the body that are distinguishable by the way in which the brain interprets them. They are described below.

Sensation of Touch

Anything from blowing gently on the skin to a gentle caress to being firmly grabbed would fall into this category. By slowly simulating the same area of the skin, it is possible to sensitize it to the point that the very slightest touch will cause a large reaction in the recipient. It is possible to reach the point where the recipient is sufficiently sensitized that any more stimulus will cause the release of endorphins in the body to minimize reactions to the stimuli. We will have loaded the sensory systems to the level that they are overloaded, and that overload is what triggers the release of the endorphins. The result is a feeling similar to the "runner's high," which is no more than a reaction to the endorphins released due to the stress of a long run. By sensitizing the skin sufficiently by simply touching it, we can cause the same reaction that is caused by forms of physical stress.

As the stimulus becomes more forceful, the sensation is still that of touch until we reach the threshold of pain.

Threshold of Pain

When the stimulus is great enough and, sometimes, quick enough, we interpret the sensation as pain. It is usually a warning that the body has arrived at the point that, if the stimulus is maintained for a time, damage may be done. If the stimulus is maintained, endorphins will be produced, but this time they will probably be produced more quickly. Again, the endorphins will serve to minimize the sensations somewhat, so that the body can endure more for longer. And the "high" or euphoria produced by the endorphins will be the same.

It is not necessary for damage to be done to produce the endorphins using pain, so one *can* arrive at the point of endorphins release quite safely, depending on the form and level of play.

Relief

How does one describe the feeling that results from the release of the endorphins? If you've had it, you know the pleasurable experience that it is. If not, you may want to consider putting your body through what is necessary to get there. This could be running to get the "runner's high," or SM play to get a similar feeling. The advantage of SM play is that you used your fantasies to get there.

Agony

Agony is the reaction to serious, damaging pain. It will likely cause the release of endorphins, but they may not be enough to keep the pain to a tolerable level. If the agony lasts long enough, the body will go to its next level of defence to excessive stimuli: unconsciousness.

Unconsciousness

When unconscious, our brain does not have to deal with the pain, and the body will do what it can on "autopilot." This is not a good state to be in, mainly because it reduces to almost zero the ways in which a person can escape from the source of the pain. But it is the body's last level of defence. If the stimulus continues to the next level, the likely result is not one any of us would like to contemplate.

Death

What's to be said? If you get roughed up too much, this is probably where you'll end up.

Agony, unconsciousness, and death are places psychotics put people.

They have nothing to do with safe, sane, and consensual SM play.

PLAY

So this is what it's all about? Well, maybe. We intend to cover the mechanics of play here, rather than the safety aspects. What, if any, is the sequence of events that must happen for successful play? Are there cues and responses that will help ensure successful play? What could we put it place to help things along?

Most good play will provide stimuli to the brain of both the Top and the Bottom at such speeds that the conscious mind will rarely be able to perform an analysis of it at the time. Nor is anyone likely to want to *at the time*; because we're usually far too engrossed in the fun we're having. The first time people play with each other, the chances are that the scene, while exciting, will not reach the heights everyone would like. When we play, we have to provide some kind of feed-back to our partner about what really turns us on, so that we can have the best scene possible. This may be done consciously or unconsciously. As players get to know each other better, the cues passing between them become more easily read and, possibly, more subtle. Eventually, a couple might become like a soloist playing an instrument: the Top is a highly skilled musician able to exact the most exquisite music from a favourite instrument, the Bottom. Doubtless there is potential for the reverse to be true; in the case of a dominant Bottom, for example. The cues and responses ultimately become a smooth, subconscious flow of energy between the players. This is when the really exciting scenes take place.

Responses to stimuli in either direction can be regarded as cues to the other player(s). They come in many forms and to all five of the senses. They can be used to heighten the anticipation of an action, and the lack of cues can be used to enhance the element of surprise.

Guy Baldwin, International Mr. Leather, 1989, has described play of all forms in the following manner: Cue, Stimulation, Assimilation, Recovery from stimuli, and, back to Cue, to complete the circle. What do these words really mean? In short, both players have to react to each other. The Top will always have to be aware of the state of the Bottom (i.e. be able to read the cues coming from the Bottom) in order to know when is the right time for the next action. Once a stimulation has been given by the Top, the Bottom has to assimilate it and then recover enough from it to be ready for the next stimulation.

All the five senses are involved in any play unless you decide to deprive the Bottom (or the Top) of one or more of those senses. Indirectly, they are likely to remain present; for example, the mind can fill in quite a lot of the blanks with the ears when the eyes have been blindfolded.

While it's not something that anyone would want to do *during* a scene, we feel that an analysis and understanding of the mechanics of play can only help to enhance the scenes we enjoy. In the rest of this section, we will to look at the various types of stimuli, the possible cues that could come from them or be used to occasion them, and the potential sequences of events involved.

After the discussion of the cues and simulations, we'll discuss how the levels of play change during a scene. Generally, you should start off slowly, reach the height of play for a certain period, and them "ramp down" out of the play back to everyday life.

Cue

One way to ensure that the scene continues for as long as both of you have the time and energy is to ensure that the stimulation only comes when the Bottom is ready. To do this the Top must be able to very accurately read the Bottom, the movements of the body, the sighs and groans, and all of the other means to know when the time is right. It may help if the Bottom consciously gives a cue to the Top, within the context of the scene, that indicates readiness for more of the same, less of the same, or none of the above.

The way in which the Bottom signals the cues to the Top will vary from scene to scene and person to person. We're going to break down some of the potential cues that could come from the Top or Bottom into the five senses so that you have an idea of which cue may be appropriate to which form of play.

Aural Cue

If you have a gag in your mouth, it's going to be pretty difficult to recite the alphabet, let alone say what you want. If the gag is loose, though, you'd be amazed what can be said and understood. (Have you ever wondered how your dentist understands you, when your mouth is jammed with instruments?) Sometimes, the vocalized reaction will be in the form of grunts and groans (or whatever), rather than words. They take many different forms; some expressed in pain, others in ecstasy. Try to vocalize your responses to the Top as much as possible, so the Top will gauge whether more or less is required (or deserved). If you're in a verbal abuse scene, the volume of the voice or crying may be the needed cue.

On the part of the Top, it may be appropriate to provide some form of sound as the cue to the Bottom that the next stimulation is coming, maybe even as a teaser. The Bottom can then brace for it. This use of anticipation can be a particularly effective form of play. The Top can see the reaction when the Bottom knows that something is about to happen. The opposite can also be true, to provide an element of surprise when the stimulation actually occurs.

Visual Cue

The Bottom may give visual clues to the Top about when he/she is ready for the next stimulation. This could be in the form of body movement or position, or maybe just the position of the hand would be enough. Basic body language is something that, even in everyday life, we have generally come to be very good at interpreting. This skill is very useful during a scene. The Top should be sure to use the body language of the Bottom as a good indication of whether and when to provide the next stimulation. In scenes where the Bottom can see the Top, the Bottom should be sure to react to the body language of the Top. Often, we provide and read body language subconsciously. It's probably best to let this happen, and go with the flow of your instincts.

That's 87, Sir!
Thank you, Sir!

Tactile Cue

If your play involves the partners touching, maybe a leg rubbed up against the Top is going to be a useful way to tell the Top that you're ready for more. Grabbing your partner harder or releasing your grip could be the cue the Top needs to proceed.

The Top may just gently touch the Bottom immediately before the next stimulation is to occur. This can put an element of anticipation into your play.

Oral Cue

There are not many oral cues that we can think of, except the verbal ones covered above. This is not to say that feeding the Bottom something pleasant (or unpleasant) could not be used as a form of cue of something else about to happen. A Bottom who sticks his/her tongue out to a Top may just be asking for a spanking.... You'll probably find some oral cues to prove us wrong.

Nasal Cue

The Bottom might use a form of sniffing as the cue, although that may be considered as an aural cue to the Top. Of course, this nasal cue could be irrelevant: if the nasal cue to the Top were an odour, it might just tell the Top that the Bottom shit his/her pants!

The Top could use smells as the way to tell the Bottom to expect the next stimulation, which might even be other smells, depending on the scene.

Stimulation

Once the cue has been given by either the Bottom or the Top, the stimulation itself occurs. This is the part of play that most people associate with SM. There is no particular reason for this stimulation to involve pain, however. A feather is a particularly effective way to torture someone.

Below we present some of the very many ways to stimulate your partner.

Aural Stimulation

Music is an effective aural stimulation. Either as a background to play, or as a foreground way of making life unpleasant for the Bottom. Have you ever tried to play Country and Western to someone who hates it? Wagner to someone who likes Easy Listening? You'll drive them nuts. (In one James Cagney film, he played a Coca-Cola executive captured by communists, and in which they try to get the formula from him. He is bound to a chair and forced to listen to a 78 r.p.m. record of "Itsy-Bitsy Teenie-Weenie Polka-Dot Bikini" played with a hole drilled off-centre. Pure torment!)

In verbal abuse scenes, the stimulation would be the next bout of abuse and/or humiliation.

One can use sound to confuse the Bottom as to what is happening, where he/she is, or where the people around him/her are situated. We know of one very effective scene where the Bottom had been made to think that there was broken glass under him as the ropes suspending him were being cut one by one. In reality, there was no danger of him falling on the glass because of the way things had been set up, but the effect on his brain was quite complete.... He describes it (with some relish) as one of the most memorable and intense scenes he has ever had.

Note that total silence can also be used effectively as a cue: for surprise or anticipation.... Equally, depriving someone of their sense of hearing can be very erotic. This could be combined with deprivation of other senses, such as taste and sight in the case of a hood which may to lead form of disorientation in the Bottom. Be careful under these circumstances at the end of a scene to bring the Bottom gently back to the "real world" at the end of the scene. It's very possible for a Bottom to lose the sense of balance and place while under such sensory deprivation. To be brought back to "reality" too quickly may prove both physically and emotionally dangerous.

Visual Stimulation

A hot man or woman in leather (or lace) is a pretty good visual stimulation for many people.

Visual stimulation usually tends to be done during the set up of play. Images are very important to some people. During play, however, visual stimulation, such as forms of deprivation and confusion, is very effective. For example, it is possible to buy glasses (more like goggles, really) that have prismatic lenses. This should confuse a Bottom quite nicely. The Bottom may end up having no idea of which way is up, down or left and right. Colour is also effective; you could keep changing the colours seen by the Bottom's eyes if you rigged things well enough. Different colours to each eye, perhaps?

A couple of safety checks before you play with visual stimuli are appropriate. First, check if the Bottom needs to wear corrective lenses, even for the anticipated scene. Second, if the Bottom has a history of abusing psychedelic drugs, make sure that such a scene will not set the Bottom into a flashback episode.

Epileptics can suffer seizures from flashing lights, so you would do well to check with your Bottom before this kind of scene.

Tactile Stimulation

This is where most of the stimulation during play happens. Whips, electricity, knives or fire (both potentially *very* dangerous), soft cloths, toothpicks, chains, feathers, mouthwash (if the Bottom is a recovering alcoholic/addict, be sure to use mouthwash containing no alcohol), catheters, forks, butt plugs, sterile needles, strawberry jam, paddles, fingers, tit clamps, hands, spoons, feet, boots, vibrators, etc.. You name it, we've seen it used.

Probably the most important implements you will use for tactile stimulation are your hands. These can slap, punch, caress, pinch, abrade, flick, squeeze, stretch, etc.. Your feet can do many of the things that your hands can, if you let them. And the mouth, lips, and teeth can also do about as much.

All of the above can be used in many situations and at many levels of stimulation. For instance, a feather is generally recognized to be an implement of gentle stimulation, but even the smallest feather can be turned around to use the sharp end. At this point, it works like the end of a toothpick, and, pushed onto a tit, cock, or labia can be quite painful. Most of your play will involve ramping up the level of stimulation to a peak and then bringing it down again. This may mean that you use different forms of your chosen implement, say, small whips up to bull whips and back again.

Technique will always provide more fun than the brute force and ignorance method. Learn how to get the best out of your toys. Play with them safely in ways they may not have been intended. After all, as you can see from the list above, a lot of the toys were never intended for sex play. For example, whips normally intended for animals with thick skins require a lot of practice on inanimate objects before being used on a person. Otherwise, you may inflict unintentional pain and cause unintentional damage.

For such things as an "abrasion trip," it seems that less is more. You may find that a far greater response can be produced with a lighter touch. Maybe this is due to the anticipation of pain by the Bottom.

Tactile stimulation can be violent in the case of a whip, or soothing in the case of caressing, or merely a touch. Some of the variations and their effects are covered in the section on Pain.

We hope that this has given you a few ideas to start off your creative juices, and you have a better idea of the care you need to take with anything you've not used in play before.

Oral Stimulation

A gag is a stimulation can help to ensure that the Bottom does not damage teeth or tongue during a scene. The taste and temperature of what is put into the mouth may form part of play. Care should be exercised in any gagging activity to ensure that the Bottom does not suffocate or regurgitate.

Certainly, forcing a Bottom to drink and hold the resultant urine during play as a form of control, can be used with prior mutual consent. Please see the sections on Scat, Watersports, & Raunch for safety when drinking urine.

When using gags, never put a dry rag or handkerchief in the mouth. It rapidly makes the mouth dry and cause unnecessary discomfort for the Bottom, who may gag at the dryness. It is also very easy to push a cloth too far into the mouth, causing the Bottom to gag. If the Bottom vomits under these circumstances, he/she may well suffocate in his/her own vomit, if the cloth is not removed as he/she gags.

Olfactory Stimulation

Smells, both bad and good, form stimuli in that they can give clues to what is about to happen to the Bottom. A snuffed match could be a clue to the Bottom that the scene will involve hot wax or fire.

Assimilation

Once the stimulus is given, the Bottom needs time to deal with it, understand what it was, and how he/she feels about it. This process will vary considerably depending on the type of stimulation and the person involved. The assimilation period may be almost instantaneous, or take a while longer.

Assimilation of Aural Stimuli

It could very well take a while for a Bottom to fully assimilate parts of a verbal abuse scene. The full effect of the abuse will have to sink in and have its effect. Conversely, a simple "Stop!" or "On your knees!" can be assimilated in a matter of a second or two.

If you've decided to use a sound as a precursor to the actual stimulation to follow, i.e., as a cue, remember that the sound, too, must be assimilated to have its best effect.

High sound levels may not only leave a ringing in the ears, but also could be damaging.

Assimilation of Visual Stimuli

Given the limited nature of visual stimuli during play, it should be fairly evident from the above description of visual stimuli that, generally, assimilation will be quick.

This may not be the case when you've designed the stimuli to confuse the Bottom. If you've found a pair of inverting glasses that make everything appear upside down, you should make allowances for the Bottom to adjust to them (but maybe not sound like you are…). Just be careful that the Bottom does not experience something like vertigo and fall over as a result. This could be quite dangerous. If you see a strange reaction in your Bottom, do something about it immediately. Lots of people don't even like blindfolds, let alone playing around with their vision in this manner.

Assimilation of Tactile Stimuli

The subsection on Pain in the section on the Body deals with the medical aspects of the body's reaction to tactile stimulation. Here, we're going to look at the way the body and brain take in and assess the stimulation that just occurred. It's going to take a lot more to assimilate a crack of a whip than a simple touch with a hand. If the skin has been sensitized, however, even the slightest stimulation may take a lot to assimilate.

If you change the form of the stimulation suddenly, this will also take a while for the Bottom to get used to. A piece of lambskin touched lightly to buttocks that have been whipped for the last hour could be quite a shock to the Bottom. The Bottom would have to work out what it is, and discard any fear that it might hurt too much. Different people have different thresholds of pain and sensation. Bear this in mind as you play. Fred may be able to take the bull whip full force, but John can only take light taps with a paddle. John may not come back for more if you use the bull whip on him. Likewise, Fred may not come back if all you do is tickle him. The aim is to make it fun for both of you. If you find that the two (or more) of you are incompatible, then just accept that and bow out gracefully. It's nobody's fault.

Seemingly innocent things such as feathers, even when used on unsensitized skin, can produce reactions that take a long time to assimilate. We know of one place to use a feather very lightly that produces a reaction that won't go away for about two minutes, even if the area is rubbed vigorously. If the Bottom doesn't know what is happening, he/she may have trouble assimilating the sensation.

Assimilation of Oral Stimuli

There is generally little to assimilate in the case of oral stimuli. If a gag is used it will be relatively obvious to the Bottom that that is what has been placed in the mouth. Food and drink, such as a Bottom being force-fed liquid, will also take little to assimilate.

Oral stimuli in the form of tastes may be assimilated quickly or they may not: consider the cases of, say, lemon juice or chilli peppers... or something the Bottom really dislikes.... Most "tasting" is actually performed by the nose, so, if you want the Bottom to taste something, it's generally best to leave the nose open (bitter tastes, however, are usually detected by the tongue, not the nose).

If you're going to give liquids that contain alcohol to a Bottom, be very aware that you, as Top, are the cause of the Bottom's losing some ability to assess risk. For this reason, we recommend that you do not administer alcohol during a scene.

Many practitioners of SM adamantly oppose the use of any mind- or mood-altering substances, including beer, before and during a scene, since any amount of such substances may compromise the player's ability to comprehend the circumstances or to communicate clearly as the scene progresses. Please see the section on Mind-Altering Substances for more on this subject and why the authors recommend abstaining from such substances during play. Also, if the player is a recovering alcoholic/addict, no mind-or-mood-altering substances should be part of the scene.

Assimilation of Olfactory Stimuli

As for oral stimuli, assimilation of stimuli to the nose may be relatively quick and easy for the Bottom. A smell is a smell; and, after a while, the mind and nose cease to react to a continuing smell, even if it's strong and repugnant.

Recovery

Recovery from Aural Stimuli

The Bottom may not recover from music that he/she doesn't like. Poor thing. It's not serious. The Bottom will just have to live with it.

In a verbal abuse scene, the level of the stimulus may vary, as will the recovery period. It is quite possible to really upset the Bottom to the extent that the scene may have to pause for quite a while or even stop. This form of play can be very tricky to do well, and should be treated with a fair amount of caution.

Be careful, also, with any aural stimulus designed to confuse the Bottom. The Bottom may lose balance, or even be utterly unable to continue because of confusion and disorientation.

If the aural stimulation is very loud, not only could recovery take a long time, but permanent damage can occur. Care should be exercised when playing music or other sounds through headphones to the Bottom to ensure that this does not happen.

Recovery from Visual Stimuli

As for aural stimuli designed to confuse the Bottom, visual stimuli that confuse should be treated with the same care. It would be very easy for a Bottom to fall over if he/she had little idea of up and down or left and right.

The use of colour may not need any time for recovery since it is just another form of mild stimulation.

If you use flashing lights, however, be very careful to avoid the lights flashing at four times or seven times per second. These frequencies can have the same effect as a *lot* of alcohol. They are the resonant frequencies of the brain. Not only can they produce a drunken reaction, flashing lights can cause epileptic seizures in some people. Be prepared for any sudden reaction in the Bottom if you use flashing lights. Stop the lights *immediately*, and remove the device that caused the effect, so that the Bottom can see "real life," if he/she wants to.

Recovery from Tactile Stimuli

A heavy stroke from a whip will take a while to be assimilated, then the body has to recover and calm down from the pain. This recovery period will allow the Bottom to fully experience the next stroke. If the Bottom is still recovering from the last stroke when the next one comes, he/she may end up experiencing a sensory overload, which may require that the scene be stopped.

We've seen some people take a cattle prod on the rump and not even notice it. Most people react so violently that they'd jump a few feet into the air or across the room. Let the Bottom recover properly from each stimulus. You'll know when this has happened because of the cue that follows from the Bottom (see below).

Recovery from tactile stimuli will depend on many things, for example, how the Bottom is feeling that night, what instrument is used to administer the stimulus and how the Bottom likes it, and at what stage of the scene the stimulus arrives. It is possible to give (or receive) a very strong stimulus, stronger than could have been borne at the beginning of a scene, after a scene is well under way. This is because the nerves of the Bottom will have adjusted with the aid of endorphins to the load and overload being put on them. The body can adjust to the level of stimulus, within reason, using those Oh-so-sought-after endorphins, but it does take some time for this to happen. The Top should be sure to let the Bottom recover enough to receive the next stimulus.

Recovery from Oral Stimuli

There is little to recover from when a gag has been put into the mouth. When a Bottom has been forced to drink or eat, it may take a little getting used to on their part to get the liquids or solids down. Playing with different pleasant and unpleasant tastes may be an interesting form of play, but some tastes tend to linger in the mouth (such as spices). It may require a lot of creativity to keep a taste scene going. Textures could also be used in the mouth.

Recovery from Olfactory Stimuli

The nose tends to get used to smells that are sent its way. This means that, unless the stimulus is very strong or poisonous, the nose will not smell a given stimulus after a few minutes. Therefore, nasal stimuli are best used in short doses.

Cue

After the recovery we come back to the beginning. The Bottom gives the Top a cue that the next stimulus can come. This cycle continues for as long as the play. During the play, the intensity of the stimuli will vary, usually increasing to a peak and then diminishing, but every time the cue, stimulus, assimilation, recovery, and cue sequence will be repeated.

Ramping Up & Down

A scene may start with nothing more than a glance across the dinner table or bar, or it may be the opening of the playroom door. This moment is like putting a car into first gear. You've started from a standstill, and now you're on your way. One by one, you're going to go through the gears until you're in top gear and the scene is humming along to the satisfaction of both of you. At this point, with luck and a bit of experience, communication between the players is instinctive and you can stay cruising along in top gear for quite a while. Like any car, however, a scene needs to come back down through the gears. In both cases, to slam on the brakes would be a jarring experience.

Some experienced players are able to drop into neutral after they have reached top gear, rest a little, and then continue from where they left off. We know of one Bottom who is fully aware of his surroundings during a scene and has often given a quick humorous quip to those who were watching the scene and whispering comments. He then goés straight back to the highest level of the scene (his back is usually quite raw by this point). For most people, a scene will be like going up and then down through the gears. At the top of a scene the Bottom, and probably the Top, will be on a form of "high" that was not induced by drugs. Often, it is this feeling for which the scene took place to start with. For the Bottom, part of this feeling may be due to any endorphins released during the scene.

If the Bottom's body does have endorphins rushing around in it, time will be needed to flush them out. So, a ramping down phase to your play is advisable to ensure that the body, let alone the brain, of the Bottom is not left wondering what happened as the stimuli were suddenly removed. Also, the process of coming back down through the gears should not be so quick that the high and the feelings of closeness generated by the scene are lost. Generally, all that is required to ramp down is a controlled reduction of the intensity and/or frequency of the stimuli given by the Top.

The state of warmth and closeness can remain for quite a while. At this point, the Top will have to ensure that good care is taken of a fatigued Bottom. It will seem like a form of spell to the Bottom, and this spell should not be broken by mundane chat. The spell is borne of the great intimacy that you will probably be feeling. For some Bottoms, this can be frightening, so, at this point of the scene, the Top should make sure to be there for the Bottom. If one partner breaks the spell, it can be a jarring experience for the other. The other may feel unwanted and stupid for having been there at all. Almost all of us have felt that let down as our partner has suddenly left for another, more pressing engagement, just as we were in need of sharing some intimacy after a scene. It's not a lot of fun.

This intimacy bonds people, SM players included, to each other. It creates moments that we can and should savour.

SAFETY

This section is, by far, the largest section of the book. Not without reason. Our intent in producing the book was to provide the reader with as comprehensive a collection of basic data as we could find, but at a level that made it easily digestible. The subsections are ordered to lead the reader through the aspects of safety, but are constructed to allow the text to be used as a reference, if required.

In matters of medicine, you should use the contents only as a guide, and in no way as a replacement for a visit to your physician. We hope that the contents will help you determine when a visit to your physician is necessary. When in doubt, go to see your physician....

If you can think of anything we missed, please fold them into your play, and then tell us about them so that we can update future editions of the book.

Hygiene

Like so many things, the ability to prevent transmission of disease depends on knowledge of the opponent. Prevention requires an understanding of the infection and a knowledge of techniques to minimize the risk of transmission. Reacting to a disease caught is of little value when *pro*-actively taking steps to avoid transmission would have avoided it in the first place. This section is about prevention: knowing the enemy and understanding the best defence.

Sexually Transmitted Diseases

In the text that follows we hope to give you an overview of the possible diseases that you can catch as a result of accidents or careless play. We have attempted to cover only the major sexually transmitted diseases (STDs), and for each one, we have given a brief summary of the disease, how it is caused, symptoms and signs, prognosis for the infected, and a very brief summary of prevention and treatment of the disease.

For some people, this section may be the hardest part of the book to read. This is partly because, for the sake of completeness, we have used the full medical terms for the diseases and organisms. If you're reading this section for general information, we'd suggest that you don't pay too much attention to the exact technical words, just try to get a better understanding of the disease and its symptoms.

This section should in no way replace a visit to your physician when you suspect that you may have caught an STD. We just want to provide you with a better understanding of the potential diseases, how to avoid them, and the long-term consequences. Where possible, we have also tried to clear up misconceptions that we have encountered in the population as a whole.

STDs range from the very annoying but not particularly dangerous afflictions such as crabs and scabies, right up to the potentially fatal Human Immunodeficiency Virus (HIV). The incidence of STDs, among the most common communicable diseases in the world, steadily increased from the 1950s to the 1970s, but stabilized during the 1980s. Diseases such as non-specific urethritis, trichomoniasis, chlamydial infections, genital candidiasis, genital and rectal herpes and warts, scabies, pediculosis pubis, and molluscum contagiosum are probably more prevalent than the five historically defined venereal diseases: syphilis, gonorrhœa, chancroid, lympho-granuloma venereum, and granuloma inguinale. Because the former group is not formally reported, however, incidence figures are not available. For gonorrhœa, it is estimated that the world-wide incidence is greater than 250 million cases per year, and more than 3 million in the U.S.A.. For syphilis, the world-wide estimate is about 50 million people per year, with about 400,000 people needing treatment in the U.S.A.. Other infections, including salmonellosis, giardiasis, amœbiasis, shigellosis, campylobacter, hepatitis A, B, and C, and cytomegalovirus infection, are sometimes sexually trans-mitted. Strong associations between cervical cancer and herpes viruses and papillomaviruses have been discovered. Since 1978, an epidemic virus, HIV, has spread rapidly though western society and Africa. This is certainly not an exhaustive list, but, as you can see, there is reason for caution when you play.

STD incidence has risen despite advances in diagnosis and treatment that rapidly render the patients noninfectious and cure the majority. Some factors influencing this paradox include changes in sexual behaviour, e.g. widespread use of contraceptive pills and devices; more varied sexual practices, including oral-genital and rectal contact; emergence of strains of organisms less sensitive to antibiotics; symptomless carriers of infecting agents; a highly mobile population; a high level of sexual activity in some homosexual men; *ignorance of the facts by the public and physicians*; and reticence of patients to seek treatment from their physician.

STD control depends on having facilities for diagnosis and treatment; tracing and treating all sexual contacts of the patients; continuing to observe those who received treatment to ensure that they have been cured; educating physicians, nurses, and the public; counselling patients about responsible behaviour; and developing methods for producing artificial immunity against infection. It's not an easy task.

For women, the most common STDs are often lumped under the term "vaginitis," which simply means an infection of the vagina. In some women (and men, where it causes urethritis and prostatitis), this is a minor discomfort. In others, there will be discharge, burning sensations, odour, body pain, and/or general malaise. If it goes systemic, you'll probably feel terrible. Vaginitis can be caused by any number of agents. Some are caused by yeasts (fungi). Others are bacterial. Some are even caused by parasites. This is also true for men. Men can catch the same infections, with or without symptoms. Sometimes the symptoms are different for the sexes. Vaginitis, like viruses, can be passed from men to women, women to men, men to men, and women to women.

Any time there is an exchange of bodily fluids that may contain the infectious agent, risk of infection occurs. Infections are most commonly spread by contact, be it oral, vaginal, or anal, with your hand, a toy, or any other contaminated material.

The only real protection that we have for gonorrhœa, syphilis, hepatitis, HIV, and other viral infections are condoms, dental dams, and rubber gloves. Dental dams are used as a barrier between your mouth and anything that you don't want your mouth to touch, be that the vagina or anus. Of course, there's also the condom. These *must* be made of latex to offer you any protection from disease. Anything else simply will not do the job. For a more complete look at prevention of disease transmission, please also see the section on Cleanliness & Disinfection.

Most STDs have made friendships with each other. That is, you don't just get one STD. Sometimes, having one disease will encourage your body to pick up another, because your resistance to infection is lower when you already have one infection. These infections may be at the same time, or one after the other.

As an aside, it's great that there are over-the-counter preparations for a number of the common ailments, such as some of those of the vagina. This is useful for those who have a recurring problem; they can go to the store, buy the necessary medication, and fix the problem. If you've caught something that you don't usually get and you don't know what it is, *get medical attention, immediately.* If it's there one day and it bothers you, and if that same thought bothers you again, that should serve as a warning to you and cause you to visit your physician. Many STDs will show symptoms just after the time of infection. However, when the symptoms disappear, it does *not* mean that you're all better. In many cases, it simply means that you've gone on to a new stage of the infection. Also, it does not mean that you're now any less contagious than you were at the time that you had the symptoms. Some illnesses go from very virulent, to not very much, to you can't pass it on at all. The main problem is that diseases vary and so does the way each individual responds to them. So, until you know what you've caught, you should assume that it's contagious. Some diseases go back and forth between being contagious and then not, "ping-ponging." For some, from beginning to end you will be contagious. Some, within hours or days, will have you able to transmit the disease to someone else. Don't assume that you can diagnose yourself.

Because of the variability of STDs and their means of transmission, you should assume that the easiest one to catch is present, and act accordingly. This doesn't mean that you have to wrap yourself in rubber body suits (unless you're into that sort of thing…), but it does mean that you should be conscious of the potential risks and know about the symptoms and treatment of the diseases you could catch.

Below, we've included a brief summary of the most common STDs, their causes, symptoms, and treatment. Please take the time to read them all. We've arranged things so that you can use the information as a reference, too. There may be some surprises in there for you. For instance, did you know that men can catch vaginitis? Read on, MacDuff....

Viruses

Viruses come in many forms. We've all had colds, most of us have had measles and mononucleosis. Some of us have HIV. As you can see, viruses come in many shapes and severities. They also come with differing ease of transmission, i.e. some, like the common cold, can be transmitted through the air, others, like HIV, need the exchange of bodily fluids to move from one person to another. Unlike the common cold, most STD viruses require the exchange of fluids. Some viruses can survive outside the body for quite a while, others die almost immediately they come out of the body.

Generally speaking, STD viruses are easy to catch if you have an opening for them to enter the body, say a tear in the lining of the rectum, a mouth ulcer, a cut in the skin, etc.. The most effective way to prevent viral STDs is to use a latex barrier in the form of a condom or a dental dam. Where condoms are concerned, *only* latex ones will do. All the other types do not stop the transmission of viruses.

HIV & AIDS

The human immunodeficiency virus (HIV) has been referred to in many ways during research and public discussion about it, namely; human T-lymphotrophic virus Type III (HTLV-III), lyphadenopathy-associated virus (LAV), and the AIDS-associated retrovirus (ARV). This is mainly due to the number of independent laboratories that performed the initial research into the virus. Today, the term human immunodeficiency virus (HIV) is the only term used by laboratories, the press, and the public, and is the one that is used throughout this book. HIV is a retrovirus that infects a major subset of human lymphocytes, known as T4 "inducer/helper" cells. After infection, these T4 cells are depleted, resulting in a reduced T4 "helper" to T8 "suppressor" cell ratio. HIV is also known to infect cells such as macrophages and nervous tissue cells. It is believed to remain present in humans until death.

Acquired immunodeficiency syndrome (AIDS) is believed to be caused by HIV, and is characterized by severe immune deficiency which results in opportunistic infection, malignancy, and neurologic disorders in people who do not have a prior history of immune deficiency. People infected with HIV do not necessarily have AIDS; they are, however, capable of infecting others.

Following infection, a wide variety of defects and abnormalities may be found in the person's T cells, B cells, natural killer cells, and monocytes/macrophages. Simply, all parts of the human immune system can be affected. All dysfunctions of the immune system of AIDS patients can be explained by the loss of the critically important T4 cells, despite the potential for other parts of the immune system to be affected. A variety of nervous system symptoms may occur as a result of infection, or as a result of direct injury of the nervous system cells by HIV infection.

HIV is *not* transmitted by casual contact or even the close, non-sexual contact that usually occurs at work, home, or in school. The transmission of the virus requires that bodily substances that contain the infected cells pass between the two people, for example: blood or plasma and plasma-containing fluids (such as saliva). While HIV has been found in semen, sweat, tears, and vaginal secretions, it must be noted that transmission by means of tears, saliva, fomites, or air has *not* been reported to date.

Transmission is usually by direct contact, e.g. blood transfusions (now rare due to screening processes) or injections with contaminated needles (common with intravenous (IV) drug users), or by exposure through mucous membranes; that is, by close, direct contact that breaks the normal barriers that the body has to infection. Any break in the skin barrier, such as lesions, provides the means for HIV to enter the body. In **homosexual men**, infection is often through the mucous membranes of the rectum, where lesions are common. Transmission from **men to women** is more common than the other way around, but cases of transmission from **women to men** are being increasingly reported. While transmission by means of an accidental needle stick has occurred, HIV transmission is less likely than transmission of hepatitis B by this means. The virus has been found in breast milk, and this route has been responsible for some cases of infection, although it remains rare.

A wide variety of problems can occur after infection by HIV. Within 2 to 4 weeks after infection some patients have a 3 to 14 day combination of fever, malaise, rash, pain in the joints, and inflammation of the lymph nodes. *For most people living with HIV there is no such phase,* they have only an asymptomatic infection, a phase that could last for years. This means that diagnosis often has to wait until one of the characteristic manifestations of AIDS is found to be present. This, in and of itself, is sufficient reason to get yourself tested regularly. This will ensure that, if you've done anything that might increase the risk of transmission *to* you, you'll minimize the risk of inadvertently passing it to someone else later. During the asymptomatic phase, people living with HIV may have a low T4 to T8 ratio. Many of these develop the signs and symptoms that suggest AIDS, but do not develop into full-blown AIDS.

AIDS-related complex (ARC) is a large group of signs and symptoms that are shown by people in groups that have an increased incidence of AIDS, but who do not show the typical opportunistic infections or Kaposi's sarcoma (KS) that characterize full-blown AIDS. These symptoms can include swelling of the lymph nodes, weight loss, intermittent fever, malaise and lethargy, chronic diarrhœa, genital or anal warts, anæmia, immunologic abnormalities characteristic of AIDS, and oral thrush (candidiasis). A subset of ARC patients have a persistent generalized lymphadenopathy (PGL), which means they have lymph nodes swollen to greater than 1 cm. for at least three months involving two or more sites in the area of the groin (in the absence of any illness or drug use known to cause such swelling). A more severe manifestation of ARC is the wasting syndrome, which is characterized by weight loss of more than 15% and is associated with fever, night sweats, oral thrush, or diarrhœa persisting for more than 3 months. Full-blown AIDS is more likely to occur to a patient with the wasting syndrome than one who only has PGL. The wasting syndrome is known as the "slim disease" in Africa.

Full-blown AIDS consists of any or all of the above symptoms with a progression to development of opportunistic infection and/or some secondary cancers known to be associated with AIDS, e.g. Kaposi's sarcoma (KS). Some patients develop the opportunistic infections without any preceding symptoms. There are several opportunistic infections that have been noted often in these people; *Pneumocystis carinii* pneumonia, candidiasis, cytomegalovirus infection, and herpes simplex infection are among them. Some other secondary diseases have also been seen, for example: herpes zoster (shingles), recurring *Salmonella* bacteria, tuberculosis, and oral thrush (candidiasis). This is by no means the whole list....

Nervous system disorders range from acute and chronic meningitis to nerve diseases with weakness and pins and needles to brain disorders with seizures, hallucinations, and progressive dementia. The central nervous system is involved in about 30% to 50% of all AIDS patients, and is probably the result of the various opportunistic infections and direct infection of the nervous tissue itself. All bodily systems are ultimately devastated by these complications and the death rate appears to be 100%, with about 90% dying from the opportunistic infections.

There are two main tests for antibodies to HIV. The first is the enzyme-linked immunosorbant assay (ELISA), in which a serum or plasma sample from the person is tested. The sensitivity of the test varies in differing laboratories, but almost all of those who are infected show a positive result. It is *possible* for the ELISA test to give a false-positive result, particularly in people who are asymptomatic. If the test is positive and the person is asymptomatic, it is advisable to repeat the test. If the second test is also positive, then the second type of test, the Western blot, is performed. This is a labour-intensive test that also tests the serum or plasma of the person. If the Western blot is also positive, the person should be considered both infected and infective. These two tests are also used to screen the blood supply.

It should also be noted that it is *possible* for asymptomatic carriers to show a false-negative result to both the ELISA and the Western blot for several months (the "window"), despite their being infected.

At the time of writing, there is no completely effective treatment for AIDS. Development of a vaccine is being pursued, but it has yet to provide fruit. This means that preventative measures are essential. Most infections result from repeated, close contact with an infected person, specifically by mucous membrane contact with infected blood or other bodily fluids of the infected person. Sexual relationships are the main source of such contacts, so safer sex practices, reduced number of contacts, and use of protective devices (condoms, dental dams, latex gloves, etc.) are all factors that can reduce the likelihood of infection. Women who know they are infected should avoid pregnancy, since there is a high likelihood that the child will be born infected. Anyone infected with HIV should not donate blood.

There is no reason for a person with HIV infection to be isolated from the rest of the population, even as a hospital patient, except when complications, such as suspected or proven tuberculosis, are present.

A few notes about people living with HIV or AIDS are appropriate here. Those who are seropositive for HIV are often at greater risk for catching a disease than those who are negative, because of their compromised immune system, so cleanliness guidelines are even more important when one or more of the partners is positive. There has been some suggestion of herpes and/or syphilis as cofactor(s) for HIV developing into AIDS, so those who are positive should be aware of their partner's herpes and syphilis status, if possible.

SM play can create a great deal of physical stress, usually more for the Bottom than for the Top. Those with HIV infection tend to be less able to take stress than those without, so seropositive players may have to expand the rôles they take to accommodate a lower amount of physical stress. The good side to this is that it presents seropositive people with an opportunity for creativity when it comes to play.

There are symptoms of HIV infection that are commonly found in people with the infection and there may be an interplay between these symptoms and the activities of an SM scene, so these should be discussed before the scene begins. Often, people with HIV will have greater skin sensitivity, implying greater susceptibility to marking or bruising. Fatigue is also a common symptom, implying consideration and adjustment of scene intensity and of scene frequency, where necessary. It is also advisable to be sensitive about the time a scene takes place because HIV may affect the times of day a person feels up to a scene. Before the scene, you should plan some recovery time and a place for the body to recover afterwards.

Alcohol, drugs, etc. are all immunosuppressors, as well as ways to diminish a person's ability to assess risk, so they are even less advisable during SM play for people with HIV.

People with HIV often have a zinc deficiency and ejaculate has a lot of zinc in it. So, men with HIV should note that many ejaculations imply the need for a zinc supplement. Fisting requires enemas and this process removes a lot of the good flora in the bowel. There is probably an imbalance of these flora in the bowel of most people with HIV, so it is important to ensure that the flora of the bowel be supplemented. Try fresh live-culture yoghurt or some of the colonic flora supplements containing lactobacilli (available in many health food stores). See your physician, if you have questions about whether to take supplements and which to take.

Hepatitis

Hepatitis is an inflammation of the liver. The main causes are the hepatitis viruses Types A, B, and non-A, non-B (the latter now identified as hepatitis C); and drugs (including alcohol). Other, rarer causes are the mononucleosis, yellow fever, and cytomegaloviruses. Parasites can invade the liver, but they do not cause true hepatitis. Hepatitis is a world-wide disease. Some people still refer to hepatitis A as infectious hepatitis and short-incubation hepatitis, and to hepatitis B as serum hepatitis, posttransfusion hepatitis, and long-incubation hepatitis. These terms should not be used.

Hepatitis B is the most well-known of the agents that cause the disease. It is associated with many symptoms ranging from asymptomatic infection, chronic hepatitis, cirrhosis (a scarring of the liver), and cancer of the liver. Hepatitis A is not known to have a chronic carrier state (unlike hepatitis B), and is not known to cause a chronic hepatitis or cirrhosis. Hepatitis due to hepatitis C is not well known, but evidence to date has implicated at least two distinct viruses. In general, its behaviour is similar to hepatitis B.

Hepatitis A spreads mainly by oral contact with fæces. Blood and other secretions may also be the cause of infection. The fæces contain the virus during the incubation period and this usually ends a few days after the symptoms of the disease begin; so, by the time a diagnosis is made, the disease is no longer infectious. The virus can be transmitted by raw shellfish. Most hepatitis A infections pass unnoticed. In some countries over three-quarters of the adult population has been exposed to the virus.

Hepatitis B is often transmitted through contaminated blood or other blood products, and is often transmitted by the needles shared by drug users. Both **heterosexual** and **homosexual** contact can result in the spread of the disease, but the rate of infection is less than that of hepatitis A and the means of acquisition is often unknown. Unrecognized infection with hepatitis B is common, maybe up to 30% of cases, though less common than for hepatitis A. (One of the authors can pin-point when he had hepatitis B to within a year, but he had no symptoms of the disease during that period....) Relatively little is known about C hepatitis transmission patterns, but it is responsible for about 80 to 90% of hepatitis after transfusions, with hepatitis B being responsible for most of the rest. Incubation periods for hepatitis A are about 2 to 6 weeks; for B about 6 to 25 weeks; and for non-A, non-B from less than 2 to about 25 weeks (on average about 7 to eight weeks).

Hepatitis varies from mild flu-like symptoms to sudden, intense, and fatal liver failure, depending on the patient's immune response and other poorly-understood factors. The phase before onset of the disease begins with sudden anorexia, nausea and vomiting, and fever. A distaste for cigarettes is a characteristic early manifestation of the anorexia. Especially in hepatitis B sufferers, nettle-like pale rashes and joint pains can occur. After 3 to 10 days the patient's urine becomes dark, followed by jaundice of the skin. At this point, any systemic symptoms die down, despite the worsening jaundice, and the patient starts to feel better. The jaundice usually peaks at about the 1 to 2 week point and fades during the 2 to 4 week recovery. The liver is usually enlarged and, in about 1 in 5 cases, the spleen is also enlarged. There are usually no signs of chronic liver disease in uncomplicated cases.

The disease is difficult to diagnose because it mimics many flu-like symptoms. Alcoholic hepatitis is due to a history of drinking and is usually suggested by a more gradual onset of the symptoms. Blood tests are usually used to determine whether the infection is hepatitis.

Hepatitis usually resolves itself within about 2 to 4 weeks. Hepatitis B is more likely to cause serious problems than hepatitis A. Chronic hepatitis is rare for cases of Type A, but it occurs for about 10 to 15% of Type B infections.

The blood of people with acute hepatitis should be handled with great care since the disease is easily transmitted by blood contact. Household contacts of a patient with hepatitis are usually given an immune globulin treatment to help protect them from infection. Vaccination against hepatitis B is probably sensible for **homosexual women** and **men** who practice anal-receptive intercourse (ass-fucking). The cost of the vaccine can be high, but not as high as treating the illness.... As of writing, there is no vaccine available for hepatitis A. Naturally, until the agents responsible for C and D hepatitis are known, there will be no vaccine for it.

No special treatment is usually required for hepatitis sufferers. The patient need not be kept in bed for the duration of the disease, nor is a special diet required. Most people can go back to work as soon as the jaundice is over.

Herpes

The term "herpes" usually refers to the herpes simplex virus, also known as herpesvirus hominis. It is a recurring viral infection that causes single or multiple clusters of vesicles (blisters), filled with clear fluid on slightly raised inflammatory bases on the skin or mucous membranes. Type 1 usually causes cold sores on the lips of the sufferer, and Type 2 causes genital infection with the transmission of the disease by direct contact with the lesions, most often during sex. In most cases, people cannot determine the exact time of infection. The virus appears to lie dormant in the base of a person's nerves until triggered by exposure to the sun, an illness causing fever, physical or emotional stress, or certain foods and drugs. Often the trigger mechanism remains unknown.

Cold Sores

For the most part, when we talk of herpes, we talk of cold sores (sometimes called fever blisters). The sores are caused by the herpes simplex virus. It causes painful blisters and lesions of the lips, and sores which can last one to three weeks. Once you've caught it, you never lose the herpes virus. It can be activated by any mild trauma, such as dental treatment, abrasion of the lips, sunburn, food allergy, anxiety, onset of menstruation, or any disease that produces a fever or an increased metabolic rate.

Patients usually have a sensation of fullness, burning, and itching before the typical vesicle develops on slightly elevated tissues of the lips. The vesicular lesion may be present for hours before it breaks and a yellowish, crusted lesions forms. The lesions seldom last more than about ten days. Inside the mouth, lesions of the palate and gums begin with many small vesicles that rupture quickly to unite and form large, superficial ulcerations with irregular edges. A large reddening usually surrounds the ulcers. You can be contagious before the virus-filled fluid of the lesions or blisters is present.

If you have herpes, genital or labial, let your partner know. They have the right to say "No, you're not going to do that," whatever the "that" may be. Even if you're playing safely, accidents can happen in the least expected ways.

Diagnosis of cold sores is usually simple, due to the characteristic appearance of the lesions and their location.

Treatment is usually more effective if started *at the first indication* of changes of sensation in the affected area. The treatment is normally for the pain involved, and to discourage spread of the disease. Sometimes, antibiotics are prescribed to guard against secondary infections. Sunscreen containing para-aminobenzoïc acid (PABA) can help to reduce the effect of the sun in causing recurrences. Corticosteroids can spread the virus, especially on mucous membranes. Topical ointments with active agents such as acyclovir discourage the lesions from spreading and act as lubricants. Ice applied to the affected areas can reduce the swelling. If the lesions and swelling interfere with eating or other regular functions, acyclovir may be prescribed orally.

There is no cure for herpes simplex.

Genital Herpes

Genital herpes is an infection of the genital and rectal areas of the body by the herpes simplex virus. It is the most common cause of genital ulceration in developed countries. It is moderately contagious and is usually spread by sexual contact. Lesions of the skin usually form about 4 to 7 days after contact and the condition tends to recur because the virus "burrows down" into the root of the infected nerves, from which it can reactivate and reïnfect the skin.

The first lesions are usually more painful than those in recurrent outbreaks of the disease. Itching and soreness usually come before a reddening of a small area of the skin or mucous membranes. A small group of vesicles then develops which erode into several superficial, circular ulcers with red ring around them. In the case of secondary infection, the ulcers may coalesce to form a larger ulcer. After a few days, the ulcers dry out, and then heal after about ten days, leaving some scarring. The lymph nodes in the groin may enlarge and be somewhat tender. The ulcers are usually painful.

The lesions may occur on the foreskin, glans and shaft of the penis in **men**; the labia, clitoris, perineum, vagina, and cervix in **women**. In the case of **homosexual men** and **women** who practice anal-receptive intercourse, the lesions may occur around the anus. In addition to the pain at the site of the infection, a general malaise, fever, and difficulty in urination or with walking may be experienced by the person.

Diagnosis is usually by taking a sample from one of the lesions and testing over a period of a day or two.

Genital herpes may be complicated by meningitis, myelitis, and dysfunctions of the nervous system. Occasionally, the patient's blood can transfer the infection to the skin, joints, liver, or lungs. It is possible for the infection to spread to areas of the buttocks, groin, and thighs through the nerves or by direct inoculation. The latter method occasionally accounts for infection of the eye or fingers. It is extremely rare for herpes to spread *into* the genitalia or urinary system. Herpes can coëxist with *Treponema pallidum, Hæmophilus ducreyi,* or *Candida albicans.* Complications and spreading of genital herpes is easier and more common in people with compromised immune systems. By far the most common complication of genital herpes is recurrent disease, usually confined to one side of the body, milder than the first attack, and with symptoms before the recurrent attack that may be severe. The recurrences vary greatly in frequency and may last over many years. Reïnfection with different strains of the virus can also occur.

The likely treatment for the *symptoms* is acyclovir. It is particularly effective for people with compromised immune systems, such as those with severe diseases or AIDS. Acyclovir does not prevent latent infection nor does it prevent recurrences.

Again, there is no cure for herpes simplex.

Syphilis

Syphilis is a disease caused by the *Treponema pallidum* organism. It is characterized by several distinct stages, and by years of symptomless latency. It can affect any tissue or vascular organ of the body and can be passed from mother to fœtus (congenital syphilis).

The syphilis organism cannot survive long outside the body, unless it is in a tissue culture. It enters the body through the mucous membranes and the skin. Within hours, the organisms reach the lymph nodes and rapidly disseminate throughout the rest of the body, causing swellings. Healing occurs with scar tissue formation. In late syphilis, hypersensitivity leads to gummatous ulcerations and death of the organs. Inflammatory changes are replaced by degenerative processes, especially in the cardiovascular and central nervous systems.

The central nervous system is invaded early in the infection and, during the secondary stage of the disease, greater than 30% of cases have abnormal spinal fluid. During the first 5 to 10 years after infection, the disease involves membranes surrounding the brain and spinal cord. Later, it damages the brain and spinal cord themselves.

Infection is usually transmitted by sexual contact, including oral-genital contact and rectal contact. Occasionally, it is passed on by kissing or close bodily contact. Recently, promiscuous homosexual men have been at the greatest risk in the United States. Untreated people with primary or secondary syphilis who have skin lesions are the most infectious. Tertiary syphilis is not contagious. Infection with syphilis does not confer immunity to subsequent reïnfection, particularly if treatment is given early in the course of the disease.

The incubation period of primary syphilis can vary from 1 to 13 weeks, but is usually from 3 to 4 weeks. The disease can appear at any stage without a history of prior stages and remote from the time of initial infection. Because the disease has diverse manifestations and is now rare in North America, physicians there may find it difficult to recognize.

Primary Syphilis: The primary lesion, or chancre, generally appears within 4 weeks of infection and heals within 4 to 8 weeks in untreated people. At the site of infection, a small red elevation of the skin soon erodes to form a painless ulcer. It does not bleed, but exudes a clear liquid full of the organism, when scratched. A red ring may surround the ulcer. Primary chancres appear on the penis, anus, and rectum in **men**; the vulva, cervix, and perineum in **women**. The chancres may also be found on the lips, tongue, tonsils, or fingers, and rarely on other parts of the body, and often produce such minimal symptoms that they are ignored.

Secondary Syphilis: Skin rashes usually appear within 6 to 12 weeks after infection and are more florid after 3 to 4 months. (About 25% of people have a healing primary chancre at this point.) The lesions may be transitory or they may persist for months. Frequently, in untreated people, the lesions heal, but fresh ones may appear in weeks or months. Over 80% of people have skin lesions, 50% have generalized enlargements of the lymph nodes, and about 10% have lesions of the eyes, bones and joints, membranes surrounding the brain and spinal cord, kidneys, liver, and spleen. Mild symptoms, such as malaise, headache, anorexia, nausea, aching pains in the bones, jaundice and neck stiffness are often present. At this stage a small number of people develop acute syphilitic meningitis, with headache, neck stiffness, cranial nerve lesions, and deafness. The syphilitic skin rashes may simulate a variety of skin conditions. Usually, they occur the same way on both sides of the body, and are more pronounced on the palms and soles. They usually heal without leaving marks, but in some people they may leave areas of hyper- or depigmentation. The surface of mucous membranes often becomes eroded in circular patches that are frequently greyish-white with red rings around them. They generally occur in the mouth, throat, glans penis, and vulva; or in the anal canal or rectum. Hair often pulls out in patches, leaving the person looking somewhat "moth-eaten." Often, there is a generalized, non-tender, rubbery, discrete enlargement of the lymph nodes. The liver and spleen may be readily visible in some people as they push to the surface of the body.

Latent Syphilis: In the early latent period (less than a year after infection) infectious skin relapses may occur, but after two years the development of further contagious lesions is rare and the person appears normal. The latent stage may last for a few years or for the rest of the person's life. About 30% of untreated cases develop late or tertiary syphilis.

Late or Tertiary Syphilis: the lesions of tertiary syphilis can be divided into three categories: 1) benign tertiary syphilis of the skin, bone, and internal organs. The lesions usually develop within 3 to 10 years of the original infection and are slow to develop and heal, leaving scarring. They often appear in the mouth, throat, and nasal passages, but can occur anywhere in the body; 2) a cardiovascular syphilis that produces a narrowing of the coronary blood vessels and problems with the valves in the aorta. This manifestation usually occurs from 10 to 25 years after initial infection; and 3) a neurosyphilis that occurs in about 5% of untreated syphilitics. It can cause poor concentration, dizziness, epileptic attacks, insomnia, incontinence, impotence, behavioural changes, and madness. Handwriting can become shaky.

For primary and secondary syphilis, your physician should explain all the implications of the disease and request a full list of your sexual contacts for the previous three months in the case of primary syphilis, and the previous year in the case of secondary syphilis. If not, give him/her a list so that the people can be examined, treated, and informed that they may be contagious. They should not have any sexual contact until they and their partners have been examined and have completed treatment. Antibiotics are usually prescribed for syphilis. People with early and late latent syphilis are treated with antibiotics to prevent the development of tertiary manifestation of the disease. About 50% of people with early infectious syphilis react within about 6 to 12 hours of initial treatment with general malaise, fever, headache, sweating, rigors, and a temporary worsening of the lesions. This reaction usually subsides within 24 hours and is not dangerous to the person apart from the anxiety it may produce.

That's 114, Madam!
Thank you, Madam!

It is very important to retest after treatment to ensure a complete cure. You should retest 1, 3, 6, and 12 months after treatment or until no reaction is found, whichever period is longer. After treatment, the lesions heal quickly. People with latent syphilis will be kept under surveillance at intervals of 3, 6, 12, and 24 months, and those who persist in positive results will be retested annually indefinitely.

Warts

Genital warts are caused by papillomaviruses and are usually transmitted sexually. The incubation period is about one to six months. You can move warts from one part of your body to another by touching the warts with, say your finger, and then touching your finger to another part of your, or someone else's, body. During the eighties, genital wart incidence in the United States grew at twice the rate of that for genital herpes. There's a 60 to 70% chance that if you have regular sexual contact with someone who has warts, you'll catch them in the near future. In **men**, genital warts usually occur on the warm, moist areas of the foreskin, the end of the penis, and on the shaft of the penis. In **women**, the warts occur on the vulva, the vaginal wall, the perineum, and the cervix; and, especially in **women**, warts can lead to precancerous conditions, e.g. cervical cancer. Many **lesbians** have warts. In **homosexual men**, they are very prevalent around the anus and in the rectum.

Genital warts generally appear as minute, soft, moist, red or pink swellings that rapidly grow into minute stalks. Usually, many of them are grouped together to give the overall impression of a cauliflower. Occasionally, they will grow on their own. During pregnancy, and in the presence of chronic discharge, they may grow more quickly and spread. They are normally identified by their appearance. Sometimes atypical or persistent warts will require a biopsy to check that there is no cancer present. Women with warts in their cervix should not be treated until the results of a Pap smear are known, to guide the necessary treatment.

At the time of writing, there is no treatment that is fully satisfactory. Podophyllin (an applied liquid) and electrocauterization, freezing, and surgery are all used, depending on the extent and persistence of the warts. The sexual contacts of the patient should be examined and a test for syphilis should also be performed at the first examination and then after three months or so. Relapse is frequent and will require retreatment. Many women with external warts go on to develop changes in their uterine cervix and potentially cancer of the cervix. This must be diagnosed early and treated. Follow up treatment will probably include yearly, or more frequent, checks for cancer. Warts are best treated within the first six months that you have them. Some physicians are loath to treat them right away because "they're not important," "they don't matter," "they're not growing," etc.. If you're not satisfied with your physician's opinion, seek the opinion of another physician. Frequently, local STD clinics may know more than some specialists about "what's going around."

As you can see from the above, warts, while they may be common, should be taken seriously.

Bacteria

Taken as a group, there are as many bacteria that could cause you problems from irritation to death as there are viruses. We've included the main sexually transmitted ones.

Gonorrhœa

Gonorrhœa is a disease of the urethra, cervix, rectum, throat, or eyes, that may be passed through the blood to other parts of the body. The cause, *Neisseria gonorrhœæ*, can be identified in discharges from the body. The disease usually spreads by sexual contact. Women are frequently symptomless carriers of the organisms for weeks or months and are often identified by tracing sexual contacts. Asymptomatic infection is also common in the throat and rectum of homosexual men, and has been found occasionally in the urethra of some heterosexual men. Gonorrhœa occurs in the vagina of prepubertal girls, most of whom are infected by adults, either through sexual contact or, rarely, by fomites (body wastes).

Men usually have an incubation period of about 2 to 14 days. The onset usually begins with mild discomfort in the urethra, followed a few hours later by painful urination and a pus-like discharge. Frequency and urgency of urination increase as the infection spreads to the back of the urethra.

Women usually show symptoms within 7 to 21 days after infection. Their symptoms are generally mild, but a few women the onset may be severe, with painful and frequent urination, and vaginal discharge. The cervix and deeper reproductive organs are the ones usually infected, followed by the urethra and rectum.

Women and homosexual men commonly contract rectal gonorrhœa. It is usually symptomless in women, but discomfort around the anus and rectal discharge may be experienced. Severe rectal infection is more common in homosexual men. Patients may notice a coating of the stool and a peeling of the rectal skin. Gonorrhœa from oral-genital contact is becoming more common. Although there are often no symptoms or signs, some people may complain of a sore throat and discomfort when swallowing.

In men, if gonorrhœa is not treated, it can lead to sterility. In women, the most common complication is inflammation of the fallopian tube. In both sexes, the infection may pass into the blood stream, but this is more common in women. A woman with gonorrhœa may pass it on during childbirth to the eyes of the newborn child.

The infectious nature of gonorrhœa is something that must be recognized, and patients *must* stop sexual activity until cure is confirmed. Men should not squeeze their penis in a search for urethral discharge. All sexual contacts of the patients should be reported to the treating physician, so that proper follow-up can be performed, by tracing, examining, and treating the contacts.

Usually, antibiotics are prescribed for gonorrhœa. Retesting has to be performed at one week and two weeks after treatment. A further test after 3 months is preferred.

Chlamydial & Ureaplasmal Infections

This group of STDs may be the most common in North America. The sexually transmitted causes of most cases of cervicitis and urethritis in women, urethritis in men, and proctitis and pharyngitis in both sexes have been identified. The terms previously used to describe the non-gonorrhœal forms of these infections, non-specific urethritis (NSU) and non-gonococcal urethritis (NGU), are not exact. the causes include *Chlamydia trachomatis* (responsible for about 50% of NGU and most cases of non-gonococcal cervicitis) and *Ureaplasma urealyticum*, but some cases still remain unexplained.

Men usually show symptoms between 7 to 28 days after infection, usually with mild pain during urination and discomfort in the urethra and a clear to pus-like discharge. Although the discharge may be slight and the symptoms mild, they are frequently more marked early in the morning when the lips of the meatus may be red and stuck together with dried secretions. Occasionally, the onset is more acute, with painful urination, frequency of urination, and a copious pus-like discharge. Inflammation of the anus and throat may occur after rectal- and oral-genital contact.

Women are mostly asymptomatic, although vaginal discharge, painful and frequent urination, and pelvic pain, as well as symptoms of an inflamed anus and throat, may occur. Cervicitis, with a characteristic yellow, pus-like secretion may be seen. You may have lower abdominal and back pains, and get a feeling of overall tiredness.

In men, complications include inflammation at the testes (especially in men over thirty-five) and constriction of the urethra. A serious complication is Reiter's syndrome (which occurs almost exclusively in men), consisting of non-specific urethritis, polyarthritis, and conjunctivitis, or uveitis. Complications for women include perihepatitis and salpingitis (Pelvic Inflammatory Disease (PID)).

Most chlamydial and ureaplasmal infections are treated with antibiotics. About 20% of patients have one or more relapses on followup and require more treatment. This is not a great problem, they will eventually be cured.

For men and women, *Chlamydia* can lead to urethral infections and arthritis. Women may experience irregular bleeding or changes in the menstrual cycle. For women, complications of *Chlamydia* include cervicitis, bleeding after sex, Pelvic Inflammatory Disease (PID), and sexually-acquired reactive arthritis. Septic shock is also a risk from *Chlamydia*, due to infection transferring into the blood stream. In men, *Chlamydia* can cause a lot of pain, discomfort, and sterility.

If appropriate treatment is not given, the signs and symptoms of the infection usually subside within about 60 to 70% of cases, but may persist in women, resulting in chronic pelvic infection and its results; pain, infertility, and pregnancy outside the womb.

You should stop having sexual intercourse until treatment is completed and symptoms subside. *All* your sexual partners should be examined and treated, where necessary. If you have been treated, you should follow up for at least three months with regular clinical examinations. Wear loose fitting clothes during treatment. Chlamydial infections can spread like wildfire: if you think you spread it to someone and he/she doesn't seek treatment, *don't* have sex with that person, at least not unprotected sex. You can get the infection right back.

Lymphogranuloma Venereum (LGV)

This is a sexually transmitted chlamydial disease that has a passing first phase followed by a pus-like swelling of the lymph nodes and serious local complications. LGV is caused by a few types of chlamydial bacteria, different from those that cause trachoma, conjunctivitis, urethritis, and cervicitis. The disease is found mainly in tropical and subtropical areas.

Small, blister-like lesions appear after the 3 to 12 or more day incubation period. These burst rapidly and heal quickly, so they may pass unnoticed. Usually, the first symptom is an enlargement of the lymph nodes in the groin, and then this progresses to form a large tender mass that sticks to the deep tissues and inflames the overlying skin. Many abscesses may form that have discharge pus or blood-stained material. Healing occurs eventually, but scarring may form. The abscesses may persist or recur. There may be backaches, headaches, joint pains, anorexia, and vomiting. Backache is common among **women**, who may get lesions initially on the cervix, or upper vagina. This may result in enlargement and discharge from the lymph nodes of the groin. If the rectal wall is involved in women and homosexual **men**, an ulcerated inflammation of the rectum may occur with a rectal discharge of pus. If the inflammation becomes chronic, the complications can be serious with gross swellings of the rectum and genitals.

Treatment is usually by antibiotics. The abscesses should *not* be cut or burst but may be cleaned out by your physician. For more advanced cases, surgery is sometimes required to dilate the swellings. Plastic surgery is sometimes required for swelling of the genitals. *All* the sexual contacts of the patient should be examined. The patient will be observed for about six months after apparently successful treatment.

Granuloma Inguinale

This is a condition that involves the genitalia and is probably spread by sexual contact. It is rare in temperate climates but is common in some tropical and subtropical areas.

The incubation period is from 1 to 12 weeks. The initial lesion is a painless, beefy-red nodule that slowly develops into a rounded, elevated, velvety growth. **Men** are infected on the penis, scrotum, groin, and thighs; **women** are infected at the vulva, vagina, and perineum; **homosexual men** are infected also at the anus and buttocks; **both sexes** are affected in the face. The disease spreads slowly by continuity and autoïnoculation and eventually the lesions may cover the genitalia. Healing is also slow and scar tissue forms. It is common for secondary infection to occur, and this can cause gross tissue destruction. In neglected cases, anæmia and death may follow. The bones, joints, and liver may also be affected.

The characteristic lesions of the infection can be scraped and examined under a microscope to confirm the disease.

Antibiotics are generally sufficient to cure the lesions. Treatment will last for about 3 weeks, or until the lesions have all healed, to minimize any relapses. Sexual contacts should all be located and thoroughly examined. Your physician will keep you under surveillance for six months or so after an apparently successful treatment.

Salpingitis (Pelvic Inflammatory Disease (PID))

Salpingitis is an inflammation of the fallopian tubes. The term pelvic inflammatory disease is used by some people to describe infections of the cervix, uterus, and ovaries, but it's not advisable to use the term for an unknown cause of pelvic infection. PID does kill women. With the advent of AIDS, PID will probably become more common.

Salpingitis occurs primarily in women under 25 and who are sexually active. It is usually transmitted during sexual activity. Women with intrauterine devices (IUDs) are especially vulnerable, probably because the device assists transport of the infectious agent. Salpingitis rarely occurs before a woman's first period, after menopause, or during pregnancy, possibly because many women are less sexually active at these times. It can be caused by a single agent or a combination of more than one. Possible agents include: *Neisseria gonorrhœæ*, *Chlamydia trachomatis*, viruses, bacteria, and tuberculosis.

In most cases, the infection starts in the vagina. The glands of the cervix provide an ideal environment for the organisms to flourish. Although the symptoms and signs may be more pronounced on one side, the likelihood is that both tubes have been infected. The infection of the tubes produces copious discharge that sticks everything together, to the extent that the tubes may become blocked. The discharge may spread to the perineum, causing a peritonitis. The ovaries generally avoid infection, but they have also been recorded as infected.

That's 120, Madam!
Thank you, Madam!

The onset of salpingitis is usually just after menstruation. Severe pain gradually increases in the lower abdomen, and discomfort increases with cervical movement. Vomiting may occur, and bowel sounds are normally heard quite early after infection. Bowel movement may cease. It is common to see high fever, and copious, pus-like discharge from the cervix.

A chronic form of salpingitis may follow an acute attack. It will leave scarring of the pelvis and fallopian tubes, chronic pain, irregularities in the menstrual cycle, and possibly infertility.

During an acute attack, abscesses may develop in the fallopian tubes, ovaries, or pelvis. If a small perforation of the tubes occurs, it may seal up again and respond to antibiotics, but, if it does not respond, the tubes will require surgical removal, usually including a hysterectomy. If a large abscess perforates, it should be treated as an *urgent medical emergency*. Toxic shock can follow perforation of an abscess. Infertility is a common result of salpingitis. It has caused death and should be attended to with this in mind.

Cultures and smears will usually be performed to determine the cause of salpingitis.

Treatment will depend on which infectious agent is found. Generally, antibiotic treatment is started even before the results of the cultures and smears have been returned. Other treatment will include rest in bed, and, possibly, intravenous fluids.

The sexual contacts of the patient should be examined for the infectious agent. Often, if the partner is not treated as well, the patient is reïnfected by the partner. Post treatment follow up of both the patient and the patient's partner(s) is required. Repeated pelvic examination and tests for gonorrhœa are usually performed.

Salpingitis (PID) is not a disease to be messed with or ignored....

Cystitis

Cystitis is a general term used to describe infections of the bladder. Any of several infectious agents could be responsible: *Neisseria gonorrhœæ*, *Chlamydia*, or viruses, or be secondary to vaginitis. This subsection can be used as an overview, but you should refer to the specific section on the specific infection for more details.

In **women**, cystitis is usually due to infection rising from the vagina through the urethra to the bladder. It often occurs after sexual intercourse. The causes of recurrent cystitis in women appear to be from a form of localized lack of defence mechanism which allows the infections to colonize the vaginal area.

In **men**, cystitis is usually the result of infection rising from the urethra or prostate to the bladder. The most common cause of recurrent bladder infection in men is chronic bacterial infection of the prostate. It is difficult to deal with the latter, because it is rare that antibiotics transfer from plasma into the prostate, so as soon as the antibiotic treatment is stopped the prostate reinfects the urine in the bladder.

Acute cystitis is often accompanied with burning or painful urination, an urgent need urinate, frequent urination, and lower back pain. There may be a lot of blood in the urine, particularly in **women**. Recurrent cystitis in both **men and women** can be associated with passage of air in the urine.

A urine sample is typically used to determine the cause of cystitis. It is possible to contaminate the urine sample during collection, so it may be necessary, particularly in women, to collect the urine with a catheter The most accurate method of analyzing the bladder urine is by taking the sample this way.

Treatment of cystitis is usually by the antibiotic most suited to the infection that is found.

Gardnerella Vaginalis

Gardnerella vaginalis is a cause of non-specific vaginitis and vulvitis. It is more bothersome than harmful and it is possible to have the infection for a long time without knowing it, i.e. it can be asymptomatic. It can be spread from partner to partner and back again. It is primarily spread by sexual contact.

The symptoms are a discharge, usually very wet, a very fishy smell (almost ammonia like in women) which varies from person to person, itchiness, and/or inflammation. The discharge will be white, grey, or yellowish. The smell will increase when the area has been washed with soap and after sex, because the vagina is more alkaline under these circumstances. This means that a rinsing with vinegar solution after washing will help to minimize the fishy smell.

Diagnosis will normally be by a smear.

Your physician will decide how to treat it. Usually sulfa creams, ampicillin, or other antibiotics will be used. It is very important to treat all the partners involved. There is no immunity to this form of vaginitis. If it is not completely cleared up in your partner, guess what? He/she could reïnfect you. Sometimes an acidic jelly is prescribed to help remove the alkalinity that causes the fishy smell. It can be prevented by proper wiping (i.e. front to back) and wearing loose fitting cotton clothes.

Chancroid

Chancroid is an acute, localized, and contagious disease that causes painful ulcers and discharge of pus from the lymph nodes in the groin. It is caused by a bacterium called *Hæmophilus ducreyi*.

The incubation period for is from 3 to 7 days. It produces small, painful spots on the skin that rapidly break down to form shallow ulcers with ragged edges. Each ulcer is shallow, soft, painful, and surrounded by a reddish border. The ulcers vary in size and often coalesce. The lymph nodes of the groin become tender and enlarged. It is possible for a person to spread the infection to other areas. Chancroid can cause severe tissue damage in the infected areas. It can also coëxist with other causes of genital ulcers.

Culture of the organism is difficult, so your physician will often have to determine the cause of your problems visually and by the progress of the symptoms. It is important to test for other STDs at this point to ensure that they are not the agents responsible for the symptoms.

Antibiotics are usually prescribed for chancroid. All sexual contacts should be checked for infection. An infected person is usually kept under surveillance for about 3 months, with regular tests for syphilis.

Anærobic Bacteria

Bacterial infections such as salmonella, shigella, and campylobacter are all transmitted very easily by oral-fæcal contact. Although these bacteria may coëxist with or cause proctitis, they usually produce symptoms that suggest an infection of the gastrointestinal tract. Asymptomatic infection can occur with all these bacteria, and are the rule when the agent is *Entamœba histolytica* (for which, please see the section on Amœbiasis). It is common for there to be multiple infections, especially in **homosexual men** with many partners. (Note that viruses such as hepatitis A and parasites such as giardia and amœba can also be transmitted by the oral-fæcal route.)

Salmonella

There are about 2200 known types of *Salmonella*. Those that affect humans almost all cause diarrhœa. *Salmonella typhi* causes typhoid. Typhoid is under control in the western world, but the other forms of *Salmonella* are not. They are passed during sexual contact by the oral-fæcal route, although they are also spread by infected meat products, poultry, eggs, and raw milk. They have even been spread in contaminated marijuana. Except for typhoid fever, *Salmonella* infections remain a significant health problem in the western world.

Although asymptomatic infection is possible, *Salmonella* generally produces some form of gastroenteritis, which usually appears after about 12 to 48 hours after the infection. The symptoms start with nausea, vomiting, and crampy abdominal pain followed by diarrhœa, fever, and sometimes vomiting. Stool is usually watery, but some people have semi-solid paste-like stools. Rarely, blood or mucous is present. Normally, the symptoms are mild, but in some cases a protracted, more severe illness similar to cholera can occur.

Diagnosis is generally confirmed by a culture from stool (preferable) or a rectal swab. Health organizations usually require the physician to report incidences of *Salmonella* to ensure that an epidemic does not occur. If you want to have oral-rectal sex, *Salmonella* is a very good reason to use a dental dam (as are hepatitis, giardia, and amœba).

Treatment is likely to be no more that a bland diet and plenty of fluids. Antibiotics can prolong the excretion of the organism, so they are unlikely to be prescribed, unless the disease becomes systemic (i.e. throughout the whole body). Carriers should not handle food until the disease has passed.

Shigellosis

These bacteria causes an acute infection of the bowel. The source of the bacteria is the fæces of infected individuals or convalescent carriers. It is also spread directly by oral-fæcal contact. Reïnfection with the same strain of the bacterium is possible, since infection does not provide people with immunity.

The *Shigella* organisms penetrate the mucous membranes of the lower intestine. In severe cases, the whole of the large and part of the small intestine are involved. The resultant and characteristic dysentery is normally preceded by watery diarrhœa. In many patients, dysentery does not occur after the diarrhœa.

The incubation period is from 1 to 4 days. Most people do not have a fever, nor do they have blood or mucous in their stool. However, the onset of the disease is characterized by gripping abdominal pain, urgency to defecate (shit), and the passage of the stool which temporarily relieved the pain. These episodes recur with increasing frequency and severity. Diarrhœa becomes pronounced and the soft or liquid stools may contain mucous, pus, and blood. The disease usually runs its course in 4 to 8 days. Severe cases might take 3 to 6 weeks. Secondary infections can occur in debilitated and dehydrated sufferers. If there are severe ulcerations of the mucous membranes, a lot of blood can be lost. It is uncommon to have other complications.

During testing, swabs will usually be taken from any ulcers and the person's stool will also be examined. It is very important that the person wash his/her hands thoroughly before handling food, and soiled clothes and bedding should be immersed in covered buckets of soap and water until they can be boiled. Sufferers and carriers can expect to undergo some form of isolation while they are infective.

The diarrhœa usually causes water and salt loss, so a fluid diet is often prescribed. Sometimes antibiotics are prescribed, sometimes not; it all depends on the severity of the disease, your age, and other factors. Also, some strains of the bacteria have started to become resistant to the available antibiotics, so they might only be of limited use, anyway. You may find that a hot-water bottle may help to relieve some of the abdominal pain. Your physician will follow up the treatment until your stool is consistently free of *Shigella*.

Campylobacter

Campylobacter infection is by a bacterium that may cause diarrhœa and localized infection. However, the only constant symptom is an intermittent fever when the infection is systemic. Abdominal pain and an inflammation of the liver and spleen are frequent. The diarrhœa is watery and is sometimes bloody.

Campylobacter is usually detected by testing blood, although it can be found by examination of stool samples.

Antibiotics, single or combined, are likely to be prescribed.

Fungus (Yeast)

Yeast travels around a lot. In women, it can happen if you wipe from the anus forward to the vagina. So, always wipe from the front to the back. Little girls are taught this, but no-one tells them why. Now you know why: you don't want to contaminate the field. If you wipe from front to back and contaminate the anus, who cares? The anus is dirty anyway. If you wipe the other way around, you run the risk of messing up your plumbing.

There is really only one fungus to be concerned about in terms of sexually transmitted diseases, namely: *Candidiasis albicans* which causes candidiasis, also known as thrush. It does not, however, require sex to travel....

Candidiasis (Monilial Vaginitis)

Yeast infections of the genital tract caused by *Candida albicans* are increasing in frequency, especially in women. Uncommonly transmitted sexually, the infection usually spreads from the person's normal skin or intestinal flora. The increased incidence is primarily due to the widespread use of broad-spectrum antibiotics and the large number of women taking oral contraceptives, although better diagnostic methods may also contribute to the greater number of detected cases. Other predisposing factors include pregnancy, menstruation, diabetes, constrictive undergarments, and use of immunosuppressive drugs. Candidiasis of the whole body is evidence of severe underlying disease or immunological abnormality and is rarely a complication of genital infection. Many of us have heard of "Thrush" in people with AIDS. Thrush is simply an overgrowth of this fungus.

Yeasts can travel back and forth on a menstrual pad, from one opening to the other. Of course, they can also be passed from mouth to vagina and vice versa in oral sex; from woman to woman contact, be it in the form of fluids, hands, or sex toy(s). Yeast infections can also be spread by wet towels or seats in saunas and hot tubs, where someone was sitting and dripping. If you sit down in the same spot, something may take a ride home with you....

Women usually develop vulval irritation and vaginal discharge. Frequently, the irritation is severe and the discharge almost non-existent. The vulva may be reddish and swollen, with peeking skin.

Men are often symptomless, but may complain of irritation or soreness of the glans and foreskin, especially after intercourse. Occasionally, there will be a slight urethral discharge. The glans and foreskin will be found to be red upon examination, and there may be vesicles (blisters) present. White, cheesy material may stick to the surface. In severe cases, the foreskin may be constricted. Treatment is usually with antibiotics. Relapse is common in either sex and may be due to reïnfection be the sexual partner or, more commonly, from the normal flora in combination with a provoking condition. Occasionally, contraceptive pills must be discontinued for several months during treatment.

Parasites

For the most part, these STDs are just annoying. If you've had one, you know just how irritating they can be. They can be tricky to get rid of, just like an infestation of ants in your home. When they invade your body, they invade anywhere you go. You'll have to follow instructions and make modifications to your style of life to make sure they're gone. If you think, or know, that you have one, and that you may have been in a situation where you could have given it to other people, let them know; even if they are not to popular with you at the moment. Otherwise, you will start a chain of infection, thereby becoming the root cause of many people catching the disease.

Trichomoniasis

Trichomonas vaginalis, a protozoa found in the genito-urinary tract of both sexes, is a common cause of vaginitis. The organism, found more commonly in females, affects about 20% of them during their reproductive years and causes vaginitis, urethritis, and possibly cystitis. It is more difficult to detect in men, probably causes urethritis, prostatitis, and cystitis, and may account for as much as 5 to 10% of all cases of male urethritis. Most infected men are asymptomatic carriers, but are infectious to their sexual partners.

Women typically have an onset of the disease that is accompanied by copious greenish-yellow frothy vaginal discharge associated with irritation and soreness of the vulva, perineum, and thighs. Some women experience only a slight discharge, and many are symptomless carriers for long periods, although symptoms may develop at any time. The infection frequently coexists with gonorrhœa. In severe cases, the vulva and perineum may be inflamed, with blistering of the labia. Complications are rare.

Men are generally asymptomatic. Some may have a transient, frothy, or pus-like urethral discharge with painful urination and frequency, usually early in the morning; mild urethral irritation; and discomfort in the perineum or deeper in the pelvis. A discharge may appear under the foreskin in uncircumcised men. A swelling at the testes and prostatitis are the only known complications of this disease.

Trichomonas vaginalis has garnered a lot of attention in the women's community. In 50% of women, a smear will show up the "trich" bug. In women, when there are too many of these protozoæ, they will start to cause discomfort. The level of discomfort will determine how vigorously you want to treat the problem. Like yeasts, they can travel on wet towels, where they're capable of living for hours. They also live on sauna seats and in hot tubs. In women, improper wiping can cause the spread of trichomoniasis.

It is generally treated with flagyl, an antibacterial (not antibiotic), anti-parasitic medication and/or other medication that can have some nasty side effects and high toxicity levels. So if you get *Trichomonas vaginalis*, you'll want to get rid of it quickly because the treatment may kill you faster than the illness…. All sexual partners should be examined and treated, and patients should abstain from sexual intercourse until a cure is confirmed for both partners.

Amœbiasis

Amœbiasis is caused by *Entamœba histolytica*. It is normally asymptomatic, by symptoms ranging from mild diarrhœa to dysentery may occur. It is spread by oral-rectal contact (and, in areas of poor sanitation, in food and water). This direct spreading is most common in sexual partners, particularly **homosexual men**. Controlling the spread of this disease is difficult, because so many carriers are asymptomatic.

The amœbæ invade the small intestine and can cause ulcers that may perforate to cause blood in the stool. They have been known to travel up to the liver and then on to the right lung and the area around the heart.

The symptoms of this disease could be so vague as to be unrecognized, but they are usually intermittent diarrhœa and constipation, flatulence, and some cramping, abdominal pain. Your stool may contain mucous and blood.

Amœbiasis can cause complications in the liver and appendix. Occasionally, the amœba can spread to the brain, lungs, and other organs by means of the person's blood.

Diagnosis of amœbiasis is normally confirmed by testing stool of the infected person. From 3 to 6 examinations may be required to be sure.

Treatment is usually aimed at relieving the symptoms, replacing any lost blood, and correcting any loss of fluid. Quinine-based microbicidal agents are normally prescribed. Some of the treatments may feel worse than the disease. Some of them can't even be given to you if you're pregnant or have heart trouble. Amœbiasis tends to relapse, so your physician will likely want to reëxamine you fairly often for the first six months or so after your treatment.

Giardiasis

Giardia lamblia causes this disease of the small intestine. The organisms attach themselves to the mucous membranes of the intestine and are passed from one person to another in fæces. The disease is found world-wide and is most common in areas of poor sanitation, among travellers, and in **homosexual men**. In the United States, about 4% of all stool analyzed for parasites contains *Giardia lamblia*.

Usually, there are few, if any, symptoms. Intermittent nausea, belching, flatulence, abdominal cramps, and diarrhœa. In severe cases, bad absorption of food can lead to significant weight loss and bulky, foul-smelling stool.

Stool will be examined to determine that the agent causing the symptoms is *Giardia lamblia*.

Quinine-based microbicidal agent are most frequently recommended for the treatment of giardiasis. The household and sexual contacts of any infected person should be tested for the disease. Pregnant women are only likely to be treated in severe cases of the disease.

Scabies

Scabies (mites) are caused by the itch mite *Sarcoptes scabiei*. Pregnant females tunnel into the skin, burying eggs along the way. In a few days the larvæ hatch and congregate around hair roots.

Scabies can be transmitted readily by skin to skin contact. It is rarely spread by clothing or bedding. The mite cannot live long off the human body.

Scabies causes an intense itching, particularly when you're in bed. There are characteristic burrows that look like fine wavy lines a few millimetres to 1 cm long. Inflamed lesions can occur primarily on the finger webs, the palm side of the wrists, the elbows, the folds of joints, around the nipples in **women**, on the genitalia in **men**, and along the belt line, and on the lower buttocks for both sexes. There can also be many sites around the torso and limbs. (One us had scabies and would wake up at nights wanting to tear the skin off his thighs....) The face is rarely affected in adults. The burrows can be difficult to find after a few weeks of scratching have obscured them.

Treatment is usually by a cream prescribed by your physician. It is easily cured and retreatment is rarely needed.

Lice

Body lice can involve the head (by *Pediculus humanis capitis*), the body (by *Pediculus humanis corporis*), and the genitalia (by *Phthirus pubis*). Head and pubic (crab) lice live directly on the body, while body lice live in underclothes.

Pediculosis capitis is transmitted by personal contact and by things like combs, and hats. Infestation is kept to the scalp, although it is sometimes found on the eyebrows, eyelashes, and beard.

The itching that is causes is severe. Small greyish-white nits (eggs) can be seen fixed to the hair shafts, sometimes in great numbers. They cannot be dislodged. The lice can be found (in smaller numbers than the nits) around the back of the head and behind the ears.

Pediculosis corporis is not common with good hygiene. Nits can be found on body hairs, but the lice eggs are easily found in the seams of undergarments, since the lice usually inhabit the seams of clothing worn next to the skin.

Itching is constant. Lesions are common on the shoulders, buttocks, and abdomen.

Pediculosis pubis (crabs) is usually transmitted during sex. They are normally found around the genitalia, but, in hairy people, they can be found elsewhere. The eggs are attached to the base of hairs. A sign of infestation is a scattering of minute dark brown specks (louse excreta) on undergarments where they come into contact with the lice around the genitalia and anus.

Treatment for all lice is normally with creams and shampoos for a couple of days. It is often necessary to repeat the treatment about 10 days later to destroy any surviving nits. Infestations of the eyelids and eyelashes may require the use or tweezers to remove the lice one by one. All sources of infestation (e.g. hats, combs, clothing and bedding) should be decontaminated by vacuuming, laundering and steam pressing, or dry cleaning. Recurrence is common.

Fleas

Fleas can jump between people when they're very close. They bite, and everyone reacts differently to the bite. Serious bites can be complicated by sensitivity reactions and infection. Treatment is simple, usually just prescribed lotions and creams.

Miscellaneous

There are some STDs that are not caused by one specific agent. These are described below.

Proctitis

Proctitis is an inflammation of the anorectal tissues. It is caused by gonococci, herpes simplex virus, primary and secondary syphilis, both LGV and non-LGV types of *Chlamydia trachomatis*, and human papillomaviruses. It is a disease of women and homosexual men who practice anal-receptive intercourse.

Complaints include rectal pain or soreness, urgent feelings of the need to urinate or defecate without the ability to do so, blood or pus coating their stool, or rectal discharge. Treatment will depend upon the cause and can vary from antibiotics to minor surgery.

Balanoposthitis & Balanitis

Balanoposthitis (balanitis, when the penis is circumcised) is an inflammation of the glans penis and the foreskin. It may be caused by complications of gonorrhœa, trichomoniasis, candidiasis, Reiter's syndrome, and primary or secondary syphilis. Other causes include types of dermatitis and psoriasis. In many cases no cause can be found. Balanoposthitis is often associated with a tight foreskin. The secretions under the foreskin can become infected with bacteria, resulting in inflammation and tissue destruction. People with diabetes mellitus are predisposed towards balanoposthitis.

About 2 to 3 days after sexual intercourse there may be soreness, irritation, and there may be a discharge from under the foreskin. The foreskin may constrict the head of the penis due to swelling on the surface of the head of the penis or the foreskin itself.

All other common STDs should be excluded by testing. If a cause is found, the appropriate treatment will be prescribed. Washing with salt water several times a day is likely to be prescribed if no cause is found. If the constriction of the penis by the foreskin persists after the inflammation has been resolved, circumcision may be necessary.

Vulvitis (Vulvovaginitis)

Vulvitis is a catch-all phrase used to describe a number of infectious diseases and other inflammatory conditions of the vagina and vulva. It is common for there to be a vaginal discharge with these conditions. This section of the book will serve merely to indicate the types of infection; please see the appropriate section of the book for a fuller discussion of any of these diseases.

Most occurrences of vulvovaginitis and vaginal discharges are caused by bacteria, most often by *Gardnerella vaginalis* in combination with other bacteria. Protozoæ such as *Trichomonas vaginalis* cause about one third of all cases of the disease. Candida infection is often the cause in pregnant women and diabetics. Occasionally, oral contraceptives have been known to cause a vulvovaginitis. Some of the less common causes are gonorrhœa, foreign bodies, and viral infections. Frequent douching, especially with chemicals, may upset the normal balance in the vaginal area, causing a discharge. Deodorant sprays, laundry soaps and fabric softeners, and bath water additives have all been known to cause vulvar irritation in some women. Tight, non-porous, non-absorbing undergarments may foster fungi and bacteria. Occasionally, latex in diaphragms and condoms, spemicides, and lubricants may cause some irritation.

The most common complaint is vaginal discharge, with or without vulval irritation. Itching and burning sensations are common, also.

General advice to sufferers is that, once they have seen their physician for any necessary prescription, they should take care to minimize irritation of the inflammation by removing any foreign bodies in the area (such as a diaphragm), douching occasionally with water, wearing loose clothing, and keeping the vulva clean (avoiding the use of soaps). Intermittent use of ice packs has been known to reduce the soreness. For more specific information about a given disease, please see the appropriate section.

Chemically Induced Vaginitis

Another group of non-specific vaginitis is caused by chemically induced vaginitis, such as those caused by perfumes, soaps, detergents, fabric softeners, feminine hygiene sprays, douching compounds, or other feminine medications. These are essentially allergic reactions. During your investigation into the causes of your problems, consider stopping the use of all these types of substances to be sure that one of them is not the cause. Failing any allergic reaction to these chemicals, you'll have to check for organisms....

Mechanically Induced Vaginitis

Mechanically induced vaginitis is caused strictly by physical irritation, for example: tight clothes, dampness, or rough sex. As for chemically induced vaginitis, you should remove any of these potential causes of vaginitis before you go beasty hunting.

Hormonally Induced Vaginitis

Hormonal causes of vaginitis could be from menopause and other variations in the menstrual cycle, or the side effects of medication. Your physician will take these potential causes into account during the investigation of the causes of your symptoms.

Cleanliness & Disinfection

The human body has evolved to the point that it has excellent protection against everyday infection. The skin is a very effective barrier to most things the world can throw at it, but the flesh under the skin and the bladder have little protection, if exposed. They are sterile areas of the body, so the slightest cut to the skin or the entry of an infected object into the bladder will put the body at risk. But before we go any further, a few definitions are appropriate:

Clean   means that the object has been washed, all visible contamination has been removed, and that an attempt has been made to remove any invisible infectious agents on or in the object.

Sterile   means that there is *no* infectious agent on or in the object.

(Procedures for cleaning and sterilizing both people and play toys are given in the relevant sections below.)

Any object placed into the sterile areas of the body has to be sterile. A pair of latex gloves taken from a fresh box is clean. A pair that has been properly autoclaved is sterile. This distinction is important. For example: a clean glove can be used in the vagina and the rectum, because these areas are not sterile; a sterile pair of gloves is necessary for piercing activities, where one might infect the open wound. Likewise, catheters and sounds must be sterile, because they pass into the bladder.

Condoms, Dental Dams, & Latex Gloves

Historically, the original use for condoms was to prevent the spread of disease, then many people realized that they could be used as contraceptives and started to think less of disease prevention. Nowadays, the reasons for condom use have gone completely full circle: they're used to prevent the transmission of diseases like HIV, herpes, etc.. We also have other latex barriers that can help us play safely: gloves and dental dams.

There are some basic things to know about latex. Number one is that you don't want to do anything that could damage the latex barrier. This generally means having your fingernails clipped short. To some people, long nails are a fashion statement, but the holes they create in a glove or a condom could kill you and/or your partner. Depending on the activities you want to perform, the choice is yours. Like facial tissues, latex gloves, usually of the surgical variety, can be bought in bulk. They can be autoclaved to keep them sterile and come pre-packaged in pairs. For more information on sterilizing things, please see the section on the Cleaning of Toys.

Avoid any forms of abrasives when playing with latex barriers. Grit can easily cause the latex to tear. Also, don't try to be cute and blow up a rubber before sex. If you put a small, invisible hole in the latex, you'll remove the protection that the rubber should provide.

Check the expiry dates on anything made of latex rubber. If the latex is old, it will also not do its job. Old latex gets brittle and can crack. So, if your local medical supply store is having a ten-for-one sale, check the expiry date before you buy. They must be fresh. Sometimes the only way to tell if bulk bought gloves are fresh is to check the lot number and ask the manufacturer. Don't count on any latex that doesn't look right. If it looks marbled, discoloured, or is cracking, throw it out. Sometimes, it's really hard to tell, so be careful.

Equally, if your latex barriers have been lying around in, say your toy bag, being bashed around by the toys for six months, the wrappers will have little mutilations on them. That means that they are no longer sterile. If the wrapper is all bent out of shape, don't count on the contents being clean or undamaged.

Never use fats or oils when you play using latex rubber. If a lubricant does not specifically state that it is water-based and is oil- and fat-free, don't take the chance. These oils and fats break down the rubber, weakening it, allowing for holes and tears to occur. Hand cream, moisturizers, cooking oils, Crisco, and other foods are fatty, so don't use any hand creams before using a latex glove. Even body film has oil in it.

Wrap anything that will end up in you or your partner. Finger cots are used by some when they play, but they have a tendency to fall off "in the heat of the moment." The last thing you want is to lose a finger cot, which is about the size of a dime. There are many big openings in which you could lose one of these.

Wrap things *before* you play with them. This goes for body parts as well as toys. If you're already hot and steamy, who knows what you could pick up and put on the toy, even as you wrap it in latex. *It doesn't matter whether you go for vaginal or anal penetration, use a latex glove.* If you intend to be there for a while, use two gloves, one on top of the other. If you damage the outside one, there is still a 50-50 chance that the inside one will remain intact.

The same goes for penile penetration, be it vaginal or anal. When in doubt, wrap it more than once. Try the prelubricated ones. You're not going to notice a great change of sensation. Some men say that, when a condom is tight around their penis, their penis feels better. Most AIDS prevention organizations recommend "double-bagging," some even suggest triple wrapping. You'll also have to make a choice between those with dry powder on them for ease of application, or those that come prelubricated with .nonoxynol-9 Some people are sensitive (allergic) to the type of lubricant they use.

Dental dams tend not to be lubricated. Some women are taking condoms and cutting them and using them in place of a dam. Condoms, however, are thinner than dental dams. It is relatively easy to put a split in a condom used as a dental dam. Dams are more like "industrial strength." Dams are now becoming available in larger sizes making them more like the area of a split condom.

Some people have used Saran Wrap instead of latex for prolonged rimming or oral-vaginal contact. This is an unsafe practice. Supposedly, Reynolds film is better than Saran, is better than Glad wrap, is better than Handi-Wrap. You'd have to be an engineer in polymer chemistry to understand why. It has something to do with micro-pores in the sheeting.

If you're in the situation where you've just got to go down on someone, *never* use a barrier that says it's microwaveable. This immediately means that there are micro-pores in the plastic. Good old-fashioned Reynolds film or Saran wrap is better.

Dildos don't come. So there's no problem putting a rubber without a reservoir on a dildo.

If you think that your play will involve one or both partners coming into a rubber, use a reservoir tip because there is a very real possibility that the act of coming can rupture the condom.

As a general rule, wrap it or whack it; lick it with latex; no glove, no love. The trick is to break the chain of disease transmission. Don't let diseases into or out of your body.

How to Put on Condoms

Just in case you didn't know, and for the sake of completeness, here is a quick description of how to put on a condom.

The penis should be hard when the condom is put on. If the condom has a reservoir tip, squeeze all of the air out of it using your thumb and forefinger. If there is no reservoir tip, the condom should be put on with about a half an inch not on the penis itself. Put a small amount of lubricant at the tip of the condom before you put it on (you should be using a water-based lubricant, preferably with nonoxynol-9, *not* Crisco, Vaseline, or any other oil-based lubricant). While holding the tip of the condom with one hand, roll it down the shaft with the thumb and forefinger of the other. If the vagina is dry, or if you have anal intercourse, the condom will need external lubrication (again, water-based).

When pulling out, hold the base of the condom with the thumb and forefinger of one hand. You should dispose of the condom by tying a knot in it and putting it in the garbage. Do not flush condoms down the toilet, nor use them more than once.

Condom Failure Rates

All condoms are not created equal. For instance, only latex condoms can prevent the transmission of viruses such as HIV. While, in theory, condoms should be 100% effective, in reality, they are not. As a contraceptive, they are about 90% effective. That's substantial, but hardly surefire, protection. Failure rates vary not only from brand to brand, but also from batch to batch – and according the users' age, education, and the amount of experience they have had with condoms. But you can take steps to enhance condom effectiveness. Researchers estimate that *when condoms are used properly, failure rates can be as low as one to two percent.*

Three problems can undermine the effectiveness of condoms: Breakage, leakage, and improper use. Lack of lubrication (or use of an oil-based lubricant) also increases the chance that a condom will break. A 1989 study showed that about one latex condom in 140 breaks. As for leakage, standard water tests have revealed that the major brands' leakage rates meet the Food and Drug Administration's requirements of fewer than four failures per 1,000.

A point to note is that in "test-tube" experiments, sufficiently high concentrations (>5%) of nonoxynol-9 can inactivate HIV, although effectiveness against intracellular virus has been questioned. It has also been suggested that very frequent use of nonoxynol-9 (150mg four times daily for two weeks) may disrupt the vaginal and cervical linings, which could be relevant to transmission of HIV.

What To Do When A Condom Breaks

Rather than exhibiting small leaks, as they usually do in laboratory tests, condoms and gloves can fail dramatically when in use. Once a minuscule hole is created, it can develop rapidly into a tear and split the condom into two, particularly if not enough lubricant was used.

What would we do if we found a broken condom on an object (penis, dildo, cucumber, etc....) that was being used for insertional play? Our main concern in all cases would be disease, be it from vaginal or rectal play. If the object was our penis and it was being used in a vagina, we'd also be concerned about pregnancy.

The first thing to do is to stop playing and do as much as possible to ensure that neither pregnancy nor disease transmission is likely to occur. The problem is that some damage may already have been done. Our task at this point is to minimize its effects.

First and foremost, and irrespective of our partner's reaction to such news, we would say what has just happened. This would allow us both to take the necessary measures to minimize the risk.

It is likely that you will have discovered the break in the condom (or glove) when the object was pulled out. Part may still be in the recipient, and any infection, pre-cum, or cum will be spilling from it.

Your first thought may be to flush out the person quickly with water, but any attempt to flush out the vagina or rectum at this point will likely push any infectious agent or semen further into the body. This puts the recipient into a risky position. The task is to try to get at anything left in the recipient's body without doing further damage. If you have spermicidal suppositories, you can put them in and let them do their work (about 30 minutes). The problem is that the spermicide may not get far enough into the person to reach all the spillage. In Canada, the suppositories are becoming more difficult to obtain (mainly because they are not nearly as effective as the alternatives, foam and jelly). Unless there is an adverse reaction to the spermicide, leave the suppositories in place. They will be flushed out by the body itself, when it is next ready to urinate or defecate.

Using a spermicidal jelly or foam containing nonoxynol-9 may push any infection or semen further into the body, but it will do so with a wall of spermicide. Nonoxynol-9 kills HIV, and, although it is rarely advertised that way, it also kills herpes, syphilis, and gonorrhœa. Spermicidal foam has a far greater content of nonoxynol-9 (about 12.5% versus 3 to 5%) than the jelly, since, as it foams, less of the product comes into contact with the body. Foam and jelly have an acidity that is balanced for the vagina (about pH 4.5), so if they are used in the rectum, they may sting somewhat due to their acidity and the sensitive mucous membranes in that area. (Some people are also sensitive to the nonoxynol-9 itself, but the alternative is potential pregnancy or disease....)

Because the spermicidal jellies and foams meet the spillage with a wall of spermicide, they are be our first choice (even if they do push things further into the body), followed by the spermicidal suppositories. Neither method will guarantee that you have destroyed any infection or sperm, so a visit to your physician the next morning is very important. If pregnancy is a concern, your physician will also be able to prescribe a "morning after" pill.

That deals with the internal concerns of the recipient, but what of the donor? If the inserted object was a penis, the man should urinate, wash his genital area thoroughly in soap and water a few times, and then smother it with lubricant containing nonoxynol-9. This should be left there for about 10 minutes and then washed off. The recipient should also wash and smother the external area in the same manner. If you're really, really concerned about disease, you may want to apply alcohol, hydrogen peroxide, or Betadine® to the external areas.

If the inserted object was a dildo or other toy, follow the procedures outlined in the section on Cleaning of Toys to clean it.

If you feel the need to see a physician, or for a visit to the Emergency department of your hospital, then go there immediately after treating as described above. As far as disease transmission is concerned, there is probably not much more that a physician can do for you at this point, other than monitor you both to determine if a disease was transmitted, and then to treat it.

If you have a concern about disease before you start, double-bagging is a good idea, as is a copious supply of water-soluble lubricant containing nonoxynol-9. If you need to use a condom or glove, you need to use lubricant.

Cleaning of Toys

One of the easiest ways to prevent the spread of diseases is to ensure that any toy you use during play is used on only one person. Anything that has contact with someone's blood, piss, shit, or cum should be restricted to that person. (Fortunately, it seems that sweat and saliva are not likely ways to transmit diseases.) One of the basic truths of immunology is that you cannot catch something from your own bodily secretions that you didn't already have. That does not mean that you can't move something like gonorrhœa from one part of the body to another. If solo use of toys is impossible, you're should ensure that the toy is properly decontaminated between uses.

Many bacteria and viruses are susceptible to drying. HIV is a fairly fragile virus if it is not in a bodily fluid, but others can live on, say, a butt plug for months, even if it stays dry. So, no matter how long your toys have been lying around since they were last played with, they should be decontaminated before being used again.

Any implement used for piercing, drawing blood in other ways, or inserting into the urethra should be sterile. These toys invade sterile areas of the body that can easily be contaminated. That means that special procedures have to be followed to ensure that no organisms at all live on these toys. The mouth, vagina, and rectum are not sterile parts of the body, so anything put there must, at the very least, be properly cleaned beforehand, but it does not have to be sterile.

Sterile implements used for play should be:

1. Thrown out after being used and replaced with a new one;

2. Reused only on the same person (*never* on another); or

3. Sterilized between uses by a method that will kill all viruses and bacteria.

Needles should always be discarded safely after the first use.

Whatever a toy is made of, if it can stand your playing with it, it can stand being washed. Use warm, soapy water, to start with, making sure that all pits, cracks, crevices, and other openings have been thoroughly cleaned out and that all lubricants and other materials have been washed away. *This washing will NOT kill viruses or bacteria.* The agents you will use to kill the bugs cannot get behind a film of lubricant or whatever to do their work. After the toy is washed, rinse it thoroughly to remove all the soap.

Many viruses and bacteria are hardy, so killing them all takes a lot. *Hydrogen peroxide and rubbing alcohol do not sterilize*, they do help to remove oils and surface muck to help prepare for sterilization.

Rubbing alcohol, peroxide, and chlorine, in the form of bleach, will help clean toys. Alcohol should be at least 25%, which means that the standard 70% isopropyl (rubbing) alcohol available at pharmacies is cheap and effective. (Some isopropyl alcohol sold in pharmacies is 90%. This is actually much less effective for killing "bugs" than the 70%, because it dehydrates and preserves the bug, rather than killing it. It is also much more inflammable than the 70%, and therefore more dangerous in the playroom. Avoid it.) Chlorine bleach should be diluted 1 part bleach to nine parts water. Hydrogen Peroxide is usually sold in 10% solution and should be used this way, directly from the bottle.

These methods serve only to clean your toys, they do *not* sterilize them. They help minimize the risk of viruses and bacteria staying on the toy, but they are no guarantee that all "bugs" have been killed.

The HIV virus can be killed by exposure to temperatures above 140°F or 60°C or higher for at least four minutes. This can either be from the dry heat of an oven or the wet heat from immersion in hot water. If your dishwasher or washing machine can reach these temperatures for four to five minutes, you could use it to *clean* your toys.

Toys such as piercing needles, straight razors, metal ass toys, enema tubes, and urethral sounds have to be sterilized using high temperature. Beware, however, that because certain toys were not meant to be treated with heat, things like dildos can melt under the temperatures required. If you have access to an autoclave (via a friendly nurse or physician) you're in luck, but there is no need for such complexities. A large pressure cooker will work well for anything that will fit into it. This covers most toys used for insertion. Pressure cookers may be a bit out of fashion, but they're still available. Follow the directions above to remove the muck and lubricant from the toy. If you have several toys, do this for all of them and then wrap them individually and well in sturdy paper "packets," such that when you touch the packet to move the toy there is no danger that you will touch the toy. (You may want to wrap things like piercing needles in small numbers suitable for a complete scene.) Lunch bags or other brown paper bags work well. Seal them with masking tape. Put the packets in a wire basket that will fit into the pressure cooker and will keep the packets out of the water at the bottom of the cooker. Follow the manufacturer's instructions to operate the cooker. Bring the pressure up to 15 pounds. Only *after* this point has been reached, "cook" the contents of the cooker for 30 minutes. While the packets are being "cooked," preheat your oven to 225°F. Carefully remove the basket from the cooker and put it in the oven. *Do not touch the packets with anything.* They cannot be handled safely until they are dry. Turn the oven off immediately the packets have been put into it. Let the packets cool and dry for *at least three hours*. Store them in a safe, dry place until you need them. Toys cleaned in this manner are sterile, as opposed to just clean or decontaminated.

If the toy you are using cannot be sterilized, and it regularly comes into contact with bodily fluids, it should be reserved for use on one person only for the whole of the toy's useful life. If it has been used on many people in the past, get rid of it and find a new one.

Toys that are difficult to clean, such as metal ass balls, eggs, or plugs with holes through them, need special care when you clean them. The holes in metal balls, eggs, and plugs require that you unstring them and use high pressure soapy water to clean the inside. You could also use Betadine, commonly used to scrub down things that can't be sterilized for the operating room, like a pair of surgeon's hands. You can get it at pharmacies; no prescription is required.

Toys made only of metal, like chromed metal butt plugs or metal ass balls with the string removed, can be sterilized in the oven at 300°F for at least half an hour (make sure that they cool to room temperature before you use them). If you intend to sterilize these toys this way, make sure to clean them first, as described above.

All toys that have to be clean, rather than sterile, should be well rinsed after decontamination. Bleach and isopropyl alcohol should not be allowed to come into contact with mucous membranes, such as those in the rectum or vagina.

Many publications have recommended covering dildos or butt plugs with condoms to help them stay clean during use. This can certainly help. Remember, however, that toys come is many shapes, many of them very different from the shape of an erect penis. The shape of the toy or any exposed stitching could cause the condom to split, tear, or otherwise malfunction, so don't rely on them to protect you from a contaminated toy. Use them, rather, to make cleaning the toy afterwards a bit easier. If you get the toy dirty when you take the condom off it, follow the cleaning instructions given above.

There is a problem for items like leather whips, leather dildos. The whip may come into contact with broken skin and the dildo will come into contact with vaginal secretions or fæces. Folds of braided leather in a whip or the stitching in just about any other leather toy are almost impossible to scrub properly, simply because you can't get into the crevices caused by the stitching or braiding. If you *can* get at the whole of a leather item, alcohol will cause less bleaching than peroxide or bleach. Alcohol, however, very rapidly dries out the leather, so it should be treated with an acceptable leather cleaner immediately *after* it has dried, or it will become brittle and crack. Vampire gloves may accidentally break the skin, but the chance of the same tooth breaking the skin on someone else may be low. Made of leather and steel pricks, these toys cannot be autoclaved and nor cleaned with the other available products. For all these toys, you will have to assess the risk you are prepared to accept.

Cleaning of People

While it may seem a strange topic for a book like this (we all know how to take a shower, after all), we've found that special cleaning of the body is needed for certain types of SM play. These are mainly for ass play and any form of blood letting play.

Cleaning the Ass for Play

This is the means to your end. If it is not clean, you will considerably reduce the number of people who want to play with it. Cleaning the ass requires that you use an enema of some form. Most supermarkets carry bags in their feminine needs section. If you cannot find them there, just ask. There are many reasons to use them other than to prepare for play, so you will not be looked at as a pervert if you go to buy one. The bags should be kept as a one-person only toy because of the nature of where they're used.

Most bags will come with a set of instructions with the kit. In effect, the instructions will tell you to use warm water, hang the bag above the rectum, take as much water as is comfortable or needed, allow the mixture into the toilet bowl, and repeat the procedure until it runs clear.

It is a good idea to purge the air out of the tube before you put the nozzle into the ass. To do this, make sure that the nozzle is lower than the bag, and run a little water out until it runs smoothly, without spitting air. Some people prefer to lubricate the nozzle before inserting it into the ass. Try to use a water-based lubricant, because it will flush out as you expel the mixture, and it will not degrade the rubber parts of the bag assembly with which it may come into contact.

If you just want to insert small objects into the rectum, you may only want to clean six or seven inches of it. Fisting will require more cleaning, deeper into the rectum. In this case, you may need to use more water and flush several times more.

Once you have cleaned yourself, don't forget to clean your toys. Your should remove the nozzle and clean it with a solution of nine parts bleach to one part water and then rinse thoroughly with tap water. Regardless of your cleaning method, this is a single-person toy. Don't use it for someone else, even after it has been cleaned.

An enema tends to remove everything from the colon, the bad and the good. If you use an enema often, you may want to restock the flora in the colon. Live-culture yoghurt is a good way to do this. Alternatively, there are also pills you can take that are designed to replace colonic flora. These contain lactobacilli and are available at many health food stores. If you have any questions about using these supplements, talk with your physician.

Cleaning the Skin for Blood Letting Play

Since you will be temporarily breaking the complete barrier that the skin provides and reaching into the sterile parts of the body, it is imperative that you use only *sterile* toys. If the skin through which a sterile toy passes is not sterile, then neither is the toy as it passes though the skin. Sterilizing toys is covered in the section on Cleaning of Toys, above.

The skin is not a toy. It is the body's largest organ and should be treated with as much respect as you would treat, say, the heart. We've all had to give blood for tests at some point. The nurse will wipe the area to clean it before putting the needle in our vein for the sample. The idea in this case is to remove any surface contaminant from the area before the needle passes through it. You will have to do the same thing.

Any part of the body that is to be cut or pierced should be thoroughly washed beforehand with soap or, preferably, an antibacterial soap, such as Hibitane® or Hibiclens®. (Antibacterial soaps can be bought at most pharmacies.) You might also want to use an unscented exfoliant, such as a rough wash cloth, to help dislodge any ground-in dirt. This will usually still leave a thin layer of soap on the surface that could attract dirt. To remove this, wipe the area with a cloth or cotton wool dipped in rubbing alcohol. Now that the surface is clean, it has to be sterilized. Since we can't put someone in an oven at 400°F for four minutes, or boil them for the same amount of time (unless you happen to be one of Shakespeare's crones in Macbeth), what can we do?

Hydrogen peroxide will help to clean the area, but will not sterilize it completely. We are left with only one practical method: Betadine® or another iodine-based cleaner. Once the skin has been prepared using alcohol and peroxide, wipe the area where you intend to play with the Betadine® (or similar) solution. This is the closest to sterilization of the skin that can be achieved. Do *not* touch that area again with anything that is not sterile until play is complete and the area has been properly recleaned and protected.

If you are going to pierce a nipple or any other area, make the cleaning motion a spiral shape working *outwards* from the area to be pierced. This will take any dirt away. Any milk from a nipple will have come from the inside of the body, so it cannot infect the owner of the nipple (note that men can secrete milk as well as women). The experience of piercers we know is that, during nipple cleaning, men secrete more milk than women.

The navel (belly-button) has unseen folds of skin inside. You will have to super-saturate the navel with Betadine on a cotton ball. Then work it around with a small circular actions, pushing it into the navel and agitating it as you go, to get right down into the folds of skin.

The foreskin has to be cleaned in a similar, very thorough manner. Pull it back and make sure that any folds are carefully cleaned. The female labia require you to get up under the hood, into the folds of the labia with a Q-tip with one end in Betadine first, then the other end dry. Repeat at least twice, then use a Q-tip with rubbing alcohol in the same way. The alcohol removes excess Betadine which is slippery and may cause you to slip when placing the piercing. Alcohol may sting briefly when it comes into contact with the mucous membranes in the female genitals.

For cleaning afterwards, you can use a spray bottle with a fine mist of a mixture of half-and-half rubbing alcohol and Betadine. Since you should not be causing anything more than small cuts and needle holes, you can treat them using normal first aid procedures. At least these breaks in the skin were made with sterile implements, unlike that rusty nail that you cut yourself on a while ago.

If you intend to whip an area of the body fairly actively, it would be a good idea to make sure that whipping area is also as clean as it would be for piercing and cutting. It won't take long and will help minimize any risks. Likewise, if your whipping might cause a cut or the whip has already cut someone, make sure that the whip has not only been properly cleaned but also that it is a single-person only toy (used only for the person whose back is being whipped). Depending on the kind of play, any toy that cannot be properly cleaned or sterilized should only be used on the person whose bodily fluids came into contact with it in the first place.

Mind-Altering Substances

The title of this section says a lot. Any substance that changes the way that the mind thinks or perceives its surroundings should be treated with a great deal of caution. It's one thing to go on a drug-induced trip when nothing else is involved, but SM play brings many other considerations to the use of drugs. We feel that, before discussing the details of the drugs in question, it is important to tell you why we attach so much importance to discussing them in the first place. (For the purposes of this book, we will use the term drug(s) to mean any non-prescription drug or prescription drug not used for the purposes for which it was prescribed.)

Drugs are taken specifically because they alter the way in which we perceive our surroundings and the effects that they can have on our moods. Some drugs are taken to give a feeling of power and joy, others for the sense of calm they bring to the user. All of them change how we perceive and measure the world and people around us.

The effects and/or benefits of the drugs should weighed against the costs. Most drugs have side and after effects on the body and mind. Often, these are not pleasant. Some drugs destroy internal organs, others will give you cancer. Some will make you think that you can do anything, others will produce wonderful dream-like states. Some bring about hallucinations and nightmares well after the user has stopped taking them.

Because drugs all alter our perception of the world, they also compromise our ability to measure the cost/benefit ratio properly *and* they compromise our ability to act properly on any correct measure we may have been able to make. Taking a drug increases risk during an SM scene precisely because the drug reduces our ability to assess risk accurately.

Most drug users know which drug they like best. Many have experimented enough to have found their drug of choice. Drug *abusers* fail to see the actual costs involved in their taking of the drug; that is, once addicted they care only about the benefits and not at all about the costs. Add to that that most people do not fully understand the true costs using of drugs and you have a recipe for problems.

In light of the diseases currently found in the western world, any way to keep our immune system functioning properly will help us. Aside from the reduction of a person's ability to assess risk, it has been shown that all the recreational, and some prescription, drugs weaken the immune system. Of these, the amphetamine family seems to do the most damage to the immune system. Other recreational drugs are also hard on the liver and kidneys. So, there is more than one reason for us not to use them in an SM scene.

Drugs also alter the way in which people respond to stimuli, so that, say, a Bottom using a depressant may seem to be able to take the flogging the Top is giving, but in reality his/her body is taking a beating with which it can't really cope. The Top may not be on drugs, but he/she may still not be able to see that there is a real problem, because the Bottom is not reacting normally. The Top has to try to "see through" the effects of the drug to know what is really going on. A Top's job is often hard enough without this added burden.

If the Top were on a stimulant like an amphetamine and the Bottom were on a depressant like a barbiturate, you'd have a real recipe for disaster. We know of one such case where, feeling all-powerful from amphetamines, the Top in a cutting scene almost went for the Bottom's jugular vein. In the end, the Top put a large cut in the Bottom's chest. The Bottom was too sedated to notice what was going on. The result is obvious. Fortunately, the scene was being done where there were others close enough who could do something about the incident, but only after the fact. Both Top and Bottom learnt an important, if painful, lesson.

The sense of power from some stimulants makes people feel that they can drop their usual, safe standards for play. Again, when mixed with SM play, the results can be devastating.

Experimentation with drugs usually starts slowly and proceeds until the user has a bad experience. It could be an arrest for driving while under the influence of alcohol or drugs; the loss of a potential play partner who is not willing to play with someone who uses drugs; or maybe just a bad headache the next morning. In the end, increased drug use starts to be noticed by people close to the user, who may try to persuade the him/her to seek some kind of help. The user may also notice problems and put him/herself into treatment, but the worst cases end up in hospital Emergency departments.

For all the reasons above, and probably some others, most (if not all) SM organizations have drug policies like the one given at the end of this book in Appendix A. They are there to protect you, so you can expect them to be enforced at any club event. Because you're reading this book, there's a fair chance that you have chosen to experiment with or engage in SM activities. You might also choose to take a mind-altering substance. Whether you choose to play Top or Bottom, you must decide whether your or your partner's decision to take a drug compromises either or both of your rights to safe, sane, and consensual play.

Now that we've looked at why we should be concerned about a person's ability to function safely while under the influence of any mind- (or bodily-) altering substance, we'll take a look at the various kinds that are used and what, individually, each can do to your mind and body. All of the following descriptions of drugs are from a general, rather than SM specific, point of view. Where relevant, we have made comments on particular relevance to SM play. We have tried not to be judgmental in reporting each of these substances, so the descriptions may seem a little technical and dry, but, to the best of our knowledge, they're accurate. Both the effects of use and dependence on the drug are described.

First, we'll take a quick look at the meaning of dependence. It's not possible, or desirable, to define dependence for all types of drugs together. They all react differently in the body and the mind, so the type of dependence and the hazards involved are also different.

Addiction refers to a style of living that includes drug dependence, usually both physical and psychologic, but mainly means continuing compulsive use and overwhelming involvement with the drug. Addiction also implies the risk of harm and the need to stop drug use, irrespective of whether the addict understands and agrees.

Drug use is only definable in terms of societal disapproval and involves different types of behaviour: experimental and recreational use of drugs; use of psychoactive drugs to relieve problems or symptoms; and use of drugs initially for the above reasons, but then development of dependence and continuation are at least partially to prevent the discomfort of withdrawal.

Drug users who do not apparently suffer harm seem to use their drug(s) in episodes with long breaks between, and in fairly small doses, well before the onset of physical poisoning and development of tolerance and physical dependence. Often, the drugs are used in a form close to their "natural" state, i.e. they contain a mixture of compounds and are not isolated psychoactive chemicals, e.g. alcoholic and caffeine-containing beverages, marijuana products, hallucinogenic ("magic") mushrooms, crude opium, and coca leaf. Usually, the drug is inhaled or taken orally. Recreational use is most often accompanied by ritualization, with a set of observed rules and is seldom practised alone. Most drugs used this way are hallucinogens and psychostimulants designed to induce a "high," rather than to relieve psychic distress. Depressant drugs are rarely used this way.

There are two major types of dependence on drugs:

Psychologic dependence	involves feelings of satisfaction and a desire to repeat the administration of the drug to produce pleasure or avoid discomfort. This mental state is a powerful factor in chronic use of hallucinogenic drugs. With some drugs, psychologic dependence may be the only factor involved in intense craving and compulsive use.
Physical dependence	is defined as a state of adaptation to a drug, accompanied by a development of tolerance and is demonstrated by a withdrawal syndrome.
Tolerance	is defined as the need to increase the dose of the drug progressively in order to produce the effect originally achieved with smaller doses. Physical dependence and tolerance do not occur for all types of recreational drug dependence.
Withdrawal syndrome	is characterized by unpleasant physiologic changes that happen when the use of the drug is stopped.

The effects of drugs concern us all when we play. Drugs that produce dependence act on the central nervous system and have one or more of these effects: reduced anxiety and tension; elation; euphoria or other mood-altering effects that are pleasurable to the user; feelings of increased mental and physical ability; altered sensory perception; and behavioural changes. Drugs that produce a sense of power may cause a Top to injure the Bottom. A depressant or hallucinogen may cause a Bottom to ignore unintentional pain and injury. The drugs can be divided into two main categories: those that produce mainly psychic dependence (e.g. cocaine, marijuana, amphetamine, bromides, and the hallucinogens, such as lysergic acid diethylamide (LSD), methylene dioxyamphetamine (MDA), and mescaline), and those that produce both psychic and physical dependence. Those in the first group do not produce a major withdrawal syndrome, but some produce tolerance, and in some cases symptoms like a withdrawal syndrome are present (e.g. depression and lethargy follow withdrawal of cocaine and amphetamine). Table 7–1 lists some, but by no means all, of the commonly used recreational drugs and their potential for the various types of dependence.

Drug	Physical Dependence	Psychologic Dependence	Tolerance
Central Nervous System Depressants			
Opioids	••••	••••	••••
Synthetic narcotics	••••	••••	••••
Barbiturates	•••	•••	••
Methaqualone (Quaalude®)	•••	•••	••
Alcohol	•••	•••	••
Stimulants			
Amphetamines	Unknown	•••	••••
Cocaine	0	•••	0
Hallucinogens			
LSD	0	••	••
Mescaline, peyote	0	••	•
Marijuana			
low dose Δ-9 THC	0	••	0
high dose Δ-9 THC	0	••	Unknown

Abbreviations: LSD, Lysergic acid diethylamide; THC, tetrahydrocannabinol; 0, no effect; • slight effect; •••• marked effect

Table 7–1. Commonly Used Drugs With Potential for Dependence

The medical world seems to be unclear about the development of drug dependence, but at least three components seem to contribute to it: the addictive drug, predisposing conditions, and the personality of the user. The progressions from experimentation to occasional use and to development of tolerance and physical dependence are poorly understood; it's much easier to determine the effects than the cause. Many people who become addicted or dependent have no known biochemical, drug dispositional, or physiologic responsiveness differences from those who do not, although many efforts have been made to find some. Use of drugs seems to be capable of happening in anyone. Before developing dependence, users did not demonstrate a pleasure-oriented, irresponsible behaviour that is usually and prejudicially attributed to addicts. Sometimes those dependent on a drug justify the use because of a crisis, job pressure, or family catastrophe that causes anxiety or depression. Most of these people have shown an abuse of alcohol and other drugs at the same time.

That's 150, Madam!
Thank you, Madam!

The following subsections attempt to describe the effects and symptoms of drug dependence so that you can determine what might happen to your ability to assess risk during play, and so that you can determine if your partner(s) is (are) using drugs and what effect *they* may have on *you*. (In the bibliography, we have included a separate list of books that address the use and effects of drugs and how they might affect safe play.)

Alcohol

Alcohol is absorbed into the blood, mainly at the small intestine. It accumulates in the blood because the absorption is quicker than the oxidation of the alcohol on its passage through the body. Depression of the central nervous system is the principal effect of alcohol: a blood alcohol level of 50mg of alcohol/dL of blood produces sedation or tranquillity; 50 to 150mg/dL, lack of coördination; 150 to 200mg/dL, intoxication (delirium); and 300 to 400mg/dL, unconsciousness. Levels of greater than 500mg/dL can be fatal. From 5 to 10% of the alcohol you drink is expelled unaltered in urine, sweat, and in your breath. The remainder is oxidized to carbon dioxide and water at the rate of about 6 to 13mg (of absolute alcohol) per hour. We'll leave it to you to work out how many drinks per hour are removed from the body. You'll be quite surprised.

Here's the answer, anyway: An average shot of spirits, glass of wine, or beer contains about the same amount of absolute alcohol, i.e. ≈ 15g alcohol per beer, 12g per wine, and 11g per shot. There are about 4L (= 40dL) of blood in the human system. Taking wine as the measure: 12,000mg per 40dL = 300mg/dL! The answer shocked us when we did the calculation, too. It means that the alcohol in a glass of wine, injected directly into the blood stream would probably knock you unconscious! Normally, alcohol taken orally will take some time to enter the blood stream and during that time some of it will be expelled in urine or be oxidized, so one glass of wine is not likely to make you unconscious, but it's effects are perhaps more severe than most people would like to think. Yet, alcohol is often thought by the public at large to be one of the least potent of the drugs available....

Some people like to play with enemas and, as part of that play, they may mix wine with the water. Since alcohol is passed into the bloodstream much quicker through the rectum than the stomach, the wine should be well diluted and the Top should be aware that the effect of alcohol introduced this way could be an enormous shock to the Bottom's body. If you decide play with wine enemas, we recommend that the Top use small quantity of alcohol the first time, to see how the Bottom reacts. Future scenes can be based upon the Bottom's reaction in previous scenes. This way you'll be able to minimize the risk of alcohol poisoning.

People who drink large amounts of alcohol repetitively become somewhat tolerant to its effects (this is also seen with other central nervous systems depressant like opioids, barbiturates, etc.). This tolerance is caused by an adaptation to the drug by the cells in the central nervous system. Tolerance has rarely allowed anyone to survive levels greater that about 700mg/dL. In all cases of tolerance, the effects of intoxication and impairment are seen. The physical dependence accompanying tolerance are profound and withdrawal from alcohol tolerance may produce adverse effects severe enough to cause death. People who are tolerant to alcohol tends to be tolerant to the other depressants, e.g. barbiturates, opioids, etc..

Withdrawal from alcohol occurs about 12 to 48 hours after intake is stopped and can cause weakness and sweating. Most other effects are not necessarily relevant to play, but they can be severe.

Long term excessive use of alcohol can produce hallucinations, often accusatory and threatening, making the person apprehensive, even terrified. We wouldn't want to be playing with either a Top or a Bottom going through this.

Amphetamines

These drugs are stimulants and anorexiants. They can produce a variety of reactions from elevated mood, increased wakefulness, alertness, concentration, and physical performance. They can also induce a feeling of well-being. Often, use of amphetamines (sometimes called "crystal" or "speed") is combined with large amounts of caffeine. Users of amphetamine are prone to accidents because of the feelings of excitation and grandiosity and the ensuing fatigue and insomnia that are produced (Bottoms beware of Tops on amphetamines). Intravenous use can produce forms of antisocial behaviour and start a schizophrenic episode.

Continued high dosage of amphetamines can cause some adverse reactions that will be very relevant to any SM play you may be contemplating. They include: anxiety reactions during which the person is fearful and concerned about his/her well-being; a form of psychosis in which the person misinterprets the actions of other people, hallucinates, and becomes unrealistically suspicious; after the stimulation phase the person has intense feelings of fatigue and need for sleep; and prolonged depression in which suicide is a possibility. Would you want to play with this person?

Withdrawal for amphetamines, if one exists, is not severe. It is usually followed by mental and physical depression and fatigue. The psychologic effects are similar to cocaine, but the dependence on amphetamines varies. Unlike cocaine and the other central nervous system depressants, amphetamine does cause tolerance. It develops slowly, and can reach the point at which the amount used is several hundred times that used at the beginning. Tolerance can cause a variety of effects: nervousness, insomnia, and eventually hallucinations and delusions. Massive doses in chronic users are rarely fatal, but users new to the drug have died on relatively small doses. As a result of long-term intravenous high doses (and sometimes for high oral doses or moderate long term use), a paranoid psychosis usually occurs. The symptoms of this psychosis include delusions of persecution and ideas of being all-powerful (again, Bottoms beware). Most people recover from even prolonged amphetamine psychosis. The worst symptoms usually go away in the first few days or weeks, although some level of confusion and memory loss and some delusional ideas may last for several months.

Usually, reassurance and a quiet, non-threatening environment permit the person to recover from dependence on amphetamine.

The commonly used amphetamines are: amphetamine sulphate, amphetamine phosphate, dextroamphetamine, methamphetamine, and phenmetrazine (Preludin®).

Barbiturates

Barbiturates produce a psychic dependence that may lead to periodic, as often as continuous, abuse. Physical dependence can only be detected after considerable doses have been taken. Barbiturates and alcohol are very similar in their syndromes of dependence, withdrawal, and chronic intoxication. When the barbiturate intake is reduced below a critical level, a withdrawal syndrome follows. Symptoms of withdrawal from barbiturates and other sedative-hypnotic drugs can be completely suppressed with a barbiturate. Tolerance to barbiturates develops irregularly and incompletely, so considerable behavioural disturbances can occur. Some mutual, but incomplete, cross-tolerance can occur between barbiturates and alcohol, as well as the non-barbiturate sedative-hypnotic drugs.

In general, those who are dependent on sedatives and hypnotic drugs like to use the ones that react fast (e.g. secobarbital and pento-barbital) Some signs of dependence are depression of the skin reflexes, decreased alertness, loss of control of muscles (especially those at the extremities), and slurred speech. As dependence progresses, there is an involuntary oscillation of the eyes as they look forward, control of the muscles becomes difficult (making the person fall over repeatedly), deep sleep, small pupils, and ultimately death. Those on high doses frequently have trouble thinking and have poor memory, faulty judgement, smaller attention span, slowness of speech and comprehension, and changing emotions. So, if you see slow thinking, slurred speech, and bruises on the extremities of someone's body, you might start to suspect a dependence on depressants. In Table 7–2, we have noted some commonly used and abused sedatives and tranquilizers and the dosages that have produced dependence.

In some people, dependence can occur in as little as a few weeks, so attempts to stop using a depressant can quickly lead to withdrawal. Stopping the drug use will worsen any initial insomnia and result in restlessness, disturbed dreams, frequent awakenings during the night, and feelings of tension early in the morning. The extent of the symptoms depends on the amount taken and the duration of use. Suddenly stopping the use of barbiturates or tranquilizers causes a severe, frightening, and potentially life-threatening illness that is very like delirium tremens (the DTs) caused by stopping alcohol consumption. Withdrawal from barbiturates frequently causes death, so it should be done under strict medical supervision in a hospital. Once withdrawal has begun, it is difficult to stop. Even properly managed, withdrawal can still cause seizures and may last as long as a month. Convulsions that may cause death occur in about 75% of cases of people who have been taking more than about 800mg/day.

People coming off benzodiazepines, particularly diazepam (Valium®), have similar withdrawal symptoms, but rarely as severe. Many of those who use these drugs are also heavy users of alcohol.

Playing with someone on sedatives and hypnotic drugs could be dangerous to your health. For them, coming off the drug(s) is no party either....

That's 154, Madam!
Thank you, Madam!

Drug	Dose Producing Dependence (mg/day)	Time Needed to Produce Dependence (Days)
Secobarbital	500-600	30
Pentobarbital ("Yellow Jackets")	500-600	30
Amobarbital ("Blues")	500-600	30
Amobarbital-secobarbital combination ("Rainbows")	500-600	30
Diazepam (Valium®)	60-100	40
Methaqualone (Quaalude®)	1800-2400	30

Table 7–2. Doses of Some Common Sedatives & Tranquilizers
That Have Produced Physical Dependence

Cannabis (Marijuana)

Chronic use of cannabis or cannabis substances can produce psychic dependence on the subjective effects, but no physical dependence. There is no withdrawal syndrome associated with discontinuing the use of cannabis. Unlike some drugs, it can be used continually or occasionally without apparent social or psychic problems. There have been reports of cannabis making schizophrenic episodes occur in some people, even those on anti-psychotic medication. The metabolized products of cannabis remain in the body for a long time.

Cannabis produces a dreamy state of consciousness in which ideas seem to be disconnected, uncontrollable, and free flowing. Time, colour, and spatial perceptions are distorted. In general, there is a feeling of well-being exaltation, excitement, and inner joyousness. Many of the psychic effects seem to be related to the circumstances under which the drug is taken. Occasionally, panic is seen in people, particularly those who have not used the drug often. Communicative abilities and muscle control are decreased by cannabis, as are depth perception and senses of timing. These can all be very hazardous to SM play partners of cannabis users.

Cocaine & Crack

Cocaine (sometimes called "snow") causes a psychic dependence, sometimes leading to a profound psychic addiction. The dependence is produced by high doses of the stimulant drug that cause euphoric excitement and, occasionally, hallucinations. Neither tolerance to the drug nor physical dependence have been reported, but the tendency to continue taking cocaine is strong.

The effects of cocaine use vary considerably with the method of use. when it is inhaled or injected, it produces a condition of hyperstimulation, alertness, euphoria, and feeling of great power (similar to the effects of injecting a high dose of an amphetamine). Since the drug is very short-acting, heavy users may resort to injecting it intravenously as often as every 10 to 15 minutes. With this repetition, toxic effects such as muscle-twitching, small visual hallucinations, sleeplessness, and extreme nervousness are evident. Hallucinations and paranoid delusions may occur, as well as violent behaviour; the person could be quite dangerous at this time. The action of the drug is sufficiently brief to prevent sustained aggressive activity, however. The pupils will be dilated to their maximum extent, and the heart and breathing rate may rise. Overdose of cocaine can produce convulsions and delirium, and can cause death from heart failure or collapse of the lungs. Severe toxic effects have been observed in heavy, compulsive users, most of whom have a history of heroïn use.

The smoking of "free-base" cocaine (often referred to as "crack") can be more dangerous to the user and those close to the user because crack requires the conversion of the cocaine to a more combustible form that is then held to a flame and the smoke inhaled. The extraction uses flammable solvents that have caused serious explosions. The speed of onset of the symptoms of crack are faster than for plain cocaine and the intensity of the high is magnified.

Procaine

Procaine, when snorted, produces local sensations not unlike cocaine and may even produce a high. Powdered procaine is used to cut cocaine and is occasionally mixed with other substances and sold as cocaine. Sometimes procaine is sold as "synthetic cocaine."

Hallucinogens

Hallucinogens include lysergic acid diethylamide (LSD, "acid"), mescaline, psilocybin ("magic mushrooms"), peyote, 2,5-dimethoxy-4-methylamphetamine ("DOM," "STP"), methylene dioxyamphetamine (MDA), 3,4-methylenedioxymethamphetamine (MDMA), and the amphetamines that are substituted for them. Other than LSD, hallucinogens are not available "on the street," despite what dealers and users believe. Recently, samples of street product called "ecstasy" (or just "X") have contained relatively pure MDMA.

These drugs induce a state of excitation in the central nervous system that is manifested by changes in mood (usually euphoric, but sometimes depressive) and perception. Responses to hallucinogens vary according to several factors, including the person's expectations (described as the "set" by Timothy Leary), the setting (also Leary), and the person's ability to cope with perceptual distortions. Rarely do true hallucinations occur. Effects can also include dizziness, nausea, dilated pupils, disorientation, space-time distortion, muscle weakness, and loss of appetite. Psychic dependence on the drugs varies greatly, but is usually is not intense. No evidence of physical dependence is found when the hallucinogens are suddenly stopped, and a high degree of tolerance occurs with these drugs, but it disappears quickly. People who are tolerant to one hallucinogen tend to be cross-tolerant to others.

LSD is one of the most powerful psychoactive drugs ever synthesized; so powerful that only 30 millionths of a gram can be effective. That amount is invisible to the naked eye. Once in the body, it is quickly absorbed and cleared out of the bloodstream. The effects of LSD (an "acid trip") usually begin about 30 to 90 minutes after the drug is taken, and can last about 7 to 12 hours. It is generally agreed that LSD works by inhibiting the transmission of the neurotransmitter serotonin, which enables the brain to make sense of the input that normally floods in from the outside world. Short term memory is reduced and the bewildering speed at which signals flood in is often called "sensory overload." Other reported effects are distractability, rapid mood swings, a sense of death or separateness from the body, and, in some cases, temporary or permanent psychosis.

Peyote has effects that include dizziness and vomiting, followed by spectacular kaleidoscopic visions, tactile and auditory hallucinations, muscular sluggishness, and an indifference to external reality.

Psilocybin mushrooms can cause effects that include muscular weakness, periods of impaired breathing, numbness of the limbs, dilated pupils, and difficulty of concentration. In high doses, psilocybin produces breathtakingly colourful and lifelike visions accompanied by auditory hallucinations. There is a general lassitude, space-time alteration, a sense of being disembodied, and the user

SM Play

may become wholly indifferent to any external reality. As with LSD, set and setting may vary the effects of psilocybin.

MDA, part of the amphetamine family, is known as the "love drug" due to its reputation for stimulating the libido. Symptoms can include nausea, tensing of the face and neck muscles, and repetitive chewing of the inside of the mouth. There are usually no perceptual distortions, although some people experience a form of visual "strobing." The most usual effects are heightened tactile awareness, increased visual acuity, and pain tolerance, accompanied by intense feelings of empathy. They last for up to 8 hours. Because the effects are milder than those of LSD, there is a higher risk of overdose.

MDMA ("ecstasy," "X") is similar to methylene dioxyamphetamine (MDA), as are its effects, although they are not as intense and they do not last as long; therefore the risk of overdose is greater. MDMA is currently popular at parties because it enables the user to dance in a trance-like state for long periods, causing a risk of dehydration. Adverse effects of high doses and prolonged use include convulsions and damage to the spinal cord.

The main dangers associated with these drugs are the psychologic effects and impairment of judgement, which can lead to very dangerous decisions and accidents. Due to the powerful effects and unpredictability of hallucinogens, it is very important to ensure that nobody in an SM scene be using them.

Bad reactions to LSD apparently have become rare, possibly due to the knowledge of how set and setting affect use of the drug. Bad reactions show up as anxiety attacks, extreme apprehensiveness, or states of panic. Usually, these reactions subside rapidly with appropriate management in a secure setting. Some people (especially after using LSD), remain disturbed and can even experience a persistent psychotic state. It is not clear whether the drug use precipitates or uncovers the psychotic potential of the individual, or whether the effect can occur in previously stable people.

After discontinuing use of hallucinogens, some people experience "flashbacks." These normally comprise visual illusions, but they can include distortions of any of the senses (e.g.: time , space, self-image, etc.) or hallucinations. Marijuana, alcohol, barbiturates, stress, and fatigue can all precipitate flashbacks. They can also occur for no apparent reason. The mechanisms that cause flashbacks are not known, but they tend to subside over a period of 6 to 12 months.

At the time of a bad experience with one of the hallucinogens, it is usually enough to reassure the user that the strange thoughts, visions, and sounds are a product of the drug, not to a nervous breakdown.

Opioids

Before we start this subsection, we should give you a couple of definitions:

Narcotic: a drug derived from opium or an opium-like substance, that relieves pain, alters mood and behaviour, and possesses the potential for dependence and tolerance.

Opioid: a generic term describing substances that bind to parts of the nervous system of the user's body.

The opioids produce a strong psychic dependence shown by an overpowering compulsion to continue taking the drug, the development of tolerance so that this dose must be continually increased to produce the initial effect, and a physical dependence that increases in intensity with increased dosage and duration of use. So it's quick to become dependent, and the more you use it, the worse it gets.

Tolerance and physical dependence develop very rapidly for these drugs: doses given by a physician can produce some tolerance in the space of 2 to 3 days, and discontinuing use after that period can cause some withdrawal symptoms. The opioid drugs do cause cross tolerance and users may substitute one type for another. During the time that methadone has been used for treatment of opioid abuse, its use as an abused drug has also risen. People who have developed a tolerance may show no symptoms and may function normally in their day-to-day lives. The tolerance to the various opioids varies from drug to drug, e.g. meperine users may tolerate the drug but show stimulant side effects whereas heroïn users may become completely tolerant to the euphoric effects but still have constricted pupils and constipation.

Opioid intoxication is characterized by euphoria, flushing, itchiness of the skin, drowsiness, and decreased heart and breathing rate.

Withdrawal effects to the opioids are often the opposite of the effects at the time they're taken, so these people tend to become hyperactive. The symptoms increase with dose and duration of the dependence.

Disease	Frequency (%)
Syphilis	15-30
Mononucleosis	20
Hepatitis	5-10
Lymphogranuloma venereum	20
Typhoid	15-25

Table 7–3. Percentage of Heroïn Addicts Entering Treatment with Positive Tests For STDs.

Symptoms of withdrawal appear as early as 4 to 6 hours after the drugs is stopped and, for heroïn, peak at about 36 to 72 hours after stopping. An initial anxiety and craving for the drug is followed by other symptoms that increase in severity and intensity. Initial signs may be an increase in breathing rate accompanied by yawning, sweating, and watering of the eyes. Other symptoms include goose-flesh, twitching muscles, hot and cold flashes, and anorexia. People who have been taking methadone develop the withdrawal symptoms slower and apparently less severely than those who take heroïn, but the user may feel like it's worse. Generally, withdrawal symptoms to the person going through them, will be very unpleasant, but the withdrawal itself is self-limiting. They will often become emotionally upset and want more of their drug. The withdrawal symptoms last for up to 7 to 10 days, although some have complained of weakness, insomnia, and severe anxiety for several months after treatment.

Many complications, but not all, are due to the unsanitary conditions under which the drug is used, e.g. needles tend not to be properly cleaned. A quick look at Table 7–3 will make it quite clear that playing with someone dependent on opioids is inherently riskier than someone who is not. Not only is a person under the influence of an opioid less able to assess the risk to others while playing, the risk is higher to start with.

A little more about specific opioids is given below.

Codeine

Codeine is derived from opium and has similar adverse effects to those created by the opioids.

Heroïn

Heroïn is an addictive narcotic powder derived from morphine.

Meperine

Meperine (Demerol®) is a synthetic opioid drug. The effects of meperine last for a shorter time than those of morphine. Meperine has a fairly high potential for abuse.

Methadone

Methadone can be taken orally, so it has been used has been used to treat heroïn addicts, but this ease of use has caused many people to start using it as a recreational drug. Its sedative effects are less than those of morphine, but methadone's effects last longer overall than those of morphine. Likewise, withdrawal from methadone is more gradual and delayed when compared to heroïn.

Morphine

Morphine, derived from opium, was one of the first drugs used for relief of pain. Its adverse effects are dose-related and include depression of the central nervous system, nausea, diarrhœa, and vomiting. For other details, see Opioids above.

Phencyclidine (PCP)

PCP appears to have had its heyday as a commonly used recreational drug. It is not easily classified because it has a bewildering set of effects on the central nervous system, and is therefore generally considered separately. The way in which PCP acts on the body is only poorly understood.

PCP was tested until about 1962 as an anæsthetic, and was once available as an anæsthetic for vets. Almost all PCP found "on the street" was, and is, illegally made (easily). Sometimes it is injected or eaten, but it is more common to see it mixed with other smoking material such as tobacco and marijuana. Since 1978, reported use has significantly declined, but so has the reporting effort.

With lower dosages, the symptoms include a giddy euphoria, often followed by bursts of anxiety or rapid mood swings. Higher dosages can cause withdrawn catatonic states, unsteadiness, difficulty of speech (from a muscular control point of view), muscular cramps, and uncontrollable single jerks of the limbs. A great deal of salivation is one way to tell a PCP user from someone using high dosages of central nervous system depressants, which produce a dry mouth. Sometimes the eyes roll, which helps diagnosis. Usually breathing and heart functions are not affected. At very high dosages, coma, convulsions, severe hypertension, and death occur, although not many deaths have been reported. Prolonged psychotic states have followed use of this drug. It (almost) goes without saying that SM play when any of these physical or psychological symptoms are present could be very dangerous.

PCP may stay in the central nervous system for long periods and can promote the production of a lot of stomach acid. The latter will require a lot of fluid to flush the stomach. Note that the fluid must be alkaline, so a visit to a physician or hospital will be needed.

Volatile Nitrites (Poppers)

Amyl nitrite is a vasodilator that was once prescribed to treat pain attacks in angina patients. It was sold in small glass ampoules that were broken open and inhaled to produce the effect of dilating the blood vessels. In recent years, it was used to alter consciousness and enhance sexual pleasure by breaking down inhibitions and prolonging and intensifying orgasm. When amyl nitrite was returned to the list of prescription drugs by the U.S. government, manufacturers started to sell other nitrites, such as butyl and isobutyl nitrites. All the nitrites were used primarily by homosexual men. They also work as muscle relaxants and have, therefore, been used for anal play.

The effects generally last only a few minutes and include sharply decreased blood pressure, dizziness, and increased body temperature (flushing).

Because of their strong dilating abilities, the volatile nitrites are dangerous when used by people with low blood pressure. The after effects include headaches, impaired breathing, and, in some cases, heart attack.

In most of the United States and Europe both amyl and butyl nitrite have been made illegal due to the health risks that they pose, such as brain and respiratory tract damage, potential for defibrillation, and other problems. We recommend that you do *not* use them.

Volatile Solvents (Glue)

It is possible to use industrial solvents and ærosol sprays to achieve a state of intoxication. These volatile solvents, which include aromatic hydrocarbons (e.g. benzene), chlorinated hydrocarbons (e.g. dry-cleaning fluids), ketones (e.g. acetone), and acetates (used in many glues) along with ether, chloroform, and alcohol produce a temporary stimulation and subsequent depression of the central nervous system. Psychologic dependence and partial tolerance to the fumes develop when the solvents are used almost everyday, but stopping their use does not produce a withdrawal symptom.

Soon after inhalation, dizziness, drowsiness, slurred speech, and an unsteady walk are common. Sometimes impulsiveness, excitation, and irritability occur. As the solvent makes its way further into the central nervous system, illusions, hallucinations, and delusions develop. Users experience a euphoric high that finishes with a short period of "sleep." Other symptoms include delirium with confusion, clumsiness when trying to use muscles, rapid mood swings, and impairment of thinking. The state of intoxication may last from a few minutes to an hour or more.

Complications may happen because of other toxic ingredients in the abused substance, such as lead in gasoline. Injuries to the brain, liver, kidneys, and bone marrow have been reported. Death can occur due to impaired breathing, irregular heart beating, and asphyxiation due to blockage of the airway to the lungs.

Usually, treatment for adults just means stopping the use of the solvent(s). This is difficult, for young people, and relapse is common.

Emotions & the Psyche

Your emotional state at the time of play can radically alter the kind of play that you will enjoy and the level of play you can tolerate. This can change from week to week or even hour to hour. "Not tonight, Josephine" is one end of the spectrum, another is when you're desperate for it. This must be borne in mind by players as the scene begins and progresses. Sometimes, a scene was just never meant to be. Maybe because you had a hard day at the office…. How you are feeling may change the way you perceive what is going on (in much the same manner as taking a drug might). This, in turn, could affect your ability to assess the risks involved in your play.

First Aid

Know your partner. This is probably the most important aspect of safety in the playroom. We know of a man who had known a friend for several years before playing with him. The friend wore a toupée, unknown to the first man. They were very close friends but the first man usually did not have such things as toupées in his immediate consciousness. When they finally played, the friend knelt in front of the first man, who put his hand on the friend's head.... Off came the toupée. The first question asked by the Top was "OK. What *else* didn't you tell me?" The reply was "I thought you knew." Despite being close friends with someone, you (Top) cannot assume that you have all the information you need and you (Bottom) must ensure that all special limitations with respect to play have been given.

For instance, if you have capped teeth, you should make very sure that the person you're about to play with knows that you have them. There's nothing wrong with a gag over capped teeth, provided that, as the Top, you know they're capped, so that you can get the pressure from the gag correct. There is nothing wrong with a blindfold over contact lenses, provided you know they're there. Etc.. This allows everyone involved to be careful where and when necessary. These don't have to be serious negotiations. Just an "Oh, by the way, I have two capped teeth." will do. You don't need to bring in Henry Kissinger....

The biggest problem in giving first aid of any sort is that people are not prepared for what may happen. So prepare for someone fainting during play. Be prepared with your equipment, by knowing your partner, and by being honest in dealing with people from whom you may need to get help.

The most important assessments for you to make in any emergency are, *in this order*:

1. Is the **A**irway to the lungs clear? (Generally not a problem in cases of simple fainting). This ensures the lungs can get the oxygen needed to pump into the blood;

2. Is there **B**reathing? The lungs may not be working to pump the oxygen into the blood; and

3. Is there **C**irculation, i.e. is the heart working? If it isn't, the oxygen has no way to make its way from the lungs to the brain.

Any person without blood flow to the brain for longer than about four minutes is likely to have some form of brain damage. It won't do much good to splint a broken arm if no blood is getting to the brain. So, you need to have your wits about you and all the information you need to do the right thing already firmly in your head. We have given more details about these things further on in this section. If you don't know how to do these things, find out *now*.

Don't be afraid to call 911. Yes, they're going to laugh at you. Yes, their dispatcher will have all of what you say on tape. Just don't let it bother you. It may make them laugh or bother them, but for those of us into SM it's everyday life. They have a job to do and will get on with it. Get the help you need. The physician amongst the authors has seen more than a few "interesting" cases in the Emergency Department. You may be quite embarrassed, but trust us, the Emergency Department has seen it all. (If they haven't, they'll be even more interested in the case.) Don't let yourself be embarrassed.

When you talk to hospital staff, don't think you're going to have to use long complicated words or ones that are "polite." Explain in your own words what happened (basic Anglo-Saxon words like "fuck" and "cunt" will do). Just get the message across to them clearly. Remember, they've heard every swear-word known to man; they may use them, too.... Tell them *everything*, clearly. Honesty *is* the best policy. It could save someone's life.

Also, remember that, if you're not sure of the meaning of one of those fancy words and you use it, the staff have only what you say to go by. They *will* believe what you say. If you use the wrong fancy word, you could all be in trouble. Use plain English where possible. Four-letter words are quite acceptable under these circumstances.

Reasons & Uses for Pain

Pain is the body's first line of defence in staying alive. Pain simply tells us that something is wrong. A lot of SM play involves pain. Whipping a back hurts, electricity can hurt, so can bondage. There is a very big difference between the pain you intend to inflict, or have inflicted, and unintentional pain. If you're in a heavy whipping scene and the recipient's thumb is being compressed because his/her body weight is on it, it will drive him/her crazy. This unintentional, as opposed to non-consensual, pain will completely draw the attention away from the intentional pain. If the Bottom is standing on a cold or jagged rock, it's possible that this will be all that he/she can think of. Someone with a back that looks like hamburger, and able to take that, could forget it all by stubbing a toe at the wrong moment, thereby screaming in pain.

Be very careful to use pain to your advantage; either intentional pain that is the purpose of the scene, or unintentional pain that is an indication that you should slow down or stop to investigate the cause before continuing. Unintentional pain is a warning.

Stop the Scene

For any incident or accident, *stop the scene*. This goes without saying, but we're mentioning it anyway. The event has to be acted upon. The reasons will become clearer as you read the sections below.

Stop a scene any time that the pain do not fit the intended *and* agreed play, or there is a perceived injury.

The decision relies on the common sense of both the Top and the Bottom. Please use it.

Incidents

Have safety equipment that matches the play and toys that you'll be using. This is not a luxury, it is a necessity; as necessary as the rope itself in rope bondage scenes. If you're using leather restraints and/or chains to suspend someone, use panic snaps. If you don't know what panic snaps are, find out (try the Glossary at the back of this book). Panic snaps can be opened with one hand by pulling down on the snap, whereas double-ended clips require that you lift the person to release the snap. A double-ended clip is like a "G" that has a little hook on it. A panic snap literally falls open.

If the Bottom is in rope bondage, have a pair of very good, sturdy scissors nearby. Ones that you *know* will cut cleanly through the rope you've used. Big heavy shears with blunt tips, not sewing scissors. Ambulance/paramedic scissors are probably the best choice. Poultry shears or large bandage shears will do at a pinch, but be careful with the tips.

Incidents also take the form of conditions that result from planned play, such as blood letting, cuts, abrasions, piercings, brandings, etc.. There could be light or heavy bruising from belts, whips, paddles, etc.. Raw, opened skin may come from planned whippings or canings. You should be prepared to take care of these intended wounds *before* you start the scene. Please see the section on First Aid for more about being prepared.

Fainting

In the playroom, probably the most common physical problem people have is fainting. Either you've shocked the living daylights out of them, or they're in such ecstasy that their blood is running to other parts of their body, resulting in their becoming light-headed.

Fainting occurs when there is a lack of oxygen to the brain. If the fainter is not losing blood by pooling it on the floor, where does it go? It goes to the blood vessels as they dilate, allowing far more blood in the vessels than normal, leaving the brain about a quarter of a litre short of what it needs.

From the Top's point of view, someone about to faint will probably appear to tremble, slump somewhat, and have cold sweats. The symptoms of a faint from the Bottom's point of view might include a sense of "greying out," a rapid heart beat, tunnel vision, and a sense of being about to pass out. A Top should insist that the Bottom communicate any signs of a faint *immediately* to the, rather than trying to "deal with it."

If someone faints (this could happen *after* the scene is all over) get him/her down to the floor. This allows the blood to flow back into the brain without having to work its way up against gravity to get there. The position of the body at the time someone faints could be relevant to the way you deal with the incident. For instance, if the person faints when suspended, put your arms under his/hers so that, as you release the panic snaps, his/her body falls onto yours. You can then fall to the floor with the Bottom on top of you so he/she doesn't get hurt as he/she falls. Once down, you may be able to raise the legs a little and lower the head. This will use gravity to help get blood to the brain. If the person faints while lying horizontally, put the head a little lower than the rest of the body.

Before you lower someone who has just fainted to the ground, be sure to check that the *whole* body is free to be lowered; i.e. tits, balls, etc. are not attached to anything else.

In case it's not just a faint, take the person's pulse. This can be done either by placing your fingers (not your thumb) lightly over the groove just inside of the bone on the thumb side of the underside of the wrist (where you usually see people taking pulses), or by placing the fingers lightly on the neck just below the jawbone, about halfway between the bottom of the ear and the bottom of the chin. Count the pulses for fifteen seconds and multiply by four to get the pulses per minute. Also check the number of complete times the chest rises and falls in fifteen seconds and multiply be four for the number of breaths per minute. Chances are that the pulse rate may be about 100 and the breathing about 28. This is higher than normal due to the messages sent to the respiratory centres and the heart calling for more oxygen. Normal rates are somewhere around 72 beats per minute and 16 to 20 breaths per minute. (Note that *very* active and fit people may have a normal rate as low as 60 beats per minute.)

Once the fainter has been lowered, it should take about 15 to 30 seconds, no longer, for them to start coming around from fainting. Once back with you, keep the person there, lying down for a while, until the body has a chance to reëqualize itself. Check that the pulse rate is close to normal before you let him/her get up. It should not be very fast or slow at the time he/she gets up.

Once you have the Bottom on the floor and just in case the Bottom is diabetic and didn't tell you, slip some orange juice, a teaspoon of sugar, or (if neither of these is available) a candy into the mouth, taking care not to let the Bottom choke. Giving a non-diabetic a candy won't do any harm, but it could save precious seconds if the person is diabetic. See the section on Diabetes Reaction below for more on diabetes.

If necessary, sit on the fainter to prevent him/her getting up on the grounds of, "Oh, I feel fine." Be sure *yourself* before you let him/her get up. Tell the person that he/she is proving nothing by trying to get up. He/she may not be in position to determine how fit he/she is to get up. Often, the fainter will be quite white and not feel like getting up, anyway, unless he/she wants to bash your skull in for letting the incident happen. Those who do try to get up often just faint again because the blood vessels are still dilated to some degree and there's not yet enough oxygen flow to the brain.

If you don't know where to take a pulse, and there are many places better than the wrists, find out now. Better yet, take a CPR course at your local college or ambulance station. It's a form of insurance premium, and time very well spent.

Keep anyone who has fainted warm. Playrooms are often in the basement of houses for the effect that they can give to the scenes (and for the sound protection...). Remember that someone from Florida may need a warmer room than someone from northern Alaska....

If the fainter doesn't come round from a faint within about half a minute, you will have to go to the next stage of treatment: CPR and then getting him/her to hospital.

Diabetes (Hypoglycæmic) Reaction

Many more people are diabetic than you might expect (in Canada it is about one in fifteen). It is a fairly complex condition caused by a lack of the hormone insulin. There are two main ways for this to happen: Type I diabetes (Insulin Dependent Diabetes Mellitus), when insulin is not secreted; and Type II (Non-Insulin Dependent Diabetes), when the transport mechanism is not working properly. In both cases, insulin is not getting into the blood in proper quantities. Insulin converts sugar into useful compounds and this takes place in the blood. Untreated, diabetes leads to a slow wasting away, as the body slowly starves. Type II diabetes can sometimes be treated by careful monitoring of the person's diet. In more serious cases of Type II and all cases of Type I diabetes, insulin is injected into the person.

Blood sugar levels are extremely important to the brain. Too high a level and the brain becomes sluggish; too low and the brain may shut down completely. It could take hours for too much blood sugar to cause problems, but only a matter of seconds to lose consciousness from too little blood sugar. If a diabetic has not eaten enough, or uses too much energy (by emotion, stress, exercise, or plain nervousness), he/she may go into a hypoglycæmic reaction and then faint. (Hypoglycæmia is when the blood sugar is too low, and hyperglycæmia is when the blood sugar is too high).

Unfortunately, there is no easy way to predict or prevent a diabetic emergency. The conditions that cause the hypoglycæmic reaction are almost exactly those that are involved in an SM scene: physical and mental stress.

There are symptoms that may help you identify when this condition is about to happen. Just before losing consciousness, the diabetic may appear drunk, nervous, hostile, jittery, or trembling. There may be slurred speech, hunger, headache, seizures, and/or confusion. The person may also exhibit full body sweating or clammy skin. If you see any of the above in a known diabetic, take precautions. Question the person, but be wary of responses like "I'm all right." There may already have been alterations to the brain function. If the diabetic says something like "No, I'm going into a reaction," act on it .

This hypoglycæmia must be treated *immediately*. Do not take any time to undo any bonds, except those that prevent you getting some sugar into the diabetic's mouth. Put the sugar into the person's mouth. Placement is not important, provided that it does not choke the person. If you knew you were playing with a diabetic before the scene began, you should have had some orange juice, glucose tablets, or (as a last resort) candies handy already. It would be a good idea to have some in your dungeon first aid kit, just in case you're playing with a diabetic who forgot to tell you about it.

Once you have administered the sugar and the Bottom has started to recover, get him/her out of or down from any bondage. You should cover and keep the person warm, i.e. treat as shock. Now all you can do is wait. That's the hard part. Stay with your Bottom. Time what is happening. If the Bottom does not respond with groans, opened or fluttering eyes, or body movements within about four minutes, you may have another problem and should start to address that. Don't panic, it could take a few minutes. Continue giving sugar and checking the airway for blockage.

As the Bottom comes round, he/she may seem to be drunk. Give more sugar if requested, because you cannot give someone too much sugar under these circumstances. It will take about twenty seconds to twenty minutes for the Bottom to *fully* recover from the reaction. Don't allow the Bottom to return to normal activities, let alone play. *"No more play, tonight. Thank you."* Some disorientation from having been unconscious may still be present. If the condition was caused by lack of food, reassure the Bottom and have him/her eat. (Often, the reassuring has to be done to the Top by the Bottom....)

If circumstances are such that the Bottom cannot swallow, place the Bottom on his/her side and ensure that breathing is not impaired, then put about a third of a tube of pre-mixed cake icing into the downside cheek. Failing cake icing mix, use honey or syrup. Wait three to four minutes and repeat. Follow this up with food after the person has recovered. If there is no response within ten minutes, call and ambulance and take the diabetic to hospital.

If possible, even if you know the person is a diabetic, treat for fainting also: raise the legs, lower the head, etc.. Even diabetics faint sometimes. Please see the section on Fainting for more on fainting.

That's 170, Madam!
Thank you, Madam!

Minor Cuts and Bruises

These can usually be dealt with using your first aid kit (see below). Anything more than minor cuts and bruises really counts as an accident and should be treated accordingly. Any cut caused by a dirty or metal object should be cause for concern about Tetanus. Check whether the injured person's Tetanus shots are up to date. If not, get them up to date immediately.

Accidents

We've mentioned it before, but it bears repeating here: the most important assessments for you to make in any emergency are, *in this order*:

1. Is the **A**irway to the lungs clear? (Generally not a problem in cases of simple fainting). This ensures that the lungs can get the oxygen needed to pump into the blood;

2. Is there **B**reathing? The lungs may not be working to pump the oxygen into the blood; and

3. Is there **C**irculation, i.e. is the heart working? If it isn't, the oxygen has no way to make its way from the lungs to the brain.

Any person without blood flow to the brain for longer than about four minutes is likely to have some form of brain damage. It won't do much good to splint a broken arm if no blood is getting to the brain. So you need to have your wits about you and all the information you need to do the right thing should already be firmly in your head. If you don't know how to do these things, find out *now*.

In any fall or major trauma, such as a car accident or falling down the stairs into the playroom, the possibility of damage to the spine must not be ignored. Only once you have checked the ABCs listed above, without moving the person, can you decide if it's possible to attend to the more obvious things like broken legs. You should not move someone who lies motionless after a bad fall or knock to the body. If there is spinal damage, any further movement could damage or cut the spinal cord, resulting in paralysis below the point at which the damage occurred. If the injury is severe enough, the paralysis can include the lungs, resulting in death. If the person is in a situation that could still endanger their life, such as close to a burning car, make every effort to immobilize the neck and back before moving them. Also, any limb that looks like it may be damaged should be made rigid before moving it or the person. This will prevent further damage to the tissues and veins from jagged edges of broken bone(s).

If the person has closed eyes, when you open the eyes, do they react to the light by contracting? If not, there may be brain damage. Unequal pupil size could also indicate brain injury. Knocks to the head can lead to bleeding in between the skull and the brain, putting pressure on the brain. This is why people are monitored so carefully in hospital for about 24 to 48 hours after a knock to the head.

Bleeding

Many of our playrooms are quite small. Someone may hit his/her head during play or as he/she faints; there may be bleeding or a fracture as a result of some other incident. For bleeding, apply pressure to the affected area. Minor cuts and scrapes can usually be taken care of right then and there using your first aid kit. If it's more serious (and you will be the one having to decide, so make sure that you err on the side of caution), get them to a hospital *immediately* after you have ensured that you have staunched the blood flow as best as possible. It may require an ambulance or that you take them there. Use your best judgement.

Bleeding should be stopped by applying firm pressure to the affected area, preferably with a clean cloth. Facial and head cuts tend to bleed more than the rest of the body, making them seem much worse than they really are. Most bleeding can be controlled by firm application of pressure. Arterial bleeding (bright red, spurting blood) requires a longer period of pressure to control and firmer pressure than venous bleeding (darker red blood, oozing or flowing smoothly).

Using a tourniquet on a bleeding extremity is rarely necessary, except in traumatic amputation (when a limb is severed from the body). In any other case, the tourniquet could do more harm than good, because it will cause tissue death at the point of application, due to lack of blood. Using a tourniquet where it's not needed could lead to loss of a hand, an arm, a foot, or a leg that might otherwise have been saved by the application of firm pressure.

If the person cuts him/herself on something of old metal or dirty, even if the cut is not severe, check that his/her Tetanus shots are up to date. If not, insist that it is brought up to date quickly. Take him/her to the local Emergency Department for it.

Dislocated Joints, Fractures, & Concussions

Simply put, a dislocated joint needs medical attention. It won't move the way that it should, and any movement will cause a great deal of pain. You'll likely be able to tell that it is dislocated because it just won't look right, for example, a dislocated shoulder looks like a sharp right-angle, rather than the smooth rounded shoulder you're used to, i.e. the contours of the joint change.

You should try to stabilize the joint so that the person can be taken to the nearest hospital. In the case of a leg joint, a good way is to tie the bad leg to the good one. Otherwise, use some form of splint.

If there is a fracture, go straight to a hospital.

If there is a concussion and loss of consciousness, as opposed to fainting, get them to the hospital as fast as you can. This is where having your CPR certificate is a good thing. Generally, the symptoms of a concussion are like a faint, but medical attention is needed to determine that it is a concussion. Treat the person as though he/she had fainted by lying him/her flat. The person will be breathing and there will be a pulse, but no consciousness. If they don't come round in about two minutes, take the person to a hospital. If breathing stops, CPR will be necessary immediately. Try to keep the person flat as you go to the hospital.

Damaged Ligaments

A damaged ligament will be painful and probably not allow the person to put full weight on the leg while standing. Go to a hospital.

Burns

Burns vary from slight damage to the surface of the skin to deep muscular damage. Except for very superficial burns, they will probably cause scarring of some sort, and, if not properly cared for, can easily lead to infections at the burn site. Shock is one of the recognized causes of death, and severe burns are easily sufficient to cause shock. Most burns in an SM scene are likely to be the result of an accident.

If any form of accidental burn occurs during an SM scene (to the Bottom *or* the Top), immediately release the Bottom. The Top will need as much attention and tender reassurance as any Bottom under such circumstances.

Burns have been categorized into several classes. The ones you'll need to know about are:

First degree   Only the dead, outermost layer of skin is burned. The living cells just underneath remain unaffected. The area may be swollen, red, and painful, but there will be no blistering of the skin. These burns will heal in a matter of a few days. A sunburn is a good example of a first-degree burn.

These burns can normally be treated by holding them under cold, running water or in a bowl (or bath) of ice-cold water. An ice-water compress can be used, but do not apply ice directly to the burn. This should be done until the coldness itself begins to hurt, which may take about ten minutes. You should repeat this procedure three or four times until the burned area no longer causes serious pain. Cover the affected area with a dry, sterile bandage for a couple of days. This treatment can sometimes stop a first-degree burn becoming a second-degree burn.

Any kind of lotion or salve will tend to trap the heat in the wound, so most experts suggest that you do *not* use them; nor should they be used during the bandaging of the wound, either, since they can attract dirt and cause the bandages to stick to the skin. *After* the cooling procedure is complete, anæsthetic spray, aloe vera, or vitamin E oil *may* help a light, superficial first-degree burn.

If the size and/or the redness have not lessened or the pain continues for more than a day, you should go to see your physician about the burn(s).

Second degree The first layer of living cells is damaged. Usually, there will be blistering, pain, and swelling. There is a risk of infection during the one to two weeks it takes to heal a second-degree burn. If the burn is bad enough it may require that skin be grafted onto the affected area.

As for first-degree burns, cool the burn until the pain starts to go away. Do *not* burst or otherwise attempt to drain any blisters. Likewise, do *not* put any lotions or creams on the burn. When you have finished cooling the area, pat it dry with a non-fluffy cloth (you don't want fibres of the cloth to stick inside the wound). Cover the area with many layers of clean cloth (sterile dressings, if you have them, or sheets, handkerchiefs, etc.). If possible, lift the area above the level of the heart. If the person is having trouble breathing, raise the head and shoulders and get medical attention right away.

Clear fluids from the wound indicate normal healing. If the liquid is not clear, you have an infection, so see your physician as soon as possible.

Third Degree   Deeper structures, in addition to all of the layers of the skin, have been damaged to some extent. There will usually be some form of charring of the skin, and the area will be firm to the touch, dry, and painless, because the nerves in the area have been destroyed by the burn. These burns almost always need medical attention. (One exception may be small, well-controlled brands.) Since the skin is hardened by the burn, it can break and leave the wound open to infection. Third degree burns are capable of causing shock, and consequent death. It might take several months for a third-degree burn to heal properly.

The first-aid for third-degree burns is slightly different from that for first- and second-degree burns. Put a clean, cold cloth over the burned area, or pour cool (but not ice-cold) water over it and then cover it with a thick layer of sterile, non-fluffy dressing. If the affected area is small you may be able to take the person to hospital yourself. If not, call an ambulance immediately. While waiting for transport to hospital, keep the person lying down and calm, to help prevent shock. Do not let the person lie on the wound, and try to have the wound above the level of the heart. If there is any problem with breathing when the person is lying on his/her back, lift the head and shoulders above the heart. To minimize the risk of shock make sure to offer reassurance and tenderness to relieve any stress he/she may be feeling. Since the protective barrier of the skin has been broken, one of the greatest long-term risks is infection. The healing process may take many months and is likely to be extremely painful.

First Aid Kit for the Playroom

There are a lot of pre-made first aid kits on the market, and most of them do a good job. To be sure that you have all that you need, we have compiled a list of the things that we feel should be present in the form of a first aid kit any time you play. Use it as a check-list.

You should also have this kit available when you play outside of the playroom, such as in a wooded area or by the beach etc.. Add anything that you feel we may have missed.

Ace bandage

Adhesive bandages

Ambulance scissors

Ammonia inhalant

Antibiotic cream

Aspirin and/or Tylenol

Assorted gauze bandages

Bleach (diluted).

Eyecup

Finger-tip bandages

First aid handbook

Knuckle bandages

Moleskin

Needle and thread

Oversize bandages

Snake Bite Kit

Sterile gauze bandages

Stretch tape

Sugar (for diabetics. Orange juice, granulated sugar (maybe even Life Savers))

Tweezers

An assortment of spray bottles with: Hydrogen Peroxide (H_2O_2), Distilled Water (H_2O), and Methyl (rubbing) alcohol

Alcohol helps clean the area wiped with it of dirt and skin oils. It has *some* disinfection capability, but by no means 100%. Hydrogen peroxide foams as it works, thereby helping to dislodge dirt, but, as for alcohol, it has only *some* disinfection capability. For the skin, a reasonable rule of thumb may be to use alcohol to clean *before* the playing and peroxide *afterwards*. This is mainly because alcohol is better at removing dirt-trapping oils than hydrogen peroxide, and hydrogen peroxide does not sting an open wound as much as alcohol. If you *intend* to break the skin, you should use an Iodine-based disinfectant, such as Betadine®, to sterilize the area and then wipe off any excess with alcohol before the skin is broken. Please see the section on Cleanliness & Disinfection for more information about the differences between "clean" and "sterile."

The alcohol you chose should be from 70% to 85% alcohol. This is because with an alcohol content of about 90%, you're just dehydrating the organisms you're trying to remove, in effect preserving them! Most store-bought rubbing alcohol is about 70% to 80% alcohol.

Distilled water should be used for washing off areas where you have used bleach or peroxide. Diluted bleach is a good way to clean play tables and chairs before and after play. It can also be used to clean toys, but may adversely affect things like rubber ones.

The above kit is only a list for first aid. Other things are required for a playroom, in fact anywhere you engage in SM play. For these, please take a look at the section on Safety Items for the Playroom.

Common Sense

This is probably the world's biggest oxymoron. Good sense is not very common, although it has to be for SM play. You will need to be constantly thinking about whether your play is safe, sane, and consensual. It's up to you, not your partner, to gauge whether what you're doing is sensible. If you have the slightest question about what you're doing, examine it with reference to what you have learnt is safe and sane. If it is not, then don't consent to it. If you think that a toy your Top is going to use is dirty, or that it is damaged, or whatever, then do what is necessary to ensure that it isn't used.

Common sense can be made common, just by being aware of what's going on. You can pass on that good sense by teaching others to be just as careful as you are. We will all benefit.

Safety Considerations During Negotiations & Play

SM play can be out on the edge. In order to stay on the safe edge, we have to learn and use techniques and practices to keep us there. One of the biggest factors in making SM play safe is that it is negotiated before it happens. By setting up the parameters and limits for play, each player assumes the responsibility necessary to ensure physical and psychological safety. It also allows us to answer our critics when they accuse us of unsafe play. We can confidently tell them that we played in the knowledge that it would be as safe as possible, because we had talked about it, first.

These negotiations might be in the form of a relaxed conversation in a bar, in or out of rôle. It's one thing to be turned on by the appearance of a hot number in the bar, but it's another to get home to find out that your intended Top wants to do an enema scene when you wanted a whipping, or *vice versa*. The same applies to safety issues. You will want to ensure that both Top and Bottom play safely.

Anyone who has safer sex will only think better of you for asking. It helps everyone to know that there is one less risk to think about during play. If your prospective partner shies away from any talk of safety, your gut will probably turn that traffic light we talk about in the section on Consent to yellow. You should be cautious, because someone who won't talk about safer play may well not practise it.

Out of rôle, any negotiation should be fairly straightforward. It's just going to be a matter of asking the questions that need answers. In rôle, just the phrasing changes. A Top might want to quell any fears that a prospective Bottom may have by saying something like "You will not touch my cock until I've given you permission, and I will not touch you with it until after I've told you to put a condom on it" or "I only have safer sex, so I won't allow us to any exchange fluids." Likewise, a Bottom, in rôle, may say something like "May I know your position on safer sex, Madam?" or "I need to be sure, Sir, that you will not leave me with any marks or diseases." You can use whichever words you feel are needed to convey your message.

If you have not informed yourself properly, you are not in a position to give consent for any play. Therefore, some form of negotiation before play is important. You need to decide what you want to know, and then ask for the information in a way that suits the scene. The reason is that there are many ways to initiate such a conversation. Anyone who is unwilling or unable to tolerate such talk cannot be presumed to practice safe, sane, and consensual sex.

Note that you must be familiar with the issues here in order to be a full participant in such a conversation. You must be familiar with the current thinking and what is safe to do and what is not. Unfortunately, there is some middle ground on the subject of safety, particularly with respect to oral sex, so familiarity with the issues is even more important.

Below, you'll find a few thoughts on things that you should think about and/or mention during negotiations and play. Be as honest as you can when mentioning things, because both of your safeties may be at risk if you aren't. We have included everything we could think of or remember, but this is almost certainly not a complete list. Circumstances may dictate that you use greater caution than that we've mentioned below. Please use your common sense if you think that we've missed something or that more care needs to be taken. (Please tell us if you think we've missed something or got it wrong. It'll go into the next edition.)

Silent Alarm

Even before you go home with a new partner you have just met in a bar, you may want to make sure that your friends know with whom you are going home. This way, should they not hear from you in a reasonable time, they can call to check up on you. Better yet, have an arrangement that if you have not called in by a certain time, they should assume that things have not gone well and that they should raise an alarm. This time at which an "alarm" goes off is called a silent alarm. Your new partner will not hear it, provided that your arrangement with your friends was made before you decided to go home with the new partner. It is a cheap and effective way to look after friends, given the potential for problems when we play with unfamiliar people. Ideally, you would meet new people through friends who can vouch for their integrity, but this is not always practical. You may be in another city, so your silent alarm could be a long distance 'phone call to your friend, who would wait for it and who knows where you should be staying, if you don't call.

Medical Conditions

Make sure that both (or all) of you know of any medical conditions that might affect your intended play. Do you have to take medication during the expected duration of the play? Are you subject to epileptic seizures? Do you have diabetes? Whatever the condition, get it out in the open before you start to play. Please see the section on First Aid for some more considerations during negotiation.

As you talk about medical conditions, it might be a good idea to offer your status with respect to some of the more common STDs. This will help put your potential partner at ease, and tell you something about them, if they avoid telling you their status after you have told them yours. People living with AIDS and other STDs are often relieved at being able to quickly reply that they are positive and that they play safely, and then being able to move onto the subject of play, rather than having to dwell on their status. You should be playing safely, anyway, but it does help to put everyone's mind at rest to know when they stand. If you play safely, you've nothing to lose by disclosing your status to your partner, and you could gain a lot from the knowledge that they avoided telling you their status. This is not an issue that any partner should force. If you play safely, you have every right to maintain your confidentiality, should you want to.

Those with HIV infection may want to tell their partners about limitations to their play. Often, those with HIV will get tired quickly, or have other symptoms that may make certain kinds of play difficult. These could be important considerations, depending on the current health of the person. The same sort of considerations are often true for people with other medical conditions. Having a medical condition is not something of which you should be ashamed, and discussing its potential effects on your play could save you many problems later.

Bondage

Position is the most important factor in any form of bondage, be it vertical or horizontal, sitting or standing, suspended or free-standing, arms and legs bent or straight, arms and legs close to the body or outstretched, etc.. Each position or combination of positions has its own set of problems. The main thing to bear in mind is the pull of gravity and/or any other tension or pressure and the way that they work on the body, be it at the attachment point or on the body as a whole. For example, a pulling of the arms across another part of the body may cause a pressure point that might impede circulation to a part of the body; the pulling force produced a pushing effect.

If you are using any form of restraints, particularly hard ones like metal, be sure that the restraint does not restrict circulation, pinch nerves, or push hard against bones that are near the surface of the skin. All of these things can cause a scene to stop, and are potentially dangerous.

If a Bottom has been restrained in a manner that he/she cannot balance, you should ensure that the first restraints used are to something solid enough to stop the Bottom falling. That way, if he/she loses balance, there will be no fall and no broken bones. For instance, falling with arms handcuffed behind your back could make for a very nasty fall, since you will have very little way to break your fall.

For people with migraines, muscular disorders, or those who are pregnant, you may need to use less rigid bondage. For those with a seizure disorder, *bondage may not be appropriate at all.* For all of these cases, lighter bondage, and perhaps even different materials would be appropriate, e.g., something softer. The bindings could also be applied to different places on the body. An impaired leg should be treated accordingly.

When used in the area of the head and neck, the toys can cause psychological problems that are more pronounced than in the case of simply restraining the body. The physical problems when restraining the head and neck range from bruising of the Adam's apple and strangulation, to choking caused by gags. The psychological problems could stem from the Bottom simply *feeling* that breathing is difficult, even though the airway is completely unobstructed. This and other effects can cause panic in people who are not used to head bondage.

Headaches can be caused by pressure from hoods, gags, blindfolds, etc. that have been put on too tightly. Excess pressure to the eyes can cause not only pain to the eyes, but also cause a sensation of flashes in front of them.

Be ready before you play for events such as the Bottom panicking. The equipment used should be such that a quick release is possible. If the Bottom is cursing and swearing, you should try to calm him/her down first (only if there is no sign that to remain in the restraints would cause harm). Do this because anyone in "fight or flight" panic will likely attack you and harm you and him/herself seriously when trying to escape, if not calmed down first. Generally, a few minutes of gentle reassurance are all that are needed to calm someone experiencing "fight or flight" panic.

The last basic consideration during bondage play, but by no means the least important, is an external emergency, such as fire, gas leak, break in, or even your mother-in-law walking through the front door. Not only could it be difficult to get the Bottom out of the restraint quickly, you may do damage while trying to do things in a hurry. *Never* leave a restrained Bottom alone. If the bondage is simple, such as a pairs of handcuffs with the Bottom sitting on the floor, the chances of problems are probably minimal; if the bondage is only a little more than this, not only are the chances of getting away from a fire greatly reduced, but, if the bondage or the Bottom changes position, the chances of suffocation or other damage could be enormous. Just because the house hasn't burned to the ground for the last hundred years doesn't mean that it won't during the five minutes you leave your Bottom to get a cup of coffee from the café next door.

As you learn and experiment with more advanced forms of bondage and the length of your bondage scenes, new considerations come to the fore. Muscles kept still for a long time tend to get sore and stiff.

Skin can be irritated by the direct application of glue from insulating or duct tape. As the scenes get longer, dehydration and heat exhaustion can become a real problem for Bottoms who have been "wrapped" or left in the sun. You should make sure that the Bottom gets liquid, wanted or not, after about half an hour and regularly thereafter. Also make sure that the bondage you apply is not too tight around the chest. It can cause the Bottom to suffocate.

Butt plugs or catheters can be used during bondage play, but, just as for any other time they are used, there is a risk of infection or internal damage. They should be checked periodically during the scene.

Finally, the strain of harsh or long term bondage can cause the Bottom great mental stress and may cause panic. You must be prepared to deal with this, to relieve and reassure the Bottom.

Generally, the precautions that you'll need to take during bondage include making sure that the restraints are not too tight (particularly for metals restraints). Limbs should be monitored about every ten minutes or so for signs of circulation problems (cool, numb, or white extremities).

During your negotiation of a bondage scene, you will want to recognize psychological issues, such as the potential for severe panic in the Bottom. Some people cannot stand being motionless for a few hours. They constantly feel the need to move at least a little bit, so mummification should not be attempted with them. The brain also tends to play tricks on itself when it has had no input for a while. The Bottom may hallucinate due to the brain "getting bored" and creating its own stimuli. In these scenes, Bottoms may need to be reassured that there is still a line of communication with the Top.

Because bondage of any form is very scary for novices, both of you should go slowly and carefully. We recommend that a Bottom should not be tied up on the first date.

Autobondage

Try to use common sense when you tie yourself up. First, do simple, not too restrictive things, so that you get used to the feelings involved. As you progress, *never* be tempted to tie yourself up so that you can't get loose. This implies that it is safest *not* to lock hoods and gags, and to be sure that a key for other locks is within reach. An external emergency as mentioned above will be even more difficult to deal with when you are alone. Equally, *never* put any tension on your neck, because the potential for suffocation and damage to the nerves in the neck is far too great to make the risk worth your while.

Collars

Collars are generally fine when in place. Very high ones may cause breathing problems when the Bottom is in a position that might push the collar against the Adam's apple, or push a stiff collar up under the chin. Pressure from the collar on the side of the neck may cause problems with the carotid sinus, which would slow the heart and possibly cause a faint, if the top of the collar pressed against the side of the neck just under the earlobe and under the back of the jaw.

Collars should not be jerked from the rear, since this could choke the Bottom and put too much pressure on the Adam's apple. Pulling a collar too hard from the front may cause the neck to jerk, thereby damaging it.

Genital Bondage

The main concerns in the area of genital bondage are that the bondage should not be on for long periods. The cock and balls need blood as much as the rest of the body, and the veins are close to the surface here. About ten to fifteen minutes should be the most that the cock and balls are bound tightly. Most genital bondage problems can be seen rather than felt, so particular care and regular checking is needed if the genitals are covered.

If the binding is tighter than a comfortable cockring, it should be taken off before the Bottom cums. The pressure generated at ejaculation may be enough to damage the tubes through which the ejaculate passes.

It is easy to cause abrasions to the cock and balls during a scene. These could cause a loss of pleasure and inhibit any more play for quite a while, so take care not to open the skin of the genitals.

Confinement of the genitals is another area of bondage, viz. the chastity belt. In these circumstances, circulation is an important safety factor. Cautious experimentation will ensure that the genitals are kept intact. Those who use butt plugs with chastity belts should make sure that the Bottom is able to move well, if taken out to a bar or sent to work. If the chastity belt is likely to be worn for more than about five hours, care should be taken to ensure that the Bottom has a way to go to the bathroom (usually a messy endeavour for anyone wearing a chastity belt). Any butt plug or dildo that is not reserved specifically for the person it is used on should have a condom on it before use.

Handcuffs, Shackles, & Other Metal Bondage

Metal restraints are very unforgiving, so great care has to be taken when they are used. They should always be loose. It is preferable to have them put on over at least one layer of clothing, if the Bottom is likely to be moving around. This is because shackles, etc. are heavy and tend to put their weight on a very small area, rather than distributing the pressure.

Anyone who falls while wearing metal restraints is liable to hurt him/herself. For instance, if you have put someone in handcuffs with the arms behind the back, not only are they less able to balance themselves, but they will probably fall awkwardly. It is very likely that the metal will jar badly against the wrists, potentially causing a lot of bruising and damage to the nerves. An awkward fall could also cause broken bones. When the limbs are restrained in an abnormal position, be careful of how you lay the Bottom down, so as not to cause circulation or pinched nerve problems.

Handcuffs are just as prone to putting pressure on a small area, so you should use only the cuffs that can be set once they have been put on. The setting mechanism should be one that requires you to push a little button into the cuff itself, using a key. These keys are of a standard size, so if you need to ask a policeman to get you out of them, you can. Handcuffs with a little lever to set them are too dangerous to play with because the Bottom could accidentally move the lever and tighten the cuffs too much.

For handcuffs and other locking devices, make sure that you know where the key is immediately before you start the scene, so you can unlock things in a hurry. A good idea is a second key nearby.

Cold metal against the skin can sometimes cause a dull ache that may grow to sufficient proportions to have the scene stopped, because all the Bottom can think about is that ache, rather than the scene. Once the ache has started, it will take quite a long time for it to subside, even if the area is warmed. So, if you're the Bottom, make sure that the Top is made aware of this before it becomes a problem.

In restraint scenes, you should be aware of the needs of the Bottom, even if you are the Bottom. If you feel a cramp coming, tell the Top, so that something can be done, before it happens. This way there will just be a slight hiccough in the scene, rather than ending it and cutting the Bottom fromthe bondage to relieve a cramp or whatever. It's surprising how these little things can grow into show stoppers.

We've met people who have used electric cord and chicken wire for bondage. Fat, round electric cord used in the same way as rope is probably safe, but thin, two-strand lighting variety is too thin; it will likely cause circulation problems, and may cause bruising. Chicken wire is also much too thin and unforgiving to use as bondage.

Hoods, Gags, Blindfolds, & Gasmasks

The head is the centre of all the senses. All stimuli ultimately reach the brain and are interpreted there, so it represents the "self" for us. Any bondage of the head can easily be interpreted by the Bottom as a bondage of the "self." For this reason, head bondage can be very powerful and threatening. It often leads to panic in novices.

In general, hoods and gags are reasonably safe to use. Tightness around the neck and adequate air supply should be of prime concern. Do not leave someone hooded and unattended.

When gagging someone, a sock or handkerchief is the most dangerous thing you can put in the mouth. Due to its size, it could reach the back of the throat and trigger the gag reflex in the Bottom. As the vomit rises, it will meet the gag, a complete barrier to its exit. The result is that the Bottom could suffocate on his own vomit. Not a very pleasant thought. If you do use a sock or handkerchief, put it under the tap before putting in the Bottom's mouth so that the mouth does not dry out quickly and trigger the gag reflex, and don't force it all the way in, if it doesn't fit easily.

The mouth is rarely open very wide for long. When it is, say at the dentist, it can be very painful as the muscles try to adjust. When you use a large gag that causes the mouth to open wide, remember that the Bottom will have the same kind of problems as a visit to the dentist may cause. Also, if a gag is pulled tightly into place from the back, it may damage the corners of the mouth.

A less obvious safety factor is that the face soon begins to swell under a hood. A nose opening large enough when the hood is first put on may soon become partially or completely obstructed as the cheeks swell. This can lead to serious discomfort for the wearer, if not a very dangerous lack of air. Also, what may at first be bearable for the wearer may cause panic as other factors such as any restriction of movement or intensity of play change.

If you use a blindfold or hood, remember to check for contact lenses. Likewise, if you use a gag or hood, check for false teeth or capped teeth. Pressure from these forms of bondage can cause the contact lenses to dig into the eye, or break the caps or false teeth.

Here is a quick check list of safety considerations for hoods and gags:

1. Breathing holes might become obstructed when the hood shifts during play, particularly if the Bottom is anchored in a way that allows the hood to move easily.

2. Mouth/eye zippers are popular with people who like a variety of opportunities. Facial hair can be a problem with zippers, so they should be opened and closed with care, and have some kind of backing, where possible. Pressure upon an opened or closed zipper can be painful and damage the skin.

4. Hoods and drugs (including alcohol) do *not* mix.

5. Poppers used with hoods can have unexpected results. Due to the restricted breathing in hoods the fumes can linger for a long time and the effective "dose" can be more powerful than expected.

6. A very tight hood can cause the wearer to bite the inside of the cheeks.

7. If the wearer of an eyeless hood is in darkness for too long, a state of disorientation may result. When the hood is removed, care should be taken because both the thought and movement of the wearer may not be predictable.

8. Under the same circumstances, light can be painful on eyes that have been in darkness for a while. Also, the wearer's sense of balance may not be good for a few minutes after the hood is removed.

9. *Never* use a hood to suspend body weight. the effect on the neck and spine can be disastrous. Also, the "D" rings on hoods are rarely designed to take serious strain.

10. Gags under hoods that have no mouth holes are not recommended. In an emergency, the whole hood will have to be removed (and laces can get knotted during the rush to remove the hood).

That's 186, Madam!
Thank you, Madam!

11. If one hood is used to cover another hood or a gag, the first hood or gag should always have a hole for breathing.

12. Be prepared to release your Bottom if claustrophobia occurs, and before any resultant panic sets in.

Finally, as a general note, more than for other forms of bondage, it is *very* important to have a pair of ambulance scissors close by you as the scene progresses, so that laces (or, in an emergency, the hood or gag itself) can be removed rapidly.

Leather

Most of the safety considerations that apply to rope bondage apply to leather. Toys range from simple thongs to full bondage suits. One extra concern is that some hard leathers, such as latigo, may have very strong edges that may cut or cause extra pressure on the Bottom's skin. Pressure points caused by leather suspension harnesses occur not only under the pelvis but the weight of the Bottom will cause the harness to squash into the Bottom's torso from the sides. If there are any small objects like D-rings or snaps between the harness and the skin, they could cause enough pain to stop the scene (usually when you least want it to).

Mummification

Considerations here usually relate to the pressure of the bondage on the Bottom, dehydration, muscle cramps, and communication with the Top. Simple body bandages (gauze tubes that cover the whole body) can be cheaply bought at your local medical supply store and can be very effective. They are not very likely to cause great dehydration or muscle cramps, nor are they too threatening to a novice They do, however, define the contours of the Bottom very well, which can be very erotic for the Top.

Sleep sacks and mummification with tape or plastic wrap should be tried as you get more experienced. If you want to apply duct or insulating tape, make sure that the Bottom has been completely wrapped in plastic film like Saran Wrap beforehand. Otherwise, the hair of the Bottom's body may make removal of the tape very painful. The Bottom may also have an adverse reaction to the glue of the tape, and if the mummification is tight, cramps and dehydration may be the most pressing issues.

Another form of mummification is to use the plaster bandage that is used to make leg casts. This should only be attempted by experienced players who have all the right tools with them. It takes a long time to do and costs a lot. As the bandage is applied (little by little), it heats up as it cures. This leads to the Bottom sweating and losing water, so the Top should be very aware of the state of the Bottom at all times during the application of this form of mummification. A proper pair of cast removal shears is the best way to ensure that the Bottom is not cut as the cast is removed.

The following is a quick check list of considerations to take into account if you mummify someone:

1. A flat position is better for long periods of mummification, because standing for long periods can cause the Bottom to faint due to circulation problems. It could be life threatening, if not detected immediately.

2. Always ensure that the bindings around the chest permit sufficient lung expansion for unimpaired breathing. Avoid putting any pressure on the windpipe and the Adam's apple at the front of the neck.

3. If using adhesive tape (e.g. duct or insulating tape), do not apply it directly to the skin. It may not only rip off hair when it is removed, but skin may come off with it, too. The Bottom's skin may also react badly to the glue in the tape.

4. After wrapping the upper part of the body (which is usually done first), make sure that the Bottom does not fall, since he/she will not be able to break any fall when restrained, and be seriously injured as a result of the fall. Always have an assistant to hold the Bottom, or secure the Bottom to a fixed object. Alternatively, wrap the lower limbs when the Bottom is lying flat.

5. If using "non-breathing" materials such as duct tape or Saran Wrap, be careful of the room temperature. If it is too hot, the Bottom will sweat profusely, but, since evaporation cannot occur, the Bottom may dangerously overheat (in a prolonged scene of a few hours). This is also a good reason not to mummify someone in direct sunlight or on a very hot day.

    Similarly, an overly cool room may cause the Bottom great discomfort, especially if the Bottom has been sweating.

6. If a mummification scene lasts several hours, mild dehydration may occur. The Bottom should be required to drink fluids under

these circumstances. Fluids can be given with a straw from a glass of water, for example. For long scenes, provision should also be made for the Bottom to urinate.

Rope

As you start playing with rope bondage, you will only need about 6 to 8 feet of rope. Silk scarves, neckties, nylon stockings, bathrobe belts, or regular belts may do just as well, so most of what follows applies to them as well. One of the main advantages of these forms of restraint is that you won't have to decide whether you should hide them from visitors. We wouldn't use our best ties or scarves, if the Bottom is likely to struggle. They could get torn or stretched. There is one other thing you will need before you start experimenting with ropes: a good pair of ambulance scissors. You could also use a sharp knife with a blade that will not harm the Bottom as it is used. These may be required to get the Bottom out of the bondage fast, and they are cheap safety insurance.

As for most types of bondage, position during rope bondage is the most important consideration, e.g. falling when tied can be very hazardous. Certain limb positions can be difficult for some people but not for others, e.g. tying both elbows together behind the Bottom's back for a long time is difficult for most people. Try gentle positions at first, until you are sure that the Bottom can stay tied up that way.

Rope bondage around the joints can cause circulation problems, so pay very careful attention to it during the scene. Ideally, your rope bondage should be on naked skin or skin that is only covered with sheer material. This will allow you to keep an eye on the limbs. The first signs that your bondage is too tight is that the limbs will go cold, clammy, and white. After that they will go red and puffy, and still later they will turn bluish purple. Beyond this point, blood poisoning and limb death may occur.

Insertional Practices

Many things can be put into many of the nine openings of the body. The rectum, in particular, can take a lot. Common wisdom is that one should use two condoms, one over the other, when ass fucking (call it "double-bagging"). If either party is known to have a disease, you may want to seriously consider triple-bagging. Yes, we know it can remove some of the sensations, but you're not going to have much sensation if you're dead, either....

Hæmorrhoids, anal fissures, women with hysterectomies or pregnancy, will require that you proceed more slowly throughout the scene. You may not even be in a position to penetrate due to the nature of the condition. If you can penetrate, check to see if a smaller diameter of toy would be needed to play the way you'd like to. Some women who have had hysterectomies may require more lubrication than those who have not, since the vaginal secretions may be diminished due to loss of œstrogen.

The level or kind of activity for insertional practices may have to be modified for those with medical conditions.

Fisting

Fisting may not even be an option for those with anal or vaginal damage (or other medical conditions). The following are thought to be elements that can increase the risk of transmission of HIV and other diseases during fisting:

1. Using non-water soluble lubricants. These encase and protect the viruses from attempts to remove or destroy them;

2. Using a single container for lubricant in multiple scenes and for many people. This provides a vehicle for the virus to move from one person to another;

3. Small breaks in the skin caused be *over*-zealous filing of the fingernails. Here, one is caught between the devil and the deep blue sea: one ragged unfiled fingernail can cause rectal damage, as can an over-filed one. This means latex gloves are a necessity;

4. Multiple partners;

5. Using dildos, etc. in the rectum on more than one person; and

6. Decreased body resistance due to fatigue, multiple minor infections, chemicals, etc..

Long-Term Scenes

People may need to remove or alter things such as artificial limbs, dentures, contact lenses, etc., before a long-term scene begins in order to make them more comfortable.

Those with diabetes may drop their sugar levels during a long scene. This is identified by sweating, a feeling of dizziness, and fainting. The treatment is sugar; use orange juice, if you have any, because candies can lodge in the throat and cause severe breathing problems. If you do have to use candies, be sure to watch over the diabetic to ensure that the candy does not move into the throat. Please see the section on Diabetes for fuller information about how to prepare for a hypoglycæmic faint.

Heart conditions and migraines may require that physical and emotional stress be kept at a lower level than for other people. Those with TMJ (Temporomandibular Joint disorder) should not be fed tough foods such as bagels, steak, or other things that are hard to chew. Also, take care when using bits, bridles, and gags.

Sleep deprivation is used by some people as part of a scene. Given that the results of this form of play can be very unpredictable, we recommend that you do *not* use it. It is very possible that some form of psychological problems may develop. Besides, if you want to have any other form of play with the sleep deprivation, the Bottom is likely to be so sleepy that it would probably spoil any plans you had.

Oral Sex

This can be affected by things such as TMJ , dentures, allergies, or asthma. Where cocksucking (fellatio) is involved and the sucker has TMJ, it may be appropriate to let the him/her determine the pace of this part of the scene. The same is true for those wearing dentures. Asthma and allergies create a need for air. People may want to take breaths and briefly stop sucking cock. This doesn't mean that the activity has to be stopped completely, just modified. The person with the condition may have to be the one to set the pace.

Gags and head harnesses should be treated in much the same manner. The problems will be similar to those when sucking cock. It is not a good idea to gag a person with a seizure disorder, nor to put a head harness on them. If they do start to seize, there will be problems, and any head restraints should be removed immediately. (It is a good idea to apply a mouth protector at, or before, the beginning of the scene so the tongue won't be bitten.)

Condoms on men, and dental dams for women are highly recommended for any play that might involve exchange of bodily fluids during oral sex.

Percussion Play

Whipping, particularly with a long whip such as a bullwhip, can mark the skin by causing cuts and abrasions. Therefore, before a whipping scene starts, it is important to negotiate about whether the Bottom is prepared to have marks as a result of play. Many do not want marks. When paddling someone, remember that a studded paddle used studs-to-skin can also break the skin. This means negotiation about marks may also be appropriate to paddling scenes.

Complications of a whipping scene may involve contact lenses, glasses, migraines, pregnancy, or scoliosis, and a number of other considerations. For scoliosis (curvature of the spine), the spine should be kept as in line as possible. If the spine is crooked, the Top might need to aim differently to get a good hit on the muscles. With the jarring that an intense whipping or paddlings can cause, contact lenses may be popped out, glasses may be knocked off, or a migraine may start.

Like other activities that break the skin, if you anticipate marks or breaking of the skin of any sort, make sure that you have the appropriate items at hand to care for the wounds at the end of the scene. This means having such things as hydrogen peroxide solution, bandages, etc. close by before the scene starts. Please see the section on First Aid for more information about the appropriate things to have at hand.

In both whipping and paddling scenes, the whip or paddle should always be well away from the joints of the body. Likewise, avoid letting any implement hit the spine. We know of cases where hitting the spine caused temporary numbness.

Ærosolization of Blood

There has been some concern that, in heavy whipping scenes where the skin is broken, blood may be ærosolized. There may be splashes of blood as the whip hits the Bottom, or blood may leave the whip as it passes through the air. This "floating" blood could be breathed into the lungs, ingested via the stomach after landing in the mouth, or enter the body of people near the whipping through exposed cuts that they may have. While this risk is thought to be minimal, it is a finite risk. To the best of our knowledge, no-one has yet measured the risk. We know that there is concern in operating rooms around the world that blood can enter the air during surgeries where, perhaps, rotating saws are used to cut skin and bone. Operating rooms have the advantage of being able to create a laminar flow of air to minimize the risk to those in the operating room. This is not possible in most playrooms. At least one SM organization has torn down its playroom to reörganize it, and has found dried blood "everywhere," in the form of minute droplets of blood that settled as dust. Many viruses cannot withstand drying, HIV is one of them. While we believe the risk from other diseases to be minimal, we feel that you should be aware of it. Both the Top in the scene and any spectators or other bystanders may want to wear surgical masks and ensure that any exposed cuts are covered. SM play *can* have its serious side, can't it?

Scat, Watersports, & Raunch

These forms of play are all based on bodily secretions. More often than not, the body will secrete viruses and bacteria in these secretions. Sometimes there is not very much; for example, there does not seem to be much HIV in urine of infected people, but it is there in small quantities.

If your play is going to include any form of contact with bodily fluids or secretions, you should be aware of your health beforehand so that you and your partner(s) can take the appropriate precautions.

Urine on unbroken skin will not cause an infection, but micro-cuts can be made in the skin that are not visible to the eye. Rough rubbing of the skin or perhaps dry skin caused by dry air could both cause these micro-cuts.

If you like stinking feet, or stinking any part of the body, remember why it stinks. It's because there is a breeding ground for bacteria, fungi, and who knows what there. If you don't want to catch anything, don't allow contact that would let you catch whatever is causing the smell. You'll probably be able to get a good dose of the smell without having to get too near it, anyway.

Suspension & Inversion

Asthma, cardiac conditions, blood pressure problems, migraines, and a variety of muscular and skeletal disorders should all be considered before suspension or inversion are part of a scene. So should things like contact lenses and cataract operations. People with high or low blood pressure may have problems being suspended or inverted.

Equally, a migraine may be started by this form of play. Someone with back problems may not take well to being hung by the feet or any other place. There is also a danger of retinal damage (this was the main reason that the popularity of inversion boots waned).

The scene will have to be modified to accommodate the condition. This may involve changing the duration or type of suspension, position, or means of getting into position.

Care should be taken to ensure that the Bottom has no seizure disorder. Should a seizure occur anyway, you should be ready for it *before* it happens. You will need to be able to get the Bottom out of the suspension or inversion quickly and safely.

Miscellaneous Considerations

For those with allergies, food should be discussed before starting a scene. Would the Bottom react badly to ingesting certain foods or other materials? Topical application of materials, such as lubricants, mouthwash, creams, etc., can also cause problems. Detergents soaps, deodorants, and nickel may also cause allergic reactions. Anything that you may put onto or into the body needs to be discussed.

Take care when applying things such as blindfolds to people with contact lenses or glasses. Contact lenses may have to be taken out before the scene begins. Glasses can be simply taken off.

Blindfolds can cause dizziness or disorientation in some people. Those with high blood pressure may find that a blindfold becomes uncomfortable, and they may get dizzier and more easily than others and have other problems with balance.

Many people get claustrophobic wearing blindfolds, masks, hoods, and even some forms of body restraint. The claustrophobia may happen only some time after the item is put on the Bottom. Therefore, care should, be exercised during the scene, as well as at the time the item is put on. When the claustrophobia occurs, the Bottom may be very anxious to get out of the restraint and he/she may panic. Do everything you can to reassure that Bottom as you rapidly remove the restraint. As a Bottom, if you feel something claustrophobic coming on, try to warn the Top as soon as possible. It may be possible to remove or change the restraint to allow the scene to continue. Your Top will not be able to do anything unless you give a warning. In the case that the claustrophobia comes on too fast, tell you Top *immediately* and try to stay as calm as possible while the restraint is removed. The time taken to remove the restraint may seem like an eternity at this point, but you'll help your Top by working at staying calm.

When using any form of toy, bear in mind that some people prefer different positions for the same activity. This is especially important when the Bottom has some form of muscle or joint disorder. They should be comfortable (reasonably, anyway), because we're here to have a good time.

Equipment

We usually use a lot of things other than our bodies when we engage in SM play. That is not to say that we can only play when we have other objects to help the play; SM players also engage in "vanilla" play, hugging, etc.. We have found that we can produce a variety of sensation for the body (and, by extension, the mind) using all manner of things that we find in sex shops, hardware stores, kitchen stores, chandleries, grocery stores, children's toy stores, forests, deserts, gardens, beaches, etc.. You get the idea.

All five of the senses, in any combination, are stimulated by these toys. Maybe the sight of your partner or the toy itself, the smell of the perfume or the chocolate syrup, the sound of a cracking whip or a crackling fire, the taste of a condom or leather, or the feeling of the forest floor or the tit clamps your Top just put on you. Sometimes the senses combine to give an atmosphere that is appreciated by the players, say a dark, dank cellar or the spray of waves at the shore. All these stimuli reach the brain in one way or another and are a turn-on to different people at different times.

At some point, you're going to have to choose your toys. What do you want to use, where do you get it, and what concerns should you have when you acquire it? Provided that you follow the guide-lines of safe, sane, and consensual play, it doesn't really matter what you play with, if you enjoy its effects. Paddles, potties, panties, porridge, and pine cones are all part of the panoply of potential playthings.

The chosen toys should be fit for your intended purpose. They should excite, be strong enough where necessary, and have a way out in an emergency. Below we've tried to show you some of the range of possibilities, along with the attendant safety concerns.

Toys

The only limits to the kinds of toys you use are your imagination and your wallet. Toys come in many varieties and purposes, many of which may never have occurred to you. Here are a few to set your mind on its imaginings.

Tit toys, cock and ball toys, harnesses, ropes, all kinds of restraints, texture toys, temperature toys, dress-up/costumes, sensory deprivation toys, suspensions, wrappings, ass toys, cunt toys, permanent piercings, play piercings, etc..

Sex shops often sell many toys, but we have found that a fertile imagination can find many more in hardware stores, kitchen stores, and tack shops. The latter are particularly useful for metal items like cock rings, etc.. All these "alternative sex shops" will tend to have lower prices than those that specialize in sex toys.

One way to get ideas for toys is to look at sex store catalogues. You may be able to find a way to simulate one of those expensive toys with something a lot cheaper. A few catalogues and a fertile imagination could take you a long way.

When shopping for toys in any of the sex shops or their alternates, be aware of the quality of the item you're purchasing. Is it really fit for what you want to do with it? Does it have any sharp edges? Will it break under the use to which you intend to put it? Remember that a lot of the alternative toys were not intended for sex play and that it will be up to you to determine their suitability. Some people have coined a word for these alternative toys: pervertibles. You'd be amazed at the kind of uses your greatest sex organ, your brain, can devise for such simple things as toothpicks and chopsticks.

Occasionally, you may take an object to modify it slightly. Take the humble chopstick. You could sharpen one end to use the point to run gently up and down the Bottom's body, you could use the point or blunt end end-on, or you could pass the flat length of the stick along the body for yet another sensation.

If you're playing in some woods, the range of possible toys changes again. Sticks, leaves, earth, water, sand, etc. can all be used to great effect. Tie your Bottom up in tree creepers, maybe to a tree. Rub pine cones or pine needles on the body. This is just one whole new world of sensations, and we'll bet that a blindfolded Bottom won't be able to identify even a small fraction of the things you've used.

That's 196, Madam!
Thank you, Madam!

In the following sections we've tried to indicate some of the potential ways to play with toys. They are by no means an exhaustive list, nor should they be considered in isolation. Grouping two or more types of toys in play can add greatly to the fun.

Gym equipment, car tools, hairdressing equipment. Have you rolled someone in carpet, lately?

Blood Letting Toys

Toys that let blood fall into two main categories: cutting and piercing. These toys should always be *sterile*. The skin in the affected area should also be sterilized before using the toy, *and afterwards*. Please see the sections on Cleaning of Toys and Cleaning the Skin for more details on how to sterilize toys and skin.

Generally, for permanent piercings, piercing needles supplied by body jewellery supply houses will be used. The material used should be one that does not oxidize, such as surgical steel or gold. Note that some people are allergic to stainless steel, so you should check this before buying the jewellery.

For temporary piercings, we have found that 20-gauge, 1" or 1½" long hypodermic needles are quite effective. Any part of the skin may be pierced, but not the parts of the body underneath the layer of skin. The needle should be double the length that you intend to pierce. 22-gauge is the thinnest needle to use when performing a temporary piercings.

One point to note is that, should a needle break or bend for any reason, as you put it back in the cap, it can punch right through the cap. We have seen this happen (in tests, no less). So, the Top should take extra care with bent and broken needles. we did a little informal testing of hypodermic needles. We found that if you try to bend needles greater than 20-gauge and less than 22-gauge, they are more likely to crease and break.

The Top *must* wear sterile latex gloves. If the Top has a delicate liver, he/she should not engage in piercing, since about one in ten piercings results in skin-breaking for the Top, even when protected by latex. It is as important for the Top to be wearing latex gloves during the removal of the piercings as it is during the insertion. The needles should be counted before and after the scene is completed, and the needles and swabs, etc. should be put into a puncture-proof container for disposal. A good way to do this is to keep the needle caps and make sure after play that each cap has a needle. It won't hurt to count the needles, regardless.

The Bottom will want the pierced area cleansed with antiseptic after the scene. Remember that alcohol is only a mild antiseptic. It can, however, be used as a wonderful method to sting the pierced area.

If you want to gently whip a temporary piercing, remember to use a whip that is less likely to snag on the needles used for the piercing. About the only whip we have see for such a purpose was made out of plastic fish tank air supply tubing. It is easy to sterilize with bleach beforehand, and will not snag on the piercing needles. You should not whip the pierced area hard, and the needles will not hurt much more than the surrounding skin. This addition to the temporary piercing play should be more of a psychological play than a physical one.

Piercing and cutting techniques are not for the novice. If you are interested in learning these skills, we suggest that you study with someone experienced in the area (failing that, a physician) to ensure safe and pleasurable play later on. With the continued presence of viruses such as HIV, piercing and cutting are considered, even by some experienced SM players, to be playing "on the edge" for both the Bottom and the Top.

Bondage Toys

Like percussion, this is a large, catch-all category. It includes wrist and ankle restraints of leather or steel, rope restraints, handcuffs, Saran Wrap, duct tape, etc.. Some involve sensory deprivation, others do not. You'll have to decide which form of play you want to investigate and then research it properly.

The simplest form of bondage is having the Bottom's eyes closed; the most common is probably to use some form of rope bondage, possibly coupled with blindfolds, gags, and/or hoods. The most sophisticated (and expensive) bondage toys are usually specialized pieces made of leather and iron, such as bondage suits and bags and steel hoods and shackles.

Any restraint made of metal will tend to be less forgiving than more pliable ones. So, if you're using metal, be sure that it is loose and that nearby you have the equipment you need, to cut someone out. Also, be careful not to cause great pressure in a single spot, or, depending where it is applied, you could break or badly bruise body parts.

Genital Bondage Equipment

This area of restraint is not only a matter of personal choice, but also of correct fit. Most items sold in sex toy stores do not adjust much, or they do so in discrete jumps (unless the closure is Velcro®). Genital bondage falls into three main categories: self-stimulation, prevention of masturbation, and enforced chastity. with the exception of chastity belts, most genital bondage is for men, since their equipment is so much easier to grab and bind.

Chastity Belts

Most people envision a clanking, rusting device of vaguely medieval construction when they think of chastity belts. Most of the ones you can see in museums are of dubious origin, efficiency, and practicality. Today they are sued in SM play as a form of real or symbolic enforced fidelity. To surrender such personal freedoms can be very erotic. Wearing the belt at home during play is one thing, but how about going to work wearing a chastity belt? This could engender feelings of anticipation of the belt being discovered as well as the sense of dependency, i.e. hours of erotic excitement.

If the aim is to prevent arousal or masturbation, you will be hard pressed to find one that works well. The problems relate to the variability of the situation, particularly in the male. A comfortable fit can rapidly become a dangerous one. Since many chastity belts are made of metal, their harshness and unforgiving nature may make everyday wearing impossible. As a fantasy or as part of a short scene they may be fine, but for longer use you should consider the potential problems carefully before you proceed. The fantasy of being welded into a cast iron jock strap is one thing; the reality of not being able to sit down in it without getting a hernia is another.

One aspect of the appeal of chastity belts is visual. The belt may be made of metal and look medieval; or perhaps it could take on the look of a Victorian corset, all horsehide and rivets. What about those shining high-tech ones in your local sex store? Another aspect is the degree of security: do you want to completely prevent masturbation, simply make sex difficult, or establish who belongs to whom? Yet another aspect is that of how long the device is to be worn. Anything practical for long periods is unlikely to be very secure.

The psychological effects of wearing the device a home are different from those of being forced to wear it under clothing in a public place.

The latter feelings are also very different from those of being forced to wear the belt in public without the cover of clothes. As you can see the possibilities of the variety of chastity belts is almost limitless. They are determined only by your imagination and consideration of safety.

Cockrings & Straps

There is some crossover between cock and ball bondage toys and those toys designed more for torture of the genitals. Merely the presence of a band, hard or supple, around the base of the cock and behind the scrotum is a powerful stimulant to many men. To others it is an everyday thing (for instance, one of the authors has worn a heavy chromed ring for over a year). If the cockring or cockstrap is comfortable, it can be worn continuously without undue effects. Your choice of material, weight, and tightness will depend on your preferences, or those of your Top.... Many of the more complex pieces of genital bondage rely on a cockring or strap as an anchor for the rest of the apparatus.

Non-adjustable rings are can be made of material including metal, leather, rubber, or chain. Simply putting on the ring can be stimulating and/or painful. personal preference and practicality will determine whether you put the testicles or the penis through the ring first. If you have not used a cockring or strap before, we recommend that you use one that is too large rather than too small. A ring that was comfortable at first can become dangerously tight very quickly.

Adjustable rings and straps are well suited to playtime. Cheap alternatives to sex toy store items include: short chains, large "Jubilee" clips, and disposable nylon "ties." You could close the chain with a padlock (the heavier it is, the more the Bottom will be aware of its presence). The Jubilee clip is cheap, but is potentially dangerous because it requires a screwdriver to tighten it. The genital area is not the place anyone would want the screwdriver to slip. The edges of the Jubilee clip should be smoothed before it is used and the screwdriver should be short. Garden supply stores and hardware stores sell nylon tie wraps very cheaply. One end of these is threaded through the other and the resultant ring is tightened around the base of the penis or behind the scrotum. Tie wraps have to be cut off, since they are designed to tighten only.

Lockable cockrings and straps have to be small enough to prevent the testicles from slipping through. If a screw lock is provided, you should take care to ensure that no skin is pinched as the lock is tightened. If you use a padlock, remember that any movement on the part of the Bottom may cause scrotal skin to be pinched between the lock hasp and the ring. A small piece of tape around the hasp and hole can eliminate this problem, at least temporarily.

"Parachute" harnesses qualify as genital bondage, but they are covered more fully in the section on Cock & Ball Toys.

A padlock large with a large hasp (about 2 3/4" diameter) can be used as a locking cockring. The weight of the lock itself will add to the sensation of the ring. Once you have checked that the lock can be worm for a reasonable time in private without problems, the Bottom can then wear it under clothes, say, to work. If you cannot find a lock big enough, try putting the padlock around only the testicles.

Covers, Cages, & Sheaths

Cages or covers for the genitals can be made of metal and/or leather and rubber. When made of latticework, these can have a very strong visual effect. Black latex sheaths work very well, but are sometimes hard to obtain. They can be a struggle to get into if a ball bag is included in the design, and if someone else tries to put you into one, it could take a while. Some of these sheaths include a drainage tube.

Ball balloons (lockable latex spheres) are also difficult to get on. They may require that a removable cockstrap is put on to stop the testicles from disappearing into the body as you try to put them into the bag. Talcum powder or lubricant can help. Pubic hair usually hinders efforts to put the bag on.

Leather ball bags encase just the testicles. Some of them are made with two layers of leather, so that they can be filled with lead shot to pull on the testicles as the bag is worn. Different weights are often available.

Penis sheaths made of leather or rubber are used to encase, restrict, or hold the penis up or down. they should be as soft as possible to allow for the rapid size changes in the penis during play. Some come with internal prickers to heighten the sensation for the Bottom. The pricker versions should be kept as single person toys, due to the risk of disease transmission if the pricks puncture the skin of the penis. The small buckles used to tighten some of these toys can cause havoc by pinching the skin if clothes are put on after the sheath.

Head Bondage Toys

Head bondage is often used by those into visual and aural deprivation. Head bondage could come in the form of no more than having the Bottom close his/her eyes but it could also be a complex iron restraint suspended from the ceiling.

When the head is "cut off" from the outside world with a hood, the Bottom can feel that the head is detached from the body, as though floating on its own, close to the body. Some people like to free their minds of input from the eyes and ears so that they can concentrate on the other physical stimuli. They can simply *be*, rather than have to think about or anticipate stimuli.

Hoods can be used successfully to "disguise" your partner during a scene. They can remove a problem that some people have when they indulge in SM play: they usually relate to their partner in a way that they feel is not the same as the relationship they want during the SM scene. During the scene, they would like to imagine that the person they are playing with is unknown to them. The hood allows one or both players person to go *incognito* during the scene, thereby making it easier to fulfil the fantasy. This is because hoods can change the look of a person, almost changing their character. This helps players to release themselves of much of any self-consciousness that they may be feeling. It also allows them to fantasize freely about the other player. For instance, you may not be turned on by your partner's looks, but you know he/she plays well. Not seeing your partner will allow you to imagine that he/she is your ultimate fantasy. (This will probably help the scene along, but you should be careful here not to mention your feelings blatantly to your partner, who may be offended by your attitude to his/her looks....)

The effects of hoods vary according to their type and affect both the Top and the Bottom. Factors such as tightness, padding, rigidity, acoustic properties, of the many types of hoods and gags all contribute to the overall effect. Whether you can speak or hear through a hood can have a marked effect on your play. One hood over another or over a gag can change the effects just as much.

Hoods worn by Tops tend to be less restrictive than hoods worn by Bottoms, e.g. the executioner's hood, which only covers the top half of the face. The Top's hood could give an appearance of a highwayman or interrogator. It may come further down than the half face by having a surface that covers the shoulders. Both Top and Bottom will react differently to the various designs. Old-style hoods are not the only ones with which to play: have you ever thought of playing with Darth Vader or storm troopers?

Fixtures and fittings of hoods and gags vary from plain leather to designs that include many rivets and attachment points. The comfort of the hood or gag will get less as more fixtures are added.

The construction of hoods can include any of the following: lacing closure versus zippers; closed or open eyes, mouth, or nose; inclusion of a collar in the hood design; a flap to keep hair out of the closure; eyelets and/or cinch rings; locks; attachment points to allow the hood or harness to be attached to something else; openings for ears, pony tails; or beards; the hood could be completely closed; blinkers; and muzzles or bridles. Another aspect of hood and head harness construction is the rigidity of the materials used. Hoods can come simply in the shape of a bag, or could be formed by wrapping the head with a bandage or, say, rubber strips. Materials for hoods include leather, rubber, canvas, and probably a few more things that we haven't even thought of.

Sports helmets, such as for boxing, kendo, fencing, etc. can provide a dramatic and practical addition to your scenes. Motorcycle helmets with face covers, soft hoods and gags work very well. The advantage of motorcycle helmets is that they can be used out of doors and noone will give you a second glance. Vintage leather flying helmets and high-altitude helmets could give you more ideas.

Rubber hoods are readily available in toy stores. They don't have to be just the black latex ones, either. Those that are moulded into well-known faces could be just as scary....

Gags come in many shapes and sizes. the ideal shape is a wedge like a slice from an orange. You could make one of wood and cover it with leather or rubber. The shape ensures that the front centre teeth do not take all the strain when the Bottom bites down. The traditional bar-shaped gag was used by surgeons before anæsthetics were commonly available. It was a piece of wood dowel that was padded with sheepskin and covered in leather. Each end of the wood was attached to thongs that were tied at the back of the head. Pony-sized bits from tack shops make great gags, but try to find rubber ones, because metal ones will quickly chip the teeth. Bits often have bridles already incorporated.

"O" ring gags do hold the mouth open wide, but some people find that they can be turned around inside the mouth. To prevent these gags from turning, the straps holding them in place should be at least 2cm wide. Also, they put all of the strain on the inner teeth, so any sudden mouth movement could be dangerous.

Tube gags incorporate a wide mouth cover with a tube passing through it. All the pressure form the mouth is on the front centre teeth, potentially a problem. A stopper for to fit the gag is a useful addition to these toys.

Gags in the form of "stuffers" fall into two categories: those that hold the mouth open and those that allow the teeth to close. Other than the gags we have already mentioned above, hand-made soft stuffers are available in leather, rubber, and moulded plastic (including penis-head shapes). You should not be able to bite through the "neck" of any open-mouth stuffer.

You can check the size of your own mouth by putting the corner of a thin plastic bag into your mouth, and adding some small pieces of fabric until your mouth is comfortably full. Then twist the bag shut and biting down to mould it into shape. The circumference and length of the result will give you a good idea of what your mouth can take.

At first, inflatable gags seem like good stuffers, but they can puncture is not strongly inflated and can press on the back of the throat if too strongly inflated. There can also be breathing difficulties because they can completely fill the mouth and partially block the windpipe. If you do use them, try putting a boxer's gum shield in first. This will allow you to use the minimum pressure required to fill the mouth and prevent the Bottom's teeth from puncturing the gag.

A boxer's gum shield can be used as a great gag and mouth immobilizer. After softening one in hot water, they are placed into the mouth and the Bottom bites hard on them. They mould to the teeth, making them a personal toy, and possibly the memento of a great scene. due to the moulding, pressure is equally distributed on the teeth. You could add a breather wedge between the upper and lower parts of the gum shield for many situations. If the mouth is closed with a shield in place, it is total immobilized. Further, if the mouth is covered, you will have an almost total silencer.

Outside dildos are a specialized piece of equipment, used by both homosexual and heterosexual men and women. There can be a very real embarrassment from being made to wear one and the implied threat that it may have to be used is a very powerful psychological device. If you intend to make the Bottom put the outside dildo into an orifice, make sure that it is well anchored to the Bottom, preferably with an extension into the Bottom's mouth, by way of a well fitting stuffer gag on its back side.

You have probably seen a small piece of adhesive tape used in many films to silence someone. In practice, it is not as simple. The mouth should be open wide as you apply the tape, or you should make sure that the jaw cannot open after the tape is applied. A Bottom can use a mouth stuffer to push the tape off. Wrapping tape around the Bottom's head is effective, but it could cause the Bottom to bite his/her cheeks. If you use fabric-based duct tape, you will have to be prepared for it to be painful as it comes off and for the Bottom to have an adverse reaction to the glue.

Hospital Restraints

This is a fantasy for many people and convincing rôle playing is a great help. There are very few manufacturers of these devices in the U.S.A. and none that we know of in Britain. Medical supply houses do stock them, but you may have to be a physician to buy them.

Since sometime around the 1920s, use of these devices was frowned upon, but now the practice of administering drugs is also being frowned upon. Some countries, notably France, have reverted to using the straitjacket or "camisole" to allow certain kinds of patients to let off excess energy or anger this way, without harming themselves or others. The Humane Restraint and Posey jackets have been sold for years to U.S. hospitals and sanitoria. They tend to be large and have to be expertly applied to be completely escape proof.

Many kinds of bed and table restraint are available. These usually come in the form of straps with locks. The high quality ones have prices to match. Those with Velcro® closures can be made secure, if the closure is placed correctly.

Splints and other surgical bondage can be great for doctor/patient scenes. Surgical collars and corsets can be quite a trial for the subject. They are very erotic, if you like them; very difficult, if you do not. These are often hand-made items, so they are expensive and difficult to find. If you can bring yourself to ask for them, second hand stores may have hospital trolleys and dentist chairs.

Bandages can be used for many things during an SM scene. There is one type we have found very effective: the full body stocking. It is a wide tube of white bandage. The Bottom can be slid into it and the ends closed off. It is not too threatening for a novice, since one can see through it to some extent, and movement is fairly free, compared to the other devices we have mentioned. From the Top's point of view, the body stocking is good because it allows easy access to the Bottom, accentuates the contours of the body, and can be taken off quickly and safely with a pair of ambulance scissors, if required.

Plaster bandage is covered in the section on Mummification and is for experts only.

There are many gadgets used in hospitals to clamp or open parts of the body, including the penis and vagina. If you can find a place to buy them, we'd bet you'd be like a kid in a candy store.

Metal Restraints

As mentioned above, these restraints are *very* unforgiving. They include simple handcuffs, leg iron and shackles, collars, and metal hoods. Your body will likely break before any of these toys. Note that metal hoods can be very hot, particularly in the sun (where is almost the same as putting your Bottom's head into a hot oven).

Mummification

Any material can be wrapped around or encase the body as a form of mummification. Usually the material used will be flexible, such as: Saran Wrap, duct tape, insulating tape, rubber stripping, cotton sheets, plaster impregnated bandages (for rigid mummification and experts only), canvas or leather sacks, sleep sacks, or any other material that will create general immobility of the entire body.

If plaster or tape is used as the mummification material, the body should first be covered with a material that will not stick to the skin, e.g. cotton or Saran Wrap. Generally, mummification should proceed from the head downwards. Make sure that the nostrils and mouth are left uncovered to facilitate breathing. Certain other parts of the body may be left exposed to enable the Top to work on the Bottom. For example, once the mummification is complete, the scene may then involve tit, genital, and/or foot play.

Rope Toys

The rope you use is the basic toy, but rope can be made cheaply into toys that can be reused many times, such as a pair of wrist restraints.

You just need to know how to tie the right knots There are several sources of basic information on how to tie knots (some are listed in the bibliography). They include books on basic knot tying and macramé. The difference when you use these knots for play is that the "sticks" you are tying together are softer and may fight back.

There are many objects about the house that can be used in conjunction with ropes for bondage. For example, thick broomsticks are wonderful as spreader bars, to keep feet or hands apart. If the broomstick is put horizontally behind the Bottom's back with the arms passed behind the broomstick and the hands tied together in front of the stomach, the powerful back muscles are next to useless. If it is put under the knees, with a rope passed outside each knee around the stick and then behind the back, pulling the knees to the chest, the Bottom will feel very exposed and with very little modesty. Using it vertically behind the back will afford you the kind of rigid bondage that may otherwise only be attainable with expensive specialty toys.

Other pervertibles around the house include railings (check for strength), closet bars (not very strong, so *never* to be used for suspension), chairs, and toilets seats. Bed frames are often the first thing that people think of, but, if the Bottom struggles, they can roll around and creak. They can also put holes in the walls; so maybe they are not the best pervertibles.

A few strategically placed eyebolts in door frames, walls, floors, and ceilings can help your rope bondage enormously. The mounting must be strong enough to withstand a struggling Bottom. For example, any wall mounting should be in the wall studs, not just to the drywall. Most of these eyebolts can be disguised as plant hangers, or other household mountings.

Chairs can be used not only to seat the Bottom, but also to have the Bottom bent over them, or maybe tied chair back to Bottom's back. Again, consider whether the Bottom will struggle and whether the chair is strong enough to withstand this.

As you graduate from scarves and ties, you will probably want to buy good rope for your scenes. We have found that $1/4''$ diameter soft nylon rope is the most versatile. Specialty leather items may sometimes make bondage easier for beginners, but the price may be too much for you, as you try to determine whether you enjoy bondage. There is not much of a market for used bondage equipment, so finding it cheaply may be difficult. Alternatively, if you buy something special, you may find that there is no market for it and that it is hard to sell, later.

When you tie off your ropes, try to keep the knots between the limbs and objects you use. This will reduce the chances of pressure points on the Bottom. For the same reason, it's a good idea to avoid twisting the rope or crossing it where it touches the Bottom's body. Any time that you pass a rope around the Bottom's limbs, you should wrap it around at least three times. This will spread the load when the Bottom struggles. For example, when tying wrists together, use about 8 feet of rope and leave about a foot dangling inside between the wrists, then wrap around both wrists until there is about a foot and a half left (usually about three to four times around), and bring the end down between the wrists, inside the loops of rope you have just made. Now wrap the two ends in opposite directions around the rope between the wrists. Tie the ends off with a reef knot (also known as a square knot). Tying off rope ends with a standard shoelace knot is acceptable, since it's just a variation of the reef knot.

To check that any rope bondage is not likely to be too tight, you should be able to pass one finger between the rope and the skin. If you cannot, then the Bottom may have circulation problems. If there is room for two or more fingers, the Bottom may be able to get free. A little practice is all you will need to the tension right.

If you tie a reef knot the wrong way, you'll end up with a Granny knot which can get tighter as the Bottoms struggles. This is not going to help you. Since the reef knot is likely to be the only knot you'll need as a beginner, it's worth the time to learn it properly. The more complicated knots can come later.

Cock and Ball Toys

There are even more ways to play with the cock and balls than the tits. Play can be external or, for advanced play, internal. Internal play is covered in the section on Catheters & Sounds and is for experienced players only. External play ranges from caressing to temporary and permanent piercings to application of pressure to cock and/or balls, and many other things in between.

The cock is endowed with a great number of very sensitive nerves, as are the balls. The ridge from the base of the balls to the anus has also been blessed with them. Almost any play in this area can enhance a scene. As with all play, it is usually best to start off slowly and work the stimulation up to the level that the Bottom can take. This is particularly true if you decide to stretch the balls, since it takes time for the suspensory apparatus inside to adjust to being stretched.

For novice players, the most common forms of cock and ball play are probably clothes pegs and cockrings. Many people play by wrapping the cock and/or balls with a leather thong to promote an erection. If the wrapping or binding is done too tightly, the cock and balls may go blue, just like if you wrap a piece of string around your finger too tightly. The blueness is the result of blood that has given up its oxygen to the tissues of the cock and balls and now needs to return to the lungs to get more oxygen. All tissues of the body need a supply of oxygen, so you should not leave the cock and balls tightly bound (blue or not) for more than about ten minutes or tissue death might occur. It is also possible that a very tight binding may cause forms of varicose veins in the scrotum. For safety's sake, use the rule of thumb of not leaving a tight binding on for more than about ten minutes.

Many men wear cockrings all day, every day. One of the authors has regularly gone through airport metal detectors with his on. He just tells the security staff where to expect the hand-held metal detector to go off. If the ring is big enough to avoid blood circulation problems, there is no reason why you should not wear a cockring indefinitely. One of the authors has had his on for well over a year. You might be able to find straps of leather or other materials that you could keep on indefinitely, if you wanted. All you have to do is ensure an adequate supply of blood.

During play, binding the cock and balls tightly can come in the form of the many and varied straps, metals rings (single, or in groups like the "gates-of-hell"), sheaths for the cock only, some with metal prickers inside (these should be reserved as one-person only toys, owing to the risk of drawing blood), and anything else that tickles your fancy (or that other part of the anatomy). Once bound, the cock and/or balls can be tied to other objects, animate or inanimate. For example, tying the balls to the end of a water bed when the body cannot move towards the bottom of the bed will allow you to set up gentle waves in the bed to pull on the balls each time a wave passes.

As on the rest of the body, clothes pegs hurt more coming off the cock and balls that going on. They can often be left on, depending on the endurance abilities of the Bottom, for about twenty minutes. There is enough space on the average male genitals for about 30 to 40 pegs. Yes, it will hurt; that's part of the fun. Some people like to put pegs on in groups of, say, ten. Once the Bottom has one peg of the next group on, the rest in that group will go on. It's an interesting endurance test for those who like this kind of play.

There are many devices for the balls alone. One of the classics is the "parachute harness." This is usually made of leather and surrounds the balls at the base of the cock, so that it looks like the point of a point-up cone has been cut off and the balls pushed downward into the volume of the cone. The hole in the cone is small enough, however, to prevent the balls from passing back through it. This means that if small chains are attached to the bottom of the cone, they can be brought together (causing the toy to look like an open parachute) and have weights hung from them. If you decide to do this, remember to give the suspensory apparatus inside the ball sack time to stretch with the weight before you add any more. Some parachute harnesses have metal prickers on the inside, designed to increase the pain as weight is added. Owing to the risk of drawing blood, these should be reserved as single-person toys.

Stretching the balls can also be done by wrapping a thong or locking metal ball weight to the balls and then pulling on that. You probably have an idea of the possibilities, by now.

There are many ways to squeeze the balls, some of which have been refined into toys you can buy in sex and "leather" stores. One of the simplest is two flat pieces of wood between which the balls are placed. Pressure is then applied by turning the butterfly nuts on bolts that pass through both pieces of wood. This can be very painful. Another way is to use three pieces of wooden dowel about one inch in diameter. The ball sack is placed between two of these and the third is pulled toward these two with the balls trapped in the centre of all three, so it looks like a bundle of sticks of dynamite with the balls on the inside. Pressure is changed by using more or less elastic bands to hold them together.

A variation on the dowels is to use copper pipe (with the ends well smoothed down) and attaching one of the electrical toys to two of the three pipes. This will cause both a squeezing and an electrical stimulation. (For more on safety and use of electrical toys, please see the sections on Electrotorture and Electrical Toys.)

The cock and balls are great places to whip, but gently. A hard cock is much more fragile than a soft one, so you should not knock it around too much if it gets hard. You can buy, or make, small penis whips specifically for the genitals. They should impart a sting rather than a thud, due to the fragile nature of this part of a man's anatomy. Given the sensitivity of this area, you shouldn't have to do much to get a reaction, anyway.

Again, the nerves in this area will allow you to use textures to produce a reaction. Try textured rubber gloves. Light chain mail gloves have an interesting, cold feeling. After a period of slow, gentle sensitizing of this area, maybe with just sheepskin, simply blowing gently will cause a far greater reaction than you may imagine.

One last type of ball play is for experienced players only. A wooden "butterfly" board of some six to eight inches across that has a hole in it through which the balls are passed. The ball sack (scrotum) is then stretched outwards to its limit and hypodermic needles are temporarily pushed through the scrotum into the board to hold it in place. The balls are *not* to be pierced, since that is *extremely* dangerous. The butterfly board, when properly used, often produces little blood and does little or no damage to the scrotum. It is no more damaging that going for a blood test. It is mainly a mind trip. It is also a technique where sterile procedure *must* be followed *perfectly*. Also, remember to count your needles both before and after the scene, to ensure that they are all accounted for and that nobody steps on one after the scene is over.

Another category of cock and ball toys is bondage. This section has addressed some of them. Please see the section on Genital Bondage for more ideas in this area.

Electrical Toys

Electricity through the body can be a lot of fun. It can also be very dangerous. It is very easy to scare someone with the idea of electricity, so introduce gently to a novice during play. It is best to let the novice play with the toy alone before you use it on him/her. This way he/she understand the feeling and potential of the device. There are rules that must be obeyed when playing with electricity. If you follow the rules, it is no more dangerous than most other SM activities. If you don't , electricity is far too dangerous.

1.   Stay away from toys that need wall outlets;

2.   Use crank or battery driven devices;

3.   Always keep electricity below the waist; and

4.   Start easy.

There are two main types of electrical toy used in SM play when electricity is passed into or onto the body. Those that pass current and those that do not.

For pleasure, use the electrical devices in low but continuous mode. For pain, a jolt is required (not recommended for an untrained individual). Most people have a threshold for electricity through the body. Below the threshold, the electricity can be very pleasurable. Above it, electricity causes the kind of pain no-one wants. This threshold varies considerably between people, but it seems to exist in just about everyone.

(There is a third type of electrical toy, but of a slightly different nature: the vibrator. It only counts as an electrical toy because it is driven by electricity. It does not pass electricity through the body.)

Current Devices

Current devices include Relax-A-cisors, magnetos, TENS (Transcutaneous Electrical Nerve Stimulation) units, and cattle prods. (The Relax-A-cisor started in one form or another in the 1890s to early 1900s, and has been used for kinky means for about as long....)

Give the pulsator, TENS unit, etc. to the Bottom to experiment on him/herself. This takes away a great deal of the fear associated with electricity passing through the body. Usually, about 10 to 15 minutes later, the Bottom has become quite excited.

The body tends to address only one form of pain at a time, so the law of diminishing returns applies rather quickly with electrical devices because only the most painful device will be felt. Therefore, there is little point in using more than one electrical device at a time, unless the Top likes the visual effect.

Bad contacts with the body cause unpleasant "hot-spots" that feel like very sharp, hot pains. They can even leave small burns on the skin, so be sure to have a good electrical contact. You can use saline solution (such as that used for contact lenses) or the electrolyte used for electrodes for heart monitoring, etc.. Saline conducts much better than plain water.

A metal washer lint trap, when unravelled, makes a great metal mesh "condom" to use as a contact. A light elastic band will ensure that it stays in place. Brillo® pads have a knot which, when undone, provides a copper mesh sheet that can be used in a similar manner to the lint trap. Aluminium tape for repairing gutters can be wrapped around, say, clothes pins for a contact. 18 gauge copper wire works well outside the cock, but we recommend that it *not* be put down a flaccid or erect cock.

The ringer circuit of an old field telephone can be used, but only very rarely can a person take the three coils of a telephone magneto. Rheostats for reducing the output of the telephone magnetos are available and should be used.

We do *not* recommend the use of cattle prods for electrotorture. The three battery version is the largest that should be used on a human subject. The reaction to a cattle prod is primarily muscular, i.e., if one is applied to the cock and balls, since there is little muscle in this area, the reaction will be almost non-existent. Anywhere else on the body will probably cause a violent muscular reaction in the Bottom. Contacts will corrode. *Never* leave the batteries in a cattle prod. Do not buy your cattle prod in a "toy store," go instead to a local farm implement store. The price is a lot less. Be very careful with cattle prods. The are only for *heavy, mature* Bottoms.

Stunguns are not worth the money. They are designed to intimidate with sparks and crackles. They have no safety switch (Tops beware).

Voltage Devices

There is only one main kind of voltage device on the market, the Violet Wand (also known as the High Frequency Unit and the Master High Frequency Unit). The Violet Wand is the *only* exception to the safety rules given above, but it has its own rules. It must not be used near the face, particularly the eyes. It is safe for use on all other parts of the body. Care should be taken, however, not apply an intense spark to the same area for a long time. It may burn the skin. It may also heat up any metal piercings, permanent or temporary, with which it makes contact.

Do not use the Violet Wand for more than about five minutes at a time because the generator in the unit will get too hot. there are now "heavy-duty" Violet Wands appearing on the market. These can be left on almost indefinitely. You should check the type before you play, since they look similar to the older types.

Vibrators

Vibrators come in two main forms, those with batteries and those that use line voltage. The latter should *never* be wet when you play with them because one or both of you may get a shock you don't want or need. If 120 or 240 volts pass through your body, it could stop your heart, or cause a violent motion of one of your limbs that may damage the limb by either its hitting something or its moving beyond its normal range.

Insertional Toys

Dildos, fingers, butt plugs, cucumbers, fists, carrots, ass balls, cocks, telephone handsets. The authors have seen them all put into the body. Objects put into the mouth, ass, or vagina need only be clean, and the ass and vagina are not sterile parts of the body, nor is the mouth. Provided you take care that any object you put up someone's ass or vagina has no sharp edges, pretty well anything can be if it is at least clean. Sharp edges can tear the delicate membranes inside those openings.

Some people have allergic reactions to certain substances, so, to be on the safe side, stick to plastics, rubber, and stainless steel,

The urethra and bladder are sterile environments, so anything put into the cock has to be *sterile*. Please see the section on the Cleaning of Toys for the difference between clean and sterile. Equally, anything put into the cock has to be very smooth. Sterile catheters and surgical sounds are about the only things that qualify to be put into that opening of the body.

Catheters & Sounds

Catheters and sounds are *not* a pain trip. Nonetheless, some people are very frightened of catheters and sounds. They are perceived as an invasion of one of the most private parts of a man's body. They are a head trip *only*. If there is pain when these toys are used, there is a major problem, and you *must* stop.

If you are interested in playing with catheters and sounds, but are inexperienced, be sure to get expert help on how to do it, and what it should feel like, *before* you start (this applies to both Tops and Bottoms). Start with catheters, and move on to sounds only when you are an expert with the rubber tube. When learning to use sounds, start with straight ones, and work up to the Van Buren sound.

We have included lots of dos and don'ts in this section. They're a measure of how important it is to be careful with this play. It has to be learned from a person, rather than a book, even one like this.

Scat and Watersports Equipment

Safe sex guidelines often dictate major changes from our fantasies, yet the fantasies can still be very satisfying. A Bottom for a scat (fæces, shit) scene can lie under a glass table and the top can fire away. For more intimate contact, the top can first wrap the bottom in *several* layers of Saran Wrap (one layer alone cannot prevent the transmission of viruses such as HIV), and then let loose. The Top *must* wear latex gloves when cleaning up. Any body opening, no matter how small, is vulnerable to infection from fæces.

If you have led your Bottom to think that a scat scene is going to happen, a single drop of butyric acid at the other side of the room will smell like a ton of fæces. There are many foods that have a consistency similar to fæces, so you could use a combination of butyric acid and food for the right effect. If you are a Top who does not like the smell of butyric acid, you could put it in the appropriate channels of a gas mask on the Bottom. Since butyric acid has such a powerful smell, you should use *no more* than the amount that would stay on the end of a pin if you touch it to the surface of the liquid.

Suspension & Inversion Toys

When suspending someone there are several considerations with respect to the toys/equipment that must be borne in mind. The toys must not only be able to cope with the weight of the Bottom, but also to the added forces when the Bottom moves or struggles. Test it, first. If it will hold your stationary weight, swing on it and then bounce around. If it still shows no signs of stress, you should be fine if your Bottom is no heavier than you. Even if you do not plan to have the Bottom moving or making any sharp movements, sometimes it can be difficult to predict what might happen. Testing is important in all aspects of SM play, but especially so for suspension. As a rough guide the suspension toy and the anchors for it should be able to take twice the weight of your Bottom to account for added strain when the Bottom moves or jerks around plus an additional 50% margin for safety on top of that. This means that any suspension toys should be able to take at least three times the weight of the heaviest person you intend to suspend (700 lbs. or 350kg. is a good rule of thumb).

Always suspend from at least two points, that way, if one breaks, the other should break the fall or at least slow it down. You should always err on the side of caution when suspending someone.

If you have access to an overhead structure such as a beam, pipe, or tree branch that can support your Bottom, you're lucky. But check it, first. Is the pipe and its anchors to the wall or ceiling sufficient for the weight? Does the tree branch have too much spring in it? If the safest method is going to be to use chain, make sure that the chain is secured with a safe link (see below). A piece of heavy felt or rubber can be used to protect the beam or branch from damage by chains.

If your playroom is in the basement and you can get to the wood beams in the ceiling, you can drill holes through the beams through which you can put rope, bolts, etc.. Most of these beams will be somewhere between 15 and 30 cm. high and about 5 cm. wide. Your holes should be drilled such that the bottom of the hole is no less than 5 cm. from the bottom of the beam. Remember to avoid any knots in the wood where you drill, since these are the weakest points in wood beams. Use large diameter washers on the bolt to sandwich the beam and spread the load. If you decide to use hooks, make sure that the length they enter the beam is at least 4 cm.. Where possible, do not use eyebolts. Eyebolts have a tendency to let things fall out of them as the Bottom twists and writhes, and they are usually weaker than hooks. Drill a small pilot hole in the wood before you insert the hooks. This will make the insertion easier and minimize the risk of splitting the wood.

If you have a finished ceiling with a wooden construction, you can use the hooks we mentioned above. It may take a bit of time to find the joists, but make sure that you do find the centre of them, otherwise your hooks may fall out.

Concrete ceilings pose a problem for anchor points. About the only safe way is to drill right through the concrete and put a bolt with a large washer on the other end. If the ceiling is the roof or the floor of someone else's home, there isn't much you can do.

Never try to suspend someone from a suspended ceiling. Remove a panel and put your anchors into the real ceiling in one of the ways mentioned above.

Also, never use towel bars, chinning bars, shower curtain rods, or closet rods. These are all very flimsy and cannot safely take the loads you will be putting on them.

Only use chain that has welded links. Do not, under any circumstances put your trust in the bent metal chain used for hanging plants and light fixtures. Likewise, don't even think of using plastic chain. Some chains have twisted links and they may be strong enough, but they tend to cut into hands, so they should be avoided. Remember that the chain should not only be strong enough, but should be able to take the hooks and snaps you will be using with it.

Do not use "S" hooks for attaching a chain looped around a beam or to hold two pieces of chain together. It could release far too easily. Use links that close around the both chain links involved.

If you use rope for suspension, rather than chain, be sure that it is strong enough and that you have tied it in a way that is will not come undone unintentionally, but also in a way that you can undo it quickly, is needs be. Get yourself a Boy Scout's or Klutz Book of Knots, and learn how to tie the correct knots. Do not use frayed or rotted rope, it is far weaker than good stuff. Use hemp rope, cotton rope, or large diameter nylon rope. Never use the cheap plastic rope, it fails.

Should you use rope as the primary means of attachment to the Bottom for the suspension, make sure that the design of the rope attachment is strong enough, that it is secure enough not to slip off, and that it is loose enough that it will no unduly affect the Bottom's circulation. Even for rope, you will want to use a panic snap at each attachment to your anchor points. This will let you release the Bottom almost instantly, should an emergency arise.

Either rope or chain can be used to attach to the many toys sold for suspension, such as padded leather cuffs, and boot hoists.

Having put your Bottom in the necessary bondage, how do you hoist the person up? You *could* just run a rope through a hook and pull, but it will be difficult if you're heavier than your Bottom, and impossible if you're not. Pulleys were invented to reduce the effort you needed to put into lifting heavy objects, however, they can cause problems for SM play. The ropes can slip off them, and they have no safety catch or cleat to stop the rope running back if you let go. Proper block and tackles and winches with cleats can be found at good hardware stores and chandleries.

All suspension gear should be checked to ensure that the Bottom's circulation is not impeded before the Bottom is raised off the ground. This is best done once before any tension is taken on the ropes/chains/bungees and then just before the Bottom's feet leave the ground. There should also be no pressure points of the suits or harness against the body that may ache during the suspension. It's possible for a ring on a bondage suit to be caught underneath a suspension harness and press against a protruding bone, thereby causing enough pain to stop a scene (as one of us found out).

Raise the Bottom slowly, making sure that the restraints are not cutting into the Bottom, and that the Bottom is strained only in ways that you intended. If the suspension is going to be upside down, be careful that the body and head are not injured as they are dragged across the floor, or as they swing off it. It is a good idea for you to put a mattress or other soft landing for an accidental fall of a suspended Bottom. It is essential if the Bottom is inverted.

Tie off the rope somewhere secure enough to take the Bottom's weight. It should be where the rope won't interfere with your play, but not so far as to be difficult to reach in an emergency.

Lowering the Bottom is effectively the reverse of raising him/her. Do it slowly and make sure that no part of the body, particularly the head, is injured during descent. The Bottom will be fatigued and, if suspended upside-down, quite probably somewhat disoriented. In the latter case simple requests to "Move your hands forward," or "Move your hands towards me" will be difficult to register. Give the Bottom the time needed to readjust to being under normal gravity.

There is no need for someone suspended to be far from the floor or another surface that can support him/her upon a fall. In the case of an accident, if something breaks, or he/she has to be let down quickly, it will help to avoid injury if the distance fallen is not great. In any suspension, ensure that the Bottom cannot fall during the set up of the suspension, i.e. if the first points of attachment are at the sides of the waist, the Bottom could easily fall forward, so we've found it's best to start at the uppermost attachment points. Try, where possible to have at least one tie high on the Bottom's body to avoid this happening. If the set up will not allow for this, have a third person hold the Bottom in place as the suspension is started and finished.

Bondage Suits

Bondage suits are generally made of leather or canvas. They are strong enough to take someone's weight, and usually come with several means of attachment for suspension; be it rings at the shoulders or multiple points at the side of the body. The suits are expensive and for experienced players only. Rope, bungee cords, and chain can all be used for suspension in bondage suits.

Inversion Boots

These come in the form of fitness gear most people have seen at some time during the Seventies and Eighties, and also in the form of a pair of sturdy boots nailed to a board.

The first kind, sometimes known as Anti-Gravity boots, are attached around the ankles and hooked over a horizontal bar with the person effectively hanging from the ankles. They are well padded, but were not meant for SM play. They can easily come unhooked during play. Where possible we'd avoid using them for this reason.

Sturdy boots nailed to a board are preferred. You'd be best to find someone experienced who has some of these before you make any. They require careful thought and construction, because if someone falls when inverted, the most likely place to meet the ground is on the head.... Properly designed and constructed, this toy has great visual appeal and allows for many kinds of play unavailable with an uninverted Bottom.

Some sex stores offer well designed and tested ankle harnesses that are meant to be put over regular boots, so you can hang your Bottom upside down. Since this form of play requires that the Bottom be upside down, we *also* take a lot of care to ensure that our Bottom is well protected from landing head first on hard ground.

Remember to check for any medical problems your Bottom may have with respect to inversion before trying this form of play.

Mailbags

You can put your Bottom in one of these for quite a while, provided provision has been made for breathing. Some mailbags are made specially for play. They are of very heavy canvas, with leather or canvas reïnforcing. Properly constructed, mailbags can be used to suspend the Bottom with the head inside or outside the bag, depending on the effect you want. Since the bags are about 2 feet wide at the bottom and about 3 feet high, the Bottom will have plenty of room for manœuvre, unless he/she is very big. You can't really do much with a Bottom in a mailbag, except leave him/her there, make him/her a bit dizzy by spinning the bag around, or, maybe you've attached some electrical toy to them before the suspension began so you can start using that now. After a while in one of these, there's little question who's the boss.

Slings

Slings are made in much the same way as some hammocks, but are made of wide strips of thick leather, canvas, or other strong material. A lattice about $2^1/_2$ by $3^1/_2$ feet is made and attachments are made at the four corners to suspend the sling from the ceiling or whatever at about the hip to waist height of the Top. The Bottom is then placed in the sling, lying on his/her back, so that the Top has access to the genitals and asshole. The legs of the Bottom are usually suspended from loops of leather or canvas attached to the chains or ropes coming from the corners of the sling. The Bottom can usually hang on to the chains or ropes suspending the sling by his/her head.

The Top can not only play with the exposed parts of the Bottom with toys but also use it for fucking the ass or vagina. The sling is widely used by those who like to fist fuck their Bottom, since it provides a comfortable position for both the Top and Bottom.

Suspension Harnesses

Suspension harnesses are made of thick strips of heavy leather with sturdy rings for attachment to ropes or chains to the suspension points of the ceiling or suspension frame. A similar construction is used for leather slings.

Parachute harnesses can also be used to great effect (the ones for real parachutes, not the ones for your Bottom's balls, that is). The advantage of using the "real thing" is that was designed to take a person's weight, and it's going to be pretty comfortable for a scene.

Temperature Toys

There are many kinds of temperature toys available for play. Some use real heat, others use the sensation of heat. For all heat scenes, the Bottom should be well restrained, because any sudden movement by the Bottom could cause the source of the heat to be applied somewhere it was not intended. It is best not to work near the face, since any accidental burns or scars in this area are harder to live with than elsewhere on the body. The risk of damage to the eyes, nose and mouth are also much too great to risk playing around the face.

All of the sensitive areas of the body will be very sensitive to any form of temperature play. These include the genitals, face, armpits, anus, and any area that have been previously injured or sensitized.

Generally, the precautions you will need to take are to ensure that the appropriate items are to hand to remove the heat. If you are using flames, you should have handy a fire extinguisher (it should be in the playroom anyway as part of basic safety equipment), a heavy blanket (to smother flames), a supply of lint-free bandage, and a supply of very cool water. All forms of real heat require that you have a way to cool any burns, irrespective of whether they were intentional. Please see the sections on First Aid and Burns to help determine the kind of burn and how to treat it.

If you're using simulated heat with things such as Tiger Balm®, Ben-Gay®, or mentholated rubs, etc., have a moist, cool towel handy to remove any excess. Liquid soap or dishwashing detergent may help to remove more of these sources of "heat." Yoghurt can also help reduce the sensations caused by these chemical stimulants.

Branding

Branding is an advanced form of play that is for experts only.

Any marking of the skin using heat can be considered a brand. They can last from a few months to one to two years, depending on the size of the brand, depth of the burn, and the healing abilities of the person. A branding will require good psychological preparation before the event itself. The Bottom will also require support afterwards, to prevent shock and because the brand will hurt more in the first few days after the branding than at the time of the branding.

We'd recommend using a small (less than two inches across) branding iron, that is not solid; for example, use initials or a simple geometric design. The branding iron should be of steel and heated to red-hot, allowed to cool until the glow just disappears, and then applied to the skin for no more than *one* second. This way, about the only variable is the amount of pressure that is applied as the branding is performed.

Old wrought-iron branding tools take a lot more to heat up and keep their heat a lot longer. Also, cattle brands are too big to be used on humans. Do not use improvised branding tools such as paperclips and coat-hangers. It is difficult to control the temperature of these and they may leave bits of varnish in the burn, causing problems during the healing process.

A branding tool that is too cool is as dangerous as one that is too hot. Skin may stick to a cool branding tool and, as it is taken away from the skin it may take some skin with it. An iron that is too hot will cause the heat to go down below the surface layer of the skin and cause serious damage.

An excellent way to practice branding is to use a grapefruit. In the way that medical students practice using hypodermic needles on oranges, a grapefruit also reacts like human skin. Once you can make good, clean brands on grapefruits, you can graduate to human skin. Don't forget that, while a grapefruit won't move as you touch it with the branding iron, a human will move quickly and, potentially, violently. Therefore, it is all the more important to have the person well restrained before the iron is applied.

The heat of the iron is likely to cauterize the wound, but it won't hurt to use a little hydrogen peroxide to wipe down the area afterwards. Be wary of using alcohol when branding. It's too risky to have it around naked flames or heat (unless it forms part of a controlled flame scene (please see the section on Flaming Heat). Likewise, remember that "poppers" are very inflammable, so this is yet another reason to keep them out of your SM play.

A good brand will have one or more clean, thin lines where the burn has taken place. Immediately after the branding is finished, clean the area with peroxide and pat the area dry with a lint-free cloth. A sterile, lint-free, breathing dressing should be applied to the area to protect it from being rubbed by clothing or anything else. Air will help the healing process. The brand should be left alone as much as possible for the duration of the healing. Any unclear fluid or pus from the area during healing should be referred to your physician immediately.

If something goes wrong with the branding, treat the burn as you would any other unintentional burn, and seek medical attention, when necessary.

Cigarettes, Cigars, & Matches

These can all cause bad scarring as a result of both their high temperature and the ash content. Matches have a large, high temperature, and very uncontrollable flame that can be very dangerous. Touching a cigar to skin will probably cause a first-degree burn; putting out a match on the skin will almost certainly cause a second-degree burn. Cigarettes burn much hotter than cigars and so should never be touched to the skin or put near to the skin for more than a fraction of a second. Any ash from cigarettes and cigars in a burn will complicate the healing process and probably cause marking after the healing is complete. Both cigarettes and cigars are much hotter just after they have been puffed than a while afterwards. If you've ever had the temptation to tape matches to the skin and them light them, *don't*. It will almost certainly cause second-degree burns, and possibly third-degree burns.

Flaming Heat

Flaming alcohol actually burns above the liquid, because it is the alcohol vapour that burns, not the liquid. Both 70- and 90-proof alcohols burn at fairly low temperatures (70-proof burns cooler than 90-proof), so, provided that only small amounts of alcohol are put on the skin and they are allowed to burn for only a one to two seconds, there should be no problem. The Top can generally put out the flames with a hand, if the motion of the hand is fast. If the flames get out of control or cannot be put out quickly with a hand, immediately use the safety blanket you have put close to you before the scene to smother the flames. Blowing on the flames will only serve to feed them by providing more oxygen at the site of the burning.

Hot Wax

Before you start a hot wax scene, ensure that any hair where the wax may fall is combed in the same direction, to allow for easier removal of the wax; or remove the hair beforehand as the first part of the scene. During the scene, you should remember that any skin shaved or waxed for the scene will be much more sensitive than usual.

The best source of wax for hot wax scenes is cheap, plain candles. Beeswax burns at a higher temperature and is therefore unsafe for play. Experiment on yourself with candles you've tried before.

The wax should be applied a drop at a time from a great height at first, until you know the effect of that particular candle. Hot wax should only cause temporary (a couple of hours at most) reddening of the skin. Never allow the hot, liquid wax to run onto the body, causing a pool of wax (this will be far too hot to handle and will burn the skin). One of the best ways is to rotate the candle as it burns. That way, you'll avoid large, soft lumps of wax falling on the Bottom.

If you place small, votive candles on your Bottom's body, make sure that any metal tab at the bottom of the wick is removed before you place the candle on the skin. The tab becomes much hotter than the wax. The flame itself should never get close to the skin, it can cause serious burns.

After the scene, if the wax is difficult to remove from hairy areas, gently cut away the hair containing the wax. If you pull the wax and hair out, you will cause many micro-punctures of the skin at the base of the hair follicles. Removing the wax and hair this way could be painful and will require that you treat the area with hydrogen peroxide to minimize the risk of infection in the follicles.

Ice

Ice can be used for a form of "heat" play. If the Bottom is convinced that hot heat such as flaming alcohol is going to be applied, an ice cube applied to the area where the alcohol was supposedly put will produce a sensation of fire. This is a great way to have a heat scene without any risk of fire. Done well, the Bottom will be wholly convinced that fire was applied.

Tiger Balm, Ben-Gay, & Other Chemical Skin Stimulants

The "heat" in these cases is caused by a chemical irritation of the skin. The sensation is that of heat, but it is not really hot. Most of these substances contain pepper derivatives, menthol (for example, mouthwash), or spirits (such as whiskey). They should never be applied to very sensitive areas, such as the eyes. Other sensitive parts of the body (the penis, vagina, anus, armpits, etc.) should be treated very carefully at first, to gauge the effect and whether the Bottom can take the "heat." All of these substances have a delayed action, so be careful about applying more until you're sure that the full effect of the first application has been reached. If you wrap the treated parts with plastic wrap, the sensation will be enhanced.

A top with sensitive hands may want to use rubber gloves to apply the stimulant, even though the fingers will be less sensitive than other parts of the skin.

Tit Toys

Clamping the nipples usually generates its effects by temporarily starving the nipples of blood. As the clamp is removed, the rush of blood back into the nipple (or anything else that has been clamped this way for more than a few minutes) will often cause more pain than when they were originally put on. This is why an experienced Top may ask a Bottom how the clamps should be removed. Fast produces a very intense sensation that goes away very quickly; slow is less intense, but lasts longer. A point to note here is that some contact surfaces of tit clamps have a rubbery texture that may stick somewhat to the skin after being there for a while. There is potential for this type of clamp to remove a small amount of the top layer of skin, if it is pulled off too quickly. This should be treated as though it was any other cut, since it is an open pathway to the Bottom's blood.

One of the best tit toys is attached to your Top. As in a lot of other activities, the fingers can do amazing things. From gentle rubbing and squeezing to harsh pulling and gripping to use of fingernails to cause the desired sensation.

You'd be surprised how many household objects can be used for tit play. The most common are clothes pegs. These come in various strengths and sizes. The smaller the area gripped, the harsher the feeling. There are plastic pegs that are used for things like drying photographs that are smaller than regular clothes pegs, but they grip a lot more. What do you do if you are in a hotel and have no toys from home with you? In most hotel rooms there are hangers with clips for trousers. These clips can be adjusted to the distance between the nipples and used to great effect. Even better, they come with a pre-made hook for attaching weights (like your shoes or boots).

Other "home-brew" toys might include toothpicks, toothbrushes, hair brushes, dental floss, or rubber gloves. Anything to cause an unusual sensation on the nipple. This is especially true if the Bottom has no idea what the source of the stimulation is (for instance, when the Bottom is blindfolded or hooded). Toothpicks and sharpened chopsticks can be used end-on for a sharp feeling and, should they accidentally draw blood, they can be thrown out since they're so cheap. Chopsticks can be used on the nipples end-on, they can be tapped on the nipples, or drawn over the nipple along their length. Each technique produces a different effect.

Emery boards, sandpaper, and textured work or gardening gloves provide a wonderful means of playing with nipples. So do ice cubes, used either before or after the nipple has been sensitized. A piece of soft sheepskin can be very effective after the tits have been well sensitized.

The Violet Wand is a great way to sensitize the nipples very effectively, so they "light up" at the merest touch. Chemical stimulants like Tiger Balm or Tabasco can be used, but go easy to start with and allow the product to take full effect before you use more. It's difficult to remove these stimulants once they're applied, and it will take a few minutes for the effect to wear off.

There are plenty of tit toys available in sex stores. They vary from innocuous clamps to alligator clips to vacuum toys (snake bite kits or pumped vacuums). Alligator clips should be treated with care, since the serrations can break the skin. They should be properly cleaned and sterilized between uses on different people, or they should be kept as a singe-person toy. Sex stores also lead weights (some leather covered), but anything that can be attached to the clamps (or any chain between them) will do. For weights, you may want to do your shopping in a fishing tackle store. To reduce your costs, remember that most toys are cheaper outside a sex store, so just think of where what you need is usually sold and shop there.

Some people have nipples that stick out enough to wrap them with dental floss to restrict the flow of blood to them. If this is done, care should be taken, as with any tit clamp, to ensure that the blood supply is restored in enough time that the cells in the nipple do not die from blood starvation. If you don't know how long this is (and it will be different for everybody) experiment slowly by applying minimal pressure, and each time you play use a little more pressure until you find a good mix between the time the binding can stay on and the sensation it produces.

If you want to know how a tit clamp feels, without actually putting it on the tit, try putting it on the skin between your first finger and thumb. If it feels fine there, then it should be good on the nipples.

Vaginal Toys

There are a few basic forms of vaginal play available: insertion, clamps, tying open/closed, temporary and permanent piercing, stretching the labia, electrical, temperature, and poky/prickly.

Because the female genitalia are more hidden than the man's, a great deal of mileage can be had from simply looking, ...closely. Successful torture of the vagina (cunt) depends on the Top paying attention to detail, because a great variation of sensation occurs over *very* small areas of the vagina.

A couple of basics before we describe the toys: Too much lubricant is not enough; and, for the most part, anything smaller than a baby will fit in the vagina. If you don't use enough lubricant, you may cause tears and rips, or a mechanically induced vaginitis. On the other hand, part of the pleasure of cunt-play is friction, so you'll have to find the right balance. Likewise, since the vagina was designed to take a baby, you should be able to put moderately large objects in it. Take care that they do not have any sharp edges, however. The inner parts of the vagina are mucous membranes, so a general rule is to make sure that your play is less aggressive in this area.

One aspect of anatomy should be remembered when you play with the vagina: every woman's cervix is in a different location. You will need to be careful not to bruise it. Some women have a tilted uterus, which may result in the cervix being, say, further up and to the front of the body. This makes for more fun when fisting, but it also make the fisting more difficult.

Tying-open games tend to be about exposure, availability, and the pleasure of looking/being looked at, while tying-closed games tend to be about control over access to the vagina. Both can be accomplished through use of clamps and temporary and/or permanent piercings.

Clamps for opening and closing play are attached to the outer labia only; you can then attach the clamps to lightweight ropes or strings, which can be anchored elsewhere. Since the clamps will probably hold, be sure that the Bottom cannot fall or pull too harshly on the attachments, because a harsh pull here could cause damage (which is extremely unerotic). To tie closed using clamps, stagger them left and right and then close the labia in a dove-tail effect, again using ties to anchor the strings. Clamps used this way can be laced closed.

The length of time that you can leave the clamps on the labia will depend on the individual and the tightness of the clamp. Penetration with the labia closed is possible, but the clamps add an intense sensation of their own as the flesh is pulled, so go slowly.

You'll find that clamped labia respond very well to your tapping them lightly.

Temporary and permanent piercings can also be used to tie the labia together. This is an intense trip for the Bottom, so care is constantly required from the Top. If you're using the inner labia, you'll find that it is a thin, highly sensitive mucous membrane, so it will not support the same level of play that piercings elsewhere can tolerate. Permanent piercings pose no problems about clamp time. Once the piercing is properly healed, inner or outer labia rings can easily be tied into position. Weights can also be tied to the rings, but, again, you'll want to take care when putting weights on the more delicate inner labia. Since the bite of flesh pulled by a piercing is smaller than that taken by a clamp, it will not support as much weight as a clamp.

When you put weight onto these tissues, some stretching will occur. This is the object of the play for some women. As for the nipples, and the scrotum, it is possible to increase the size of the labia somewhat this way. You should look for gradual sensations, not sudden, tissue-tearing forces. Weights have a tendency to slide off, especially as the Bottom becomes wet, so you will have to reposition them periodically. At the last second of a clamp coming off, all its bite is in a very small area, causing *intense* pain. So, unless you intend to have a screaming Bottom, make sure that they are kept properly in place. You could use clamps that are so tight that they will never come off, but the pressure required to do this will probably be too much for most Bottoms, thereby cutting your play short.

Insertional sex toys for the vagina come as dildos, strap-on dildos, and "Japanese" balls, but you can also use a speculum (great for doctor's office scenes) or "labia spreaders." Starting with fruits and vegetables, depending on your tastes, is a good idea. Be sure that they are properly washed and that they have no sharp edges (the sharp edge of a broken carrot can be quite nasty).

Dildos come plain or with a vibrator built-in. Other than the wide variety of shapes and sizes, there's really not a lot to say about dildos that is not covered in the section on Cleaning of Toys. Vibrators, however, come designed for the vagina, rectum, and even the clitoris. You should be able to find vibrators for all three places at once, each at a different speed (not your average triple play...).

Strap-on dildos are designed to fit onto a harness around a woman's hips. This lets a woman have intercourse in almost the same way as a man would with his erect penis. The advantage for women is that they can choose the size and shape of the penis. The strap-on should be treated as though it were any other dildo for cleaning purposes.

Of course, fingers, hands, toes, and feet can all be used as insertional toys. Their advantage is that they can move so many ways, and that they can react to the reaction their movement causes.

Japanese balls or other types don't have to be attached to each other for the vagina. The vagina is a dead-end, whereas the ass is not, so you can't lose them in the same way. Women often use chrome-plated balls about 2" to 3" across.

As far as temperature toys for the vagina go, ice cubes can be wonderful, and they will do no harm. If you decide to use Tiger Balm® and other chemical stimulants like Tabasco®, be careful to use a small amount at first, because the closed nature of the vagina may amplify the sensations and it can take a while for the full effect to take place. Many women like to use mentholated rubs for this kind of play. If you think that full strength may be too much for the Bottom, you can try diluting the rubs and liquids with either water for the water-based stimulants, or maybe Vaseline® for the oil-based ones like Vick's Vapo-Rub®.

Not only should you be careful about waiting for the full reaction to the first application to occur, you should also be aware that it may be more difficult to clean away too much of an oil-based stimulant than to clean away a water-based one. They will also damage latex gloves and condoms. We've found that a mentholated mouthwash can work wonders, properly applied. It has both menthol and a little alcohol in it, so it should both sting and be quite "warm." Try these all of these toys in moderation and slowly, at first.

Overall, the likelihood of successful vaginal play depends on the Top's willingness to move slowly to generate fairly symmetrical sensations, and to realize that the border between pleasure and pain in this area is razor thin.

Whips, Paddles, Rods, & Other Percussive Toys

To say that these come in many varieties would be an understatement. The rigidity, material, width, and technique all play major rôles in the effect created by these toys. The area on which they are used also changes the manner and intensity in which they should be used. Whips, paddles, hands, rods, etc. all fall into the group of percussive toys.

There are several major things that contribute to the effect of a flogging instrument. Tony DeBlase has summarized them as follows:

- The flexibility of toys you might use varies considerably. From inflexible clubs and paddles to somewhat flexible rubber hoses, riding crops, etc. to very flexible cats and bullwhips.

- The weight of the implement, combined with the muscle power put into the stroke gives the force of the blow. This becomes readily apparent when one considers the following pairs of implements: a baseball bat versus a chopstick; a fly-swatter versus a paddle; a shot-loaded bullwhip versus a cheap, paper-filled Mexican bullwhip; and a deerskin cat versus a latigo leather cat.

- The nature of the contact surface of the toy will make a great difference, due to the area it provides for the force of the blow to be transmitted to the body of the Bottom. Generally, for equal force, the thinner the implement the more damage is done. Don't forget, also, that the surface characteristics (e.g. a studded versus smooth paddle; flat versus rounded whip tails; knotted versus unknotted whip tails; smooth deerskin versus rough hemp rope; etc.) will also change the force and feel of the toy.

- The stroke of the implement has two distinct aspects that can be called the sting and the thud. Sting is the surface feel (things like welts and cuts) and thud is the deep, penetrating action of the stroke. It often results in bruising when combined with the three characteristics above. A light cat will give lots of sting but little thud, whereas a heavy rubber hose will give little sting and lots of thud. The way a flogging instrument is used can also vary the amount of sting and thud in the stroke. For example, a heavy whip laid across a back will give some sting and lots of thud, but, worked so only the cracker at its tip will hit the same back will give virtually no thud but will cut the skin bloody.

All whips and paddles can be used, to a greater or lesser extent, on most of the whippable areas of the body. (Common sense tells us that a bullwhip to the penis is not a good idea....) When whipping lightly, the eyes are the only major area to avoid. Make the toy fit the play.

The sound of percussive toys can be an integral part of the scene. For instance, one bottom may be blindfolded, but able to hear a whip as it strikes another, and the cries from that Bottom. Simply hearing sounds from a crop as it swishes through the air can be very erotic.

As you can see, the variety of applied strokes is many times greater than the variety of toys. So, if you're into percussion play, or intend to be, you'll have a lot of learning to do to determine which works best for you and what the attendant safety issues are; and you'll need to practice a lot before you start on a person.

Safety Items for the Playroom

The equipment you will need will depend simply on the kind of play. A few things are essential, however. You *must* have a first aid kit no matter what you like to do in the playroom (please see the section on First Aid). Everyone in the playroom *must* know where it is. In fact, it is a good idea to ensure that everyone knows where every emergency tool is, including the light switch, just in case it is needed. A pair of ambulance scissors is good for cutting ropes, leather, and many other things that might need freeing to release someone in a hurry.

If there are chains in the playroom, make sure that there are bolt cutters; for rope, you'll need rope shears or ambulance scissors. You'll also need these scissors if you put someone in Saran Wrap, duct tape, or a leather or canvas bondage suit, sleep sack, or mailbag. If you play with fire, you'll need a blanket to smother flames, a supply of cold water to cool things such as a burn, and enough sterile bandages for any burns. Plaster mummification will require proper plaster cutting shears that are designed not to cut into the skin as the cast is removed.

Other useful items include a readily accessible flashlight and fire extinguisher, condoms, dental dams, latex gloves, contraceptive jelly with 3% nonoxynol-9, spermicidal foam, and water-soluble lubricant with nonoxynol-9.

The simplest way to determine what is needed is to examine your intended play and ask "What might I need during play or to get out of this safely and in a hurry?" The answers are usually fairly obvious.

Cues & the Need for Them

Elsewhere we have mentioned that it is important for the Top to be aware of the state of the Bottom. Some people refer to it as "reading" someone. This is really just responding to subtle cues from the other player. A Top should try to observe theses cues, many of which will be involuntary, to know as best as possible what the scene feels like to the Bottom, and whether he/she can take more, less, or continue at the same level.

A Bottom can also observe cues from the Top. Sometimes, the cues will only come in the form of body language. Maybe the Top wants to go further, but the Bottom is not yet ready for it. The Bottom, on reading these cues, can make sure that the Top doesn't go too far by giving some kind of signal.

If all the players properly read the cues, express or involuntary, there should be few occasions where one player is going to feel that the bounds of safety and sanity were broken.

ETIQUETTE

In any social interaction, there are codes of behaviour. They range from polite respect at English high tea to the formalized ritual of the Japanese tea ceremony; from black tie state functions to spending the weekend at your friend's cottage; from dealing with the family at Christmas to putting on your leathers and going out to the bars; etc.. In SM play, the codes of behaviour that govern one's conduct before, during, and after play amount to little more than common courtesy They start with the initial contact, continue through the negotiation, and, with luck, they help take all parties to the play that follows. This interaction is where trust is built. Total honesty and respect for your partner are very important at all times.

SM, by it's very nature, entails many potential risks, physical as well as psychological, that are very real, and in some cases, potentially lethal. As stressed in all sections of this book, safety must be of prime consideration. Since unethical behaviour may result in your being hurt (physically as well as emotionally), it follows that ethical behaviour is also a basic necessity.

There are many aspects to SM: technique, power exchange, playfulness, thought, analysis, preparation, and, of course, lots of practice. It can also involve spirituality. In each aspect, we all have differing levels of skill and confidence. If someone is not careful, or doesn't care, he/she could easily bruise your ego or hurt your feelings with a misplaced word or two.

The Top must first be honest with him/herself. To do so, he/she must be aware of ego, and must try to recognize and accept the skills and limits of all the players. It must not be thought that, because the Top is skilled in one area, that he/she is an expert at everything. Likewise, the Bottom must be honest about his/her expectations and limits, and be clear about the responses given to the Top. The Bottom is, after all, responsible for giving many of the cues which will modify or stop the SM play.

Beginners often have outrageous fantasies that can cloud their perception of what can realistically be accomplished. We've covered some of this subject in the section on Other Implications of Reality. A fantasy is one thing, but you can't cut parts of yourself off during play and expect them to be there as usual the next morning. You can't hang yourself and expect to go to work the next day. Nor can you play unsafely and expect to have no risk to your health. If the play is something that your partner(s) don't want to do, or can't do, then it's not possible this time. The only fantasies that can be played out are ones that are not going to injure you, mentally or physically. Often, this means modifying the fantasy to fit reality. It doesn't mean that the Bottom has to think it's less than the entire fantasy. The scene simply has to be done safely, but in a way that the Bottom *thinks* the fantasy is being played out.

Negotiation is an area where honesty plays an important part. As a Top, one must double-check interests before proceeding and always be on the alert for genuine requests to stop. As a Bottom, if one has medical or other problems that might affect the scene, you must make the Top aware of these before play starts.

During the negotiations, each partner must communicate to the other his/her preferred style of play. If you have a verbally motivated Top with a non-verbal Bottom, you need to work out ways to give and receive the signals necessary for a successful scene. Without a willing and knowing partner, all the power and control count for nothing. Each of you needs the other.

The Bottom *influences* the scene; its direction, pace, and intensity. The Top *controls* the scene within the limits agreed during negotiation. The Top has licence, within the agreed parameters of the scene, to improvise, expand the limits of the Bottom, provide variations, be creative, and get his/her own satisfaction, too.

The Top should try to be aware of hidden agendas. Maybe what is requested is different from what is wanted or needed. The Bottom may ask for more or less than can be handled. Maybe the Bottom is trying to get some form of punishment for an unrelated transgression a long while ago. There may be forces outside the scene driving the Bottom's requests. A good Top will not allow these to drive a scene, because it can sabotage the play.

Another form of hidden agenda lies in advertisements. Between the lines of advertisements, you can often make out either lies or gross misrepresentations of reality. The copy says "27," but the person is 47. "Heavy, experienced Bottom," may actually be an advertisement by a novice trying to attract someone truly into SM, rather than someone who just likes to put on a pair of handcuffs. Once you get to the playroom, the reality may make him/her run away as fast as his/her heels can take him/her. These distortions of reality in advertisements occur quite regularly. Both Tops and Bottoms should be aware of them and take sufficient care to ensure that the advertiser really is "as advertised."

A Top must be sensitive to the needs the Bottom. If the Bottom has given the Top a list of likes and dislikes, but, during the scene, the level of the Bottom's arousal, the sounds or movements of the Bottom change to indicate a change in the flow of the scene, the Top must recognize this, and, where possible, go with the flow. This can be as simple as dealing with a "willing" Bottom, someone who is trying to please the Top and to explore the edges of his limits with the possibility of expanding them. The opposite is dealing with the "unwilling" Bottom. Here, the Top is doing what pleases him/her, and the Bottom is forced to accept it. We must emphasize, however, that there are still limits to what an unwilling Bottom should be made to do. As a Top, you must force only those who want to be forced, and you must make certain of your Bottom's major limitations before you begin, so that you do not exceed them.

SM play has another factor that needs to be discussed here. A Top can feel that a scene has failed because he has exhausted his/her "bag of tricks," and the Bottom didn't achieve orgasm. Conversely, the Bottom can feel that he/she has done everything possible, taken as much as he/she was able (maybe more), and the Top didn't achieve orgasm. SM play does not have to be overtly sexual, although, at its least, it should represent a bond between the partners, based on power, respect, instruction, and learning. Both partners must be aware of the importance of sex in the scene for the other. Some Tops like to see and use a hard cock. Most Bottoms need the physical touch of or a verbal communication with their Top. In some scenes, actual sex between partners may not be desired, or it may be wanted at the end of the scene, completely out of the context of the scene.

Honesty

A theme that you will have noticed running through this book from the first page is that of honesty; honesty to yourself, honesty to others. It is one of the most important contributors to a great scene. If you accept the kind of play that turns you on, regardless of "what others think," then you are ready to ask for it. If you were not honest to yourself, then you are likely to ask for something that is not the best thing to turn you on, and you'll end up asking yourself why all of your scenes don't seem satisfying. You lied to the person who probably means the most to you and who can best find what you want: yourself. Lies of commission, or lies of omission, they will all mess things up for you.

If someone told you he/she wanted a real thrashing with a flogger, when what was really wanted was an abrasion scene, you're going to be disappointed by an aborted scene when the flogger gets too much for the Bottom; and the Bottom will end up wondering why it all hurt so much. It all seems so obvious, but we find people who are dishonest with themselves, and by extension others, all the time.

If you are a novice to a field of SM play, you will be able to take yourself and your partner on a wonderful journey as you explore the field and your limits. This applies to both Tops and Bottoms. A Bottom *can* teach a Top, even within the context of a scene. All it takes is an admission during negotiations that you want to explore this form of play and that you'd like to try it today.

Scene is Failing

When a scene starts to falter, it could just be because one of the players is not in the mood, or simply does not like this type of play. Whatever the reason, both Top and Bottom should try to be aware of whether a scene is working. If it is not, then, within the context of the scene, it is quite possible to change the direction of the scene. It is not a reflection on anyone's abilities, simply that today things are not working right. The recognition of a failing scene and doing something about it in time to redirect the play is really just another form of honesty: "This isn't working well (read: it's not fun for me any more), let's try doing this instead, if that's OK with you." The words you use will probably be different, but the message is that you would like the scene to be a turn on for both of you.

Also, you may be having a great time, but you notice that your partner is not. This is just as good a reason to try to modify the scene, as mentioned above.

Bar Etiquette

Bar etiquette is something that is not exclusive to the SM scene; it bridges all groups of society. If someone comes up to you, says "Hi!" and mentions getting together, but you're not interested, a simple "Thanks, but no thanks." is the correct response under all circumstances. Don't waste his/her or your time giving meaningless answers like "Oh, sure we'll have to get together one of these days." There is nothing wrong with turning someone down (you probably won't be the first or the last). Just do it politely and unambiguously.

At this point, we would ask that you at least be aware of your reasons for picking your partners. Do you base your choice on looks: must the Top always look like a Norse god(dess) in leather? Is age an important factor for you? Remember that, in SM, experience usually goes with the years of practice. Conversely, the older ones of us must realize that, in the nineties, some of the young players we see climbed into their first sling or participated in their first SM scene while still in their teens. By the time they reached their twenties, they had done as much experimenting as their much older counterparts, sometimes much more. If you expect too much, you may never get what you want. To use a phrase that may mean more to people in England that those in North America: People who put people on a pedestal rarely "knock them off."

Bedroom Etiquette

Etiquette, etiquette. Just where *is* Miss Manners when you need her? With luck, she's on your shoulder giving you good advice. If you've just brought someone home, how are you going to feel if he/she uses your favourite toy or puts on your best leather without asking you? You'd probably feel somewhat resentful you were not asked first. Miss Manners would never let someone get away with that. She'd give a witty rebuke to say that he/she should have known better.

Etiquette and manners are simply a matter of putting yourself in the other person's place and asking "How would I feel if he/she did something like this?" It's no more and no less than a mark of respect for the person with whom you'd like to play. You really have no right to use someone else's property without permission. How you ask for that permission will depend on the situation, but please do ask.

There is at least one safety-related reason for asking permission to use someone else's toys: the toy may be broken, but not obviously so. You could easily do some damage to the toy or your partner, if you didn't know about the problem beforehand.

Below, we have broken out playroom etiquette for the situations where there will be many players in the same play area, be it a club playroom, a special club event, or any other place with many players all doing their own thing. It's very similar to bedroom etiquette, but there are some significant differences.

Playroom Etiquette

Due to the space requirements for some of the equipment for our play (and due to the expense of some of it), organizations have sprung up with "playrooms." The organizations sometimes have "runs" where many players will congregate for a weekend or even a week of play. Often, these playrooms and runs will be set up with five to ten or more pieces of equipment in the same room, tent, or basement. This has resulted in situations of many people playing in close proximity, with all the attendant problems. Individually, we may not be playing with more than one partner, but this form of play is definitely "group play," in the sense that others are present. We should accord them the courtesies we would like from them, such as relative quiet. Some scenes lend themselves well to public play, while others do not.

We also have to become used to the idea that we, and others, will be nude or semi-nude while we play and watch the play. In these circumstances, we still have to respect each other's right to privacy. For some of us, it will take time to become comfortable with the idea of being nude or playing in the presence of more people than our partner(s). To help those new to playing in places where there are others and who feel this way about nudity or playing in "public," we must try to find ways to help them feel at ease with our presence and their bodies. Unfortunately, this sense of ease is not something that can be forced.

It is up to us to promote high standards in SM play, both by example and instruction. We should encourage others to do the same. We have included a set of guide-lines to be followed by players in a group scene as Appendix B.

When you are watching someone else's scene and unless there is evidence to the contrary, give the Top the benefit of the doubt. Instruct, where necessary. And always give and show respect for the people you are playing with and around.

If you're not in your own playroom, it may be appropriate to ask for permission to use any of the equipment. Again, it's just a matter of simple common courtesy. It could also be a safety issue, should a piece of equipment be broken: you may not notice the problem and then have an accident due to the faulty equipment, whereas asking would have avoided the safety problem entirely and been considerate of the other person's feelings.

FURTHER READING & VIEWING

Most of the following books and videos are by and originally intended for homosexual men and women. The information held in their pages will be valuable to you, no matter what your sex or orientation. For example heterosexual men will be able to learn a lot about SM play with women from the Lesbian S/M Safety Manual by Pat Califia. SM is one area where we can all benefit from each other.

The reason that most of the books and videos are by homosexual authors is simply that, historically, they seem to have been better organized as an SM community. This is probably because their community was based on sexuality to start with. We are starting to see more and more contributions coming from the heterosexual community as time passes. No doubt things will all even out in the near future.

Please note that we have tried to include those publications that are specifically about SM activities or are about a subject that crosses over into SM for some players. In Canada and the U.K., some of these titles are not available. Inclusion of a publication here is not an endorsement, it is merely an indication that we know that it contains information relevant to people who enjoy SM.

Books

There is a great variety of books available to those seeking information about SM. We have gathered a list of those of historical interest and those that deal with safety and SM, and the reasons why people enjoy it. These reasons can range from spiritual to sexual.

Coming To Power

A path-breaking work, this mostly non-fiction collection was originally published in 1981 by Samois, a now-defunct lesbian SM group that flourished in San Francisco in the late 1970s. It single-handedly raised the discussion of SM to a new level of political and psychological sophistication. If nothing else, Samois deserves the credit for defining SM as "a form of eroticism based on a consensual exchange of power." With thinking and polemics honed in confrontations with anti-SM feminists—who first tried to deny that lesbian SM ever existed, then did all they could to suppress it—the more than two-dozen contributors to *Coming to Power* tackle the diverse implications of that definition in terms of not only individuals but also of the communities and society within which they exist and interact. If parts of *Coming to Power* seem dated, it is only because the book raised consciousness about SM and this, in turn, helped transform the SM scene to the one we know today.

Learning The Ropes

This book by Race Bannon, a well-respected expert in SM sexuality, is a wonderful introduction to the possibilities of SM. It has many, good examples of how couples might enjoy SM play. The book is designed to educate at a basic level.

It's also a great way to help explain to friends the pleasure you derive from SM play, because it does so in such a non-threatening manner. It properly shows how SM play and lovemaking are one and the same for many people.

Leatherfolk

Edited by Mark Thompson, this book is an examination of some of the history of SM in the United States, and the emotional and other reasons involved for many and varied players. Leatherfolk is a collection of essays from 25 authors with a broad range of backgrounds: men, women, heterosexual, homosexual, spiritual, political, etc.. It covers SM topics as diverse as spirituality, politics, and important historical events and places.

Leatherman's Handbook I & II

This book is of great historical importance to the SM scene. We all owe Larry Townsend a debt for writing one of the first important books on the subject.

The first edition, however, contained many inaccuracies and may seem to promote the use of drugs and "poppers." Much of this was updated in the second edition. The deficiencies in the book were mainly due to general lack of prevailing knowledge at the time. The SM scene has come a long way since the book was first published.

The book is important for anyone who wants to learn about the history of the scene, and to gain an appreciation of how things have changed over the years.

Leathersex

Joseph Bean, a well known practitioner, will be publishing this guide in 1993. Given Mr. Bean's experience, we anticipate that it will be worth your while to examine it.

The Lesbian S/M Safety Manual

Covering safety in a very broad sense, from first aid for physical accidents to rules for emotional self-preservation for both Tops and Bottoms, this slim book by Pat Califia contains much that will be useful to anyone involved in SM, irrespective of gender or orientation. The didactic articles are interspersed with very short sex stories by Dorothy Allison.

Macho Sluts

Imaginative, well written erotic fiction from Pat Califia, including short stories and one novella, all with SM action or sensibilities. Most are exclusively lesbian, but one story has only gay male characters, and one involves some shenanigans between a leatherdyke and a trio of gay/bisexual leathermen. An introduction discusses political and social issues around lesbian and SM pornography, and there is an afterward about lesbians, AIDS, and safer sex.

Permanent Partners

A book about homosexual relationships and how to make them last. There is a section dealing with power and control issues that could be of great interest to those who enjoy SM relationships. The book is easy to read and provides examples of how to solve problems in a relationship. It deals with the effects of homophobia on relationships. You may be experiencing similar effects from people who do not understand SM on your SM kinkiness.

Sir! More Sir!

Master Jackson from San Francisco has published this guide for those who enjoy SM. At the time of printing, we have not been able to obtain a copy for review.

The S/M Resources Guide

This list is compiled by author Race Bannon. It is a frequently updated list of where to find things, from bars to art to accommodations, etc., in Canada and the United States. While the guide is not a recommendation of the resources it lists, most of them are well known to the SM community in the local area, if not nationally. It is pan-sexual in nature and, where possible, notes whether the establishment caters to heterosexual, homosexual, and/or bisexual customers. Mr. Bannon has produced a catalogue that should become as important a resource to SM players as the Gayellow Pages™ are to the homosexual community. The guide is a good place to start looking for that "perfect" toy or, maybe, perfect mate....

SM 101

Mr. Wiseman has produced a thorough and very readable look at SM play and its safety aspects. The book looks at most of the major SM activities and the techniques involved, and safety is well addressed. He has also taken a look at some practices related to SM, and has provided information on how and where to get help in the U.S. for problems that are related to SM play. *SM 101* will become an important part of every SM library.

That's 244, Madam!
Thank you, Madam!

Ties That Bind

This book is a collection of articles written by Guy Baldwin, M.S. in *Checkmate, Drummer, Frontiers,* and *Manifest Reader* magazines. The original articles were very well received and those of you who have any form of SM library will want to include this book in your collection, if the magazines are not. Using his experience counselling people in his psychotherapy practice, Mr. Baldwin investigates the many and varied possibilities of SM relationships, from the details of scenes to the way other people react to SM players. Consent and the use of drugs during scenes are discussed intelligently and thoroughly. We learned a lot from these articles.

The Urban Aboriginal

A pioneering work by Geoff Mains, a gay leatherman, trained scientist, and spiritual seeker, who sought to reveal the roots of the SM subculture to both that subculture and to the outside world. Although he may have over generalized from his experiences in the pansexual fisting community of San Francisco in the early 1970s, he provided the first, widely available, serious discussion of the varieties of altered consciousness promoted or exploited by SM and their relation to bodily manipulations from bondage to piercing. Many of the themes that are common in today's thinking about SM were first explored in this book, including endorphin release, spiritual euphoria, rites of passage, tribalism, ritual psychodrama, bondage and inner peace, celebration of the hidden animal, and so on (the quoted phrases are chapter titles).

Periodicals

There is a wide variety of periodicals available in Canada and the United States for those of us interested in SM. They are not always available in other countries, although limited supplies sometimes become available. We have tried to include the most established ones in the list. There may appear to be a heavy emphasis on the homosexual male magazines, this is simply because there are more of them. Most of the magazines contain articles about safety or technique. For some, this is their sole reason for existence. They can *all* be used as sources of information and/or fantasy for men, women, heterosexual, bisexual, and homosexual alike.

Bear

Bear magazine's title describes its intended audience. It covers body type as fetish for those who like men with a bear-like body. It is not an SM magazine at all, but many who enjoy SM read it.

Bound & Gagged

This magazine is specifically for bondage aficionados. Other aspects of SM are secondary, here. It is a good outlet for people to describe their real bondage experiences.

Checkmate

This is a fairly new publication, and it comes from experts in the scene. The idea is to provide factual safety information written by experts in their field. There are no advertisements in *Checkmate*, but a companion paper carries them with each publication. The first issues we have seen indicate that it is succeeding very well in its intents. The articles are well written, so the collection will provide a very useful resource for the future.

Cuir

Cuir is fairly new magazine that we have not been able to review. It is a brother to *The Leather Journal*, and is aimed at a younger market than it's older brother.

Daddy

Like Bear magazine, Daddy caters to a particular fetish: the daddy-boy fetish. Unfortunately, we have been unable to review any copies, we just know of its existence.

Drummer

The magazine has for a long while been one of the bastions of homosexual male SM. It combines articles about safety with photo-spreads, fiction, and news of SM events. One of the oldest surviving SM magazines, it has recently changed ownership. It is well worth picking up previous issues as you come across them, for the informative articles as well as the fiction and photo-spreads. In Canada, regular supplies have been difficult to find in bookstores. Past issues carried Guy Baldwin's *Ties That Bind* articles that have now been collected and published as a book of the same name (see above).

Dungeon Master

This magazine is designed to provide sensible advice on SM technique and safety. It is an excellent source of information from electricity to abrasion, to playroom construction, etc..

The Leather Journal

The Leather Journal is a magazine designed to keep the pan-sexual leather/SM community informed about the latest news with respect to SM. It covers competitions, political events, and has one of the more up-to-date listings of SM organizations in North America.

Mach

This magazine is intended to have fewer advertisements and more stories and articles than most of the SM magazines. Some of the stories are not for the faint-hearted.

Manifest Reader

This is one of the most widely distributed erotic fantasy magazines with SM content. The publisher has also released many other magazines with SM content.

Piercing Fans International Quarterly (PFIQ)

This is an informative magazine produced by Jim Ward of Gauntlet in Los Angeles. It is safety-oriented and is about the only regular publication available for those of us into piercing.

Powerplay

This magazine is reputedly has content that is "sleazier" than many of the other magazines with SM content. It is targeted at homosexual men. We have not been able to find copies for review in Canada, but we know of the magazine's existence.

Sandmutopia Guardian

Like *DungeonMaster* and *Checkmate*, the *Sandmutopia Guardian* exists to provide information about safety during SM play. The articles are written by experienced players and are a gold mine of information on technique as well as safety.

Skin II

A leather, vinyl, and rubber fetish clothing and toys magazine targeted mainly at heterosexual men and women. It is a "glossy" magazine with significant female dominance throughout. It is also a well-written and thoughtful look at the pleasures of kink.

A Taste of Latex

An intentionally cutting-edge, radical sex magazine. Its pan-sexual content covers both SM and fetish. It has built its own category in the magazine market, because there is nothing quite like it. Many younger readers will relate to its content. Contributors have included Pat Califia, a well respected author of SM material.

Videos

We have included a summary of the videos that may be of historical interest, or are important in their field of SM. In the last few years, videos showing safer SM have appeared. These include those that aim to educate, as well as those designed as "adult entertainment."

Born to Raise Hell

This was a film that played for only one night only in Los Angeles. (Slaves for Sale was possibly the first video.) It is now available, if you look for it, in video format. It was radical in its day, and parts of it can still be regarded that way. There are some very violent scenes and watersports, both of which are regarded as unsafe today. It shows a lot of fisting without protection. For many, it was the first serious look at SM in practice, rather than pornography, simulated or otherwise. If you enjoy SM, you should see this film to see how things used to be done.

Bound For Europe I, II, & III

These videos were made by the same team as made Born To Raise Hell and were made a couple years after the Dungeons of Europe series. North American actors in European settings.

The Dungeons of Europe I, II, III, & IV

This was one of the first series of SM videos designed to show safe, sane, and consensual SM play. It was made by the same team as made Born to Raise Hell. There is play ranging from suspension to piercing to tit and cock and ball torture. They show a variety of playrooms, so you might find some ideas for your playroom, here. Some interesting bondage.

Palm Drive Videos

Some specialized technique demonstration videos, e.g. punching, tit work, etc.. Lots of cigars, daddies, teddy-bears, etc.. These are not "pretty-boy" videos. They deal with a lot of fetishes, and play such as wrestling.

Sandmutopia Series

There are three videos in the series. They all start with a lecture. (As a result, the lecturer has sometimes been referred to as the Julia Child of the dungeon.) The lecture is then followed by a demonstration, and the last part of each video shows the technique in practice in the form of a real scene.

The first video is about *Topical Torture*. The main subjects are forms of skin sensitization, so the videos show play such as Violet Wand and hot wax techniques.

The second video, *Rope That Works*, goes into the many and varied techniques of rope play.

The final video in the series is called *Whips I* and has a lot of spanking and paddling.

Slave Dungeon Hamburg & Slave Dungeon Los Angeles

These videos, made by Europeans with European actors, show a variety of SM scenes. Unusual for SM videos, there is a lot of sex when compared to the North American offerings. These European videos also tend to be rougher than most North American videos.

USSM I, II , III, & IV

These videos show a lot of whippings and excellent clothes-pin play. The whipping scenes have had the tenderness between the actual whippings removed to make a film that caters more to fantasy, although tenderness can be seen for brief moments.

These videos show combinations of experienced SM players in various flogging, bondage, and clothes peg scenes.

Zeus' Tightrope Series

These videos are made for an audience of body builders and body worshippers and there are many depictions of fantasies of body builders in bondage. They are basically bondage videos.

FUTURE PUBLICATIONS

We intend to publish more books like this for those of the SM community who would like to delve more deeply into particular subjects. This book should have given you a fairly firm grounding in the basics of SM play, the rest of the books in this series will go into the subtleties of SM play, the toys and techniques used, the attendant safety aspects, and provide more sources of information relevant to the subject.

Because this is the first edition, we expect that, unintentionally, we have omitted subjects or not covered some as well or as accurately as possible, even though we tried to be as thorough as possible. We'd very much like to have feedback about the style and content of this edition so that future editions can improve on this one. Please feel free to write to us with any suggestions and/or criticisms. We'd like to continue to update the book to keep it up to date with changes in the scene. For instance, given the way things have been changing in the last ten years, it is conceivable that spirituality and SM will come to play a larger part of the scene in the next ten.

Each of the topics we have covered can be addressed in much greater detail. If you have a topic that you would like to see discussed in one of the future books, please drop us a line, care of the publisher.

That's 251, Sir!
Thank you, Sir!

APPENDIX A

SAFER SEX & DRUG POLICIES

The following policies are based upon successful ones that were written by Tony DeBlase and have been used for many years by one of the premier north American SM organizations. You may want to use them for any group that you start or of which you are already a member.

Safer Sex Policy

Unsafe sexual practices are defined as rimming; blood-to-blood contact between persons; sharing of sex toys which come into contact with any bodily secretions; fæces, semen, or urine of others in the mouth or on broken skin; fisting without latex gloves; anal intercourse without a condom; the use of petroleum-based lubricants; and shared lubricants from other than a proper dispenser. Unsafe sexual practices are prohibited at all times in the Clubhouse and at any Club-sponsored activity.

Also prohibited are patently unsafe SM activities. These include:

1. No device which sends electrical charges into the body will be connected to any portion of the anatomy above the waistline, with the exception of both electrodes on the same arm. The violet wand may be used above the waist, but not near the eyes.

2. No needles, pins, catheters, sounds, or any other device intended to break the skin or invade a body orifice may be used on a second individual unless it has been sterilized between uses.

3. No object made of glass or other breakable material shall be inserted into the anus, urethra, vagina, or other body cavity.

Any member of the Club observing any person violating these prohibitions shall immediately ask that they cease. Failure to coöperate with this request, or repeated violations, may result in the offender being prohibited from attendance at the Clubhouse or participation in other Club activities. Should there be a disagreement, the person designated by the Club shall make the final decision.

Drug Policy

The possession or use of any illegal or non-prescription drug or other substance in the Clubhouse or at any Club-sponsored activity is absolutely prohibited.

Any person unable to function in a safe and responsible manner due to drug or alcohol use will be asked to leave the activity and may be prohibited from attendance at the Clubhouse or further participation in Club activities.

Note: In the light of recent legislation and on the advice of attorneys, "poppers" (e.g. amyl or butyl nitrite) and other forms of "room odourizers" and inhalants are considered by the Club to be illegal drugs.

APPENDIX B

GROUP SM COURTESY

What follows is based upon a successful set of guide-lines that was written by Tony DeBlase and has been used for many years at one of the premier North American SM runs. You may want to use it for any run or group event that you hold.

We are all here to experience SM, but area of interest and levels of experience vary. We therefore ask that you observe the following guide-lines for group SM.

1. Double check interests before proceeding and immediately accede to genuine requests to stop.

2. Some like one-on-one and others like group activities. If you want to join a scene already under way, don't just butt in, but don't just go away, either. Check with the Top running the scene and join in or not, as he/she says.

3. If you're in the vicinity of action or watching a scene in progress, keep out of the way and keep quiet. In the playroom and other play areas, keep what you say to appropriate subjects and to an appropriate level.

4. If you are into heavily verbal trips, avoid places where your loud shouts, curses, etc. may disturb someone else's scene.

5. As a Top, force only those who *want* to be forced, and make certain that you know your Bottom's major limitations and turn-offs before you begin.

6. As a Bottom, if you have a medical or other problem that might affect the scene, make certain that your Top is aware of them *before* you begin.

7. We know that all participants in a large SM event cannot be experts. We must all serve as keepers of our fellow players, for their safety and our own. If you see an activity that you truly feel is dangerous, or that is being forced upon an unwilling Bottom, please notify someone in charge at once!

8. If someone in charge asks you to stop an activity, do so at once. If you disagree with his/her appraisal of what you are doing, discuss it (quietly) with him/her *later*.

9. Observe the limitations of the Club policies on Safer Sex and Drugs.

10. No piss or scat scenes are permitted in the play area.

11. No electrical shock device may be used above the waistline. Violet wands may be used anywhere on the body, except the face.

12. Items used to pierce the skin or draw blood in any way may not be used unless sterile. Needles may not be re-used.

13. No photographs, videos, or other recording may be taken in the play area without the permission of the organizers and the consent of *everyone* recorded (this includes people in the background for both pictures and sound). Posed shots for photography or video require a written release from everyone shown in the picture.

14. Offering or agreeing to an act of prostitution is prohibited.

15. NO SMOKING in the play area.

APPENDIX C

SM QUESTIONNAIRES

The following questionnaires are designed as a way to communicate your preferred SM play to both yourself and your partner(s).

The first questionnaire can help you determine where you stand with respect to SM. There are no right or wrong answers. Put down a rating for each item as honestly as you can. Then review the whole sheet. The resultant sheet may surprise you. Don't worry about that. The whole is usually somewhat different from the sum of the parts. It may lead you to explore things you've yet to try or even admit to.

Exchanging such a questionnaire can be an amusing way to perform a scene negotiation, because it should provoke some very "stimulating" conversation.

Answer the questions by writing a number from 0 to 10 in the appropriate column. As a guide, you could use the following system for choosing numbers:

0   Not under any circumstances
1   Total turn-off, likely to spoil the scene
2   Not a turn on, but I can live with it
:
5   Neutral
:
8   Turn-on, but not essential
9   Really wild turn-on
10 Essential

We've taken the liberty of filling out the section on unsafe practices. It's one thing to fantasize about them, but entirely another to practise them. After you've read this book, we hope that you'll only indulge in safer sexual practices.

	Fantasy		Experience	
	Top	Bottom	Top	Bottom
Aromas	——	——	——	——
Ball Stretching	——	——	——	——
Belts	——	——	——	——
Big Men/Women	——	——	——	——
Bikes/Bikers	——	——	——	——
Blindfolds	——	——	——	——
Bondage	——	——	——	——
Bondage (Painful)	——	——	——	——
Boot Cleaning	——	——	——	——
Bootlicking	——	——	——	——
Boots	——	——	——	——
Branding	——	——	——	——
Breath Control	——	——	——	——
Buttplug	——	——	——	——
Cage	——	——	——	——
Cane	——	——	——	——
Castration Scenes	——	——	——	——
Cat O' Nine Tails	——	——	——	——
Catheter	——	——	——	——
Chains	——	——	——	——
Cock & Ball Play	——	——	——	——
Cockrings/Cockstraps	——	——	——	——
Cold Room	——	——	——	——
Cowboys/Cowgirls	——	——	——	——
Cuffs (Leather)	——	——	——	——
Cunt Licking	——	——	——	——
Denim	——	——	——	——
Dildos	——	——	——	——
Dog Training	——	——	——	——

Domestic Chores	—	—	—	—
Electricity	—	—	—	—
Enemas	—	—	—	—
Exhibitionism	—	—	—	—
Fellatio (cock sucking)	—	—	—	—
Fucking (Fist)	—	—	—	—
Fucking (Rectum)	—	—	—	—
Fucking (Vagina)	—	—	—	—
Gag	—	—	—	—
Gasmasks	—	—	—	—
Hair (Body)	—	—	—	—
Hair (Crew Cut)	—	—	—	—
Hair (Facial)	—	—	—	—
Hair (Long)	—	—	—	—
Handcuffs	—	—	—	—
Harness (Leather)	—	—	—	—
Harness (Rope)	—	—	—	—
Harness (Suspension)	—	—	—	—
Heavy Men/Women	—	—	—	—
Hood	—	—	—	—
Immobilisation	—	—	—	—
Lace/Lingerie	—	—	—	—
Leather	—	—	—	—
Leg Irons	—	—	—	—
Marines	—	—	—	—
Marks (Permanent)	—	—	—	—
Marks (Temporary)	—	—	—	—
Massage (Rough)	—	—	—	—
Medical Scenes	—	—	—	—
Mud	—	—	—	—
Mummification	—	—	—	—

Muscle	—	—	—	—
Neck Bindings	—	—	—	—
Oil/Grease	—	—	—	—
Outdoors	—	—	—	—
Pain (Heavy)	—	—	—	—
Pain (Light)	—	—	—	—
Physical Exercise	—	—	—	—
Piercing (Permanent)	—	—	—	—
Piercing (Temporary)	—	—	—	—
Piss	—	—	—	—
Police	—	—	—	—
Public Bondage	—	—	—	—
Restricted Breathing	—	—	—	—
Rope Bondage	—	—	—	—
Rubber	—	—	—	—
Sex Without SM	—	—	—	—
Shaving (Body)	—	—	—	—
Shaving (Genitals)	—	—	—	—
Shit	—	—	—	—
Short Men/Women	—	—	—	—
Shorts	—	—	—	—
Sling	—	—	—	—
Small Men/Women	—	—	—	—
Sound Control	—	—	—	—
Spreadeagle	—	—	—	—
Sucking Cock	—	—	—	—
Suspension	—	—	—	—
Tall Men/Women	—	—	—	—
Tawse	—	—	—	—
Tit Torture	—	—	—	—
Training With a Second Top or Bottom	—	—	—	—

Uniforms	—	—	—	—
Unsafe Sex	—	—	0	0
Urethral Sounds	—	—	—	—
Uncircumcised Men	—	—	—	—
Verbal Abuse	—	—	—	—
Videos	—	—	—	—
Wax (Depilatory)	—	—	—	—
Wax (Hot)	—	—	—	—
Whips	—	—	—	—
Wrestling	—	—	—	—
Other (Specify)	—	—	—	—
Other	—	—	—	—
Other	—	—	—	—
Other	—	—	—	—

I use the following (rate third column as in the previous part):

	Quantity	Frequency	How essential to my play
Alcohol	—	—	—
Cocaine	—	—	—
Marijuana	—	—	—
MDA	—	—	—
Poppers	—	—	—
Speed	—	—	—
Tobacco	—	—	—
Other _____	—	—	—

In combination with the previous questionnaire, the following one could be used by both Top and Bottom to determine where the Bottom stands with respect to any scenes you both (all) may play out. The Top should give a blank form to the Bottom to fill out, the Bottom should give the Top a completed form. Some of the information gathered here is important from a point of view of safety, while some is for use by the Top to make the scene interesting, since it will give the Top some idea of the Bottom's history and desires. The answers to the questions should be accurate, otherwise there's no point in filling it out.

You could add any questions you want that may be relevant to the way that you like to play. The questionnaire is a compilation of our thoughts and several other questionnaires we have encountered over the years.

Questionnaire For A Bottom

Note that all information may be checked by your Top for accuracy.

Name (Full name preferred) _____

Who sent you to me? _____

Telephone number: _____

Date of birth: _____

Height: _____

Weight: _____

Waist: _____ Leg: _____ Style: _____

Cock size: _____ ❏ Cut ❏ Uncut

Bust: _____

State any medical conditions or medications of which your Top should be aware (e.g. contact lenses, antibiotics, diabetes, false/capped teeth, toupée, joint problems, asthma, anæmia, etc.):

_____

What is your safeword? _____

State maximum time you have worn the following:

Dildo: _____ Size: _____

Cockring: _____ Size: _____

Buttplug: _____ Size: _____

Handcuffs: _____

Hood: _____

Gag: _____

Do you masturbate? _____ If so, how? _____

List and sex toys you own and put an asterisk by any that you have worn in public:_____

_____

State any practice(s) that turn(s) you off completely:

_____

SM Play

Are we having fun, yet? _____

State your three greatest turn-ons:

1. _____
2. _____
3. _____

List and describe and tattoos, piercings, brandings, or other permanent features of your body: _____

_____

Where do you shave regularly? _____

_____

Overnight clothing when sleeping alone: _____

What is your favourite nursery rhyme? _____

Pick the one of each of the following three pairs of words that best describes *you*:

Dominant ❑	❑ Submissive
Aggressive ❑	❑ Passive
Sadist ❑	❑ Masochist

Describe your exercise program and rate your general fitness: _____

_____

On a separate piece of paper, describe your best SM experience to date.

On another piece of paper, describe your favourite SM fantasy.

As in the additions to the first questionnaire above, a Bottom may want to give a variant of the following list of questions to a Top to fill out. A Top may want to give a completed set of responses to a potential Bottom. This questionnaire could be given by a Slave to a Master/Mistress, or some parts of it could be removed to make it a general questionnaire from someone into less strictly defined rôles during play. The questionnaire is largely based on one we have seen from SM Gays in London.

Questions From a Respectful Bottom to a Top

1. Sir/Madam, do you have any medical conditions or take any medications of which I should be aware?

2. Sir/Madam, what is your safeword?

3. Sir/Madam, what facilities do you have for playing?

4. Sir/Madam, is there a playroom?

5. Sir/Madam, will my rôle as Bottom begin as soon as I/you arrive?

4. Sir/Madam, what will you wear while you play with me?

5. Sir/Madam, what will you require me to wear while you play with me?

6. Sir/Madam, will you require me to wear anything in particular when we meet? I have

   ❏ _____   ❏ _____
   ❏ _____   ❏ _____
   ❏ _____   ❏ _____

   or I can be naked, Sir/Madam.

7. Sir/Madam, if allowed, how shall I eat, piss, and/or shit?

8. Sir/Madam, if allowed, under what circumstances shall I be allowed to sleep?

   ❏ Alone   ❏ With you, Sir/Madam
   ❏ In Bondage   ❏ Free

9. Sir/Madam, if I disobey orders or otherwise displease you, how will you punish me? _____

10. Sir/Madam, if I wish to please you especially, is there anything in particular that turns you on? _____

11. Sir/Madam, is there anything in particular that turns you off?
   _____

12. Sir/Madam, will you be taking any photographs or home video, or otherwise recording our play?

   ❏ Yes   ❏ No.

   If so, I would like a copy, Sir/Madam.

   Or:

   Sir/Madam, I respectfully request that no photographs or video be taken of our play.

13. Sir/Madam, do you approve of or use any of the following:
    ❏   Alcohol
    ❏   Poppers
    ❏   Any other mind-altering substance (please specify, Sir/Madam): _____

14. Sir/Madam, please indicate (0 = Not at all, 1 = Potentially a little, 10 = Very Much) whether the following might form part of your play with me:

    ____   _____

    ____   _____

    ____   _____

APPENDIX D

THE $35 TOYBAG

Groceries, hardware stores, tack shops, and chandleries are great places to find "pervertibles." As soon as you start to look at everyday objects in a different light, you'll be surprised what can be done with them. We decided that it would be a good idea to look for some familiar objects both to stir your imagination, and to ensure that you could put together a toybag for use when travelling that should be light and that all the toys should be easy to replace should you lose one or all of them.

This is by no means an exhaustive list of items that might be found in a basic toybag. What is in yours will very much depend on your tastes and ideas. If you're going to play in a hotel room, you might call the housekeeper and ask for some old sheets that were going to be thrown out: these could be cut into strips and used as bondage, blindfolds, etc.. And they're free! Hotel clothes hangers with clamps for pants (often rubberized) serve well as tit clamps. The hook can be used to hang weights on, or to pull upwards with your teeth if you're on your own.... So, on to *our* list.

Clothes pins: lots of places to put them. You might only put on just a few of them, or put on many in groups of five or ten. A string might be passed through a group of them so that the whole length could be pulled off at once. They can be used on just about any part of the body.

A drop sheet to cover play area (hotel bed, hosts' carpet, etc.) is very versatile. They are generally made of thin plastic and can be readily cleaned. Also you can wrap someone in a drop sheet as a form of bondage (make sure they can breathe, though).

Textured, rubberized gloves for handling glass produce an interesting sensation on the skin and it will be difficult for the Bottom to determine what is being used.

Thick black rubber gloves, the ones used for plumbing the depths of the bathroom plumbing can be used with lubricant to produce a very effective massage (Use only water-based lubricant on these, and don't leave them out in the sun). They can also be used dry with a light touch so that the rubber "catches" on the skin as it is gently stroked across the skin.

Bamboo skewers have a sharp point. They can be applied as drum sticks to a drum; in the same manner, but with the edge of the skewer rather than the tip; the long edge can be passed both along its length and sideways across the skin; and the tips can be pointed (gently) straight down onto the skin for a sharp feeling. The tip can also be moved gently over the surface of the skin. This latter can, on sensitized skin, feel like electricity. If you do accidentally break the skin, they're disposable.

Elastic bands on clothes pins can help to increase or decrease pressure. If not put on too tightly, they can be used as cock rings, and even as tit toys (if you're prepared to fiddle about a bit). Flicking them onto the skin can be fun, too.

Clothes brush is great for sensitizing the skin, as are many other kinds of brushes that you almost certainly have lying about the house. They all produce a slightly different sensation. Feather or sheepskin dusters have a totally different feel and can be used to produce a gentle current of air across previously sensitized skin.

Bandannas are great for blindfolds, gags, or to wrap around a cock. They can also be used to tie wrists or ankles together.

Cheap paraffin candles are the perfect thing if you like hot wax scenes. The cheaper the candle, the lower the burning temperature and, therefore, the safer it is.

Stir sticks for paint can usually be had free from your hardware store, particularly if you buy paint from them. They make excellent paddles. Check for splinters before using.

Mousetraps are an unusual pervertible, but they have many uses other than catching mice. Do *not* let a mousetrap snap onto the skin. The motion of the "blade" can cause great damage. The trap should be used by gently letting the blade onto the desired part of the body. They can be used for the tits, cock, or balls. When applied slowly, they produce surprisingly little pressure. They're more of a mind fuck. *If properly sterilized*, they can be used as a piercing board.

Toothbrushes with a little rubber pick have all manner of uses. The bristle can be used to sensitize the nipples, the cock, etc.. The smooth side can produce quite a surprise to previously sensitized skin, simply because it feels cold just as it touches the skin. The little rubber "gum massager" can also be used in many places about the body.

A tracing wheel for drafting provides a wonderful sensation if rolled up and down the skin, especially when run along the side of the body. Do not scrape the wheel across the skin; this may break the surface. .

Snake bite kits work well to provide suction on the nipples. The larger the cup, the greater the effective tug on the nipples. They can produce quite a bit of pain in some people. They work best if there is no chest hair.

A cheap paintbrush, on its own or in combination with other implements, can be used to sensitize the skin.

Bungee cord can folded in half with the bend wrapped in electrical tape to form a handle. The ends can then have their outer cover removed. to make a great little genital whip.

Mentholated rubs produce sensations from warmth to burning hot. Consequently, you have to be careful with some of them. If you take a little bit of the stronger ones in your palm and "water it down" with some lubricant and then put it on, it will reduce the effective strength. If it gets under an uncut man's foreskin, it will *burn*. A little bit will go a *long* way. You can use Ben-Gay®; Vick's Vapo-Rub® Tiger Balm®, etc. but remember that they all have different strength. If you have done, say, a full mummification in duct tape, with the cock and balls or tits exposed, you might want to try some of the rubs on the exposed areas. Mouthwash, particularly the mentholated type, has a wonderful effect if poured liberally over the cock and balls.

Leather thongs can be used to tie things more numerous than we can mention here. Shoes, cocks, and wrists should give you an idea of the scope.

Good cotton rope is starting to get expensive. Sash cord is one of the few ways to get 100% cotton rope these days, but it is awkward because it needs to be put into the washer several times before use to soften it up. Boiling it a few times also helps to soften it up. 100 feet will do a lot. To learn how to use rope well, try going to a macramé class. You can make restraints with rope that are *very* effective.

An important one-time cost (not part of the toybag cost) is a *good* pair of ambulance scissors. These are an absolute necessity if you use rope or cloth bondage of any sort.

So, what does all the above cost? We went out for an hour to our local hardware store and a few other places, and came back with the following:

Hotel clothes hanger	0.00
Clothes pins	1.89
Drop sheet	1.89
Textured, rubberized gloves	1.79

Thick black rubber gloves	3.29
Bamboo skewers	1.89
Elastic bands	0.89
Clothes brush	3.50
Bandanna	0.99
Cheap paraffin candles	0.14
Stir stick for paint	0.00
Mousetraps (20)	1.00
Toothbrush	1.50
Tracing wheel	2.50
Snake bite kits	1.50
Cheap paintbrush.	1.50
Bungee cord	0.89
Mentholated rub	2.69
Leather thongs (2)	3.00
Cotton rope	3.99
	$34.84

Ambulance scissors are approximately $35.

Here are a few more pervertibles commonly found around the house: plastic cooking wrap, duct tape, insulating tape, rope, ice cubes, wide leather belts, nail files, enema bags, feathers, dusters, fur, hair dryers, paddles (ping-pong and canoe), rulers, scarves, fruit, vegetables, laces, tweezers, cooking oil, wooden spatulas and spoons, etc., etc..

As you can see, it really doesn't take much to set yourself on the way to a great time.

APPENDIX E

HANKY COLOUR CODES

We have tried to garner as many sources as possible for the following codes. Although we have heard of differences between the colours and their associated meaning from country to country, we have not yet found any differences. Generally speaking, anything worn on the left means the wearer is a Top for the activity, on the right means Bottom. There is nothing to stop you from wearing any combination of colours and sides, if you're into many activities. (Novices to the SM scene should note that there is no rule that requires you to use the hanky codes. Using them, however, can sometimes make meeting someone with similar interests that bit easier. The last four items should be taken in the fun with which they were intended.) While use of the codes seems to be more prevalent in the homosexual community, we have seen evidence of it in the heterosexual community, also.

There is one code that has been omitted from the main list. It is the zip-lock bag (left has drugs, right looking for drugs). Given that drugs can easily impair your ability to assess risk, we'd recommend that you stay clear of anyone sporting a zip-lock bag, whichever side it's worn.

The list has been printed so that you can photocopy it for reference while in that dark, steamy bar.... While this may not be the complete list, we still think that you'll need a good source of light and either a complete set of paint chips or a Pantone® colour chart to make any sense of the subtleties when you're in a crowded bar....

Worn On Left		Worn On Right
Heavy SM Top	Black	Heavy SM Bottom
Leather Fetish Top	Leather	Leather Fetish Bottom
Bondage Top	Grey	Bondage Bottom
Latex Fetish Top	Charcoal	Latex Fetish Bottom
Fucker	Navy/Dark Blue	Fuckee
Cop	Medium Blue	Cop-sucker
69er	Robin's Egg Blue	69ee
Wants Head	Light Blue	Expert Cocksucker
Cock & Ball Torturer	Teal Blue	Cock & Ball Torturee
Hustler	Kelly Green	John
Military Top	Olive Drab/Khaki	Military Bottom
Daddy	Hunter Green	Hunting for Daddy
Dines Off Trick (Sex w/Food)	Lime Green	Dinner Plate
Catheter Top	Lemon	Catheter Bottom
Cums in Scum Bags	Cream	Sucks It Out
Spits	Pale Yellow	Drool Crazy
Watersports, Tearoom Top	Doily, or Yellow	Piss Freak
Rimmer	Beige	Rimmee
Two Looking for One	Gold	One Looking for Two
Has 8" or More	Mustard	Wants a Big One
Two Tons O' Fun	Apricot	Chubby Chaser
Suck My Toes	Coral	Shrimper
Anything, Anytime	Orange	Not Tonight, Josephine
Cowboy	Rust	His Horse
Spanker	Fuschia	Spankee
Fist fucker	Red	Fist Fuckee
Dildo Fucker	Light Pink	Dildo Fuckee
Tit Torturer	Dark Pink	Tit Torturer
2-Handed Fister	Dark Red	2-Handed Fistee
Razor Top	Burgundy	Razor Bottom
Likes Menstruating Women	Maroon, or Red Polka Dots	Menstruating Woman
Into Navel Worshippers	Mauve	Has Navel Fetish
"Suck My Pits"	Magenta	Armpit Freak
Piercer	Purple	Piercee
Likes Drags	Lavender	Drag
Scat Top	Brown	Scat Bottom
Has Uncut Cock	Brown Lace	Likes Uncut Men

Circumcised	Brown Satin	Likes Circumcised Men
Actually Owns a Suit	Grey Flannel	Likes Men in Suits
Beat My Meat	White	I'll Do Us Both
Shaver	Red/White Stripe	Shavee
Likes Black Bottoms	Black/White Stripe	Likes Black Tops
Likes Latino Bottoms	Brown/White Stripe	Likes Latino Tops
Likes Oriental Bottoms	Yellow/White Stripe	Likes Oriental Tops
Likes White Bottoms	White Lace	Likes White Tops
Wears Boxer Shorts	Paisley	Likes Boxer Shorts
Bestialist, Top	Fur	Bestialist, Bottom
Starfucker	Silver Lamé	Star
Likes Bottom Musclemen	Gold Lamé	Likes Top Musclemen
Has Tattoos	Leopard	Likes Tattoos
Smokes Cigars	Tan	Likes Cigars
Cuddler	Teddy Bear	Cuddlee
Chicken	Kewpie Doll	Chicken Hawk
Wears Dirty Jock	Dirty Jockstrap	Sucks 'em Clean
Stinks (Raunch Top)	Kleenex	Sniffs (Raunch Bottom)
Gives Hot Motor Oil Massage	Handywipe	Wears It Well
Rides Motorcycle	Chamois	Likes Bikers
Bartender	Cocktail Napkin	Bar Groupie
Top for Outdoor Sex	Mosquito Netting	Outdoor Bottom
Negotiable	Keys	Definitely Bottom
Japanese Bondage Top	Rope	Japanese Bondage Bottom
Shocker	Electric Plug	Shockee
Abrasion Top	Wire Brush	Abrasion Bottom
Your Place or Mine?	Toothbrush	Your Place Only
Foot Fucker	Red Sock	Foot Fuckee
Voyeur	Sheer	Exhibitionist
Wrestling, No Rules	Sweat Band	Wrestling, Rules
Offering Dinner	Plastic Fork	Seeks Dinner
Offering Brunch	Celery	Out To Brunch
	Hanky Around Head	Disco Injury
	Hanky Around Neck	Goes Divinely With My Outfit

APPENDIX F

CONTACT AD TERMS AND ABBREVIATIONS

A

AC/DC – Bisexual

Accident Prone – Usually refers to a preference for piss or shit "accidents," normally while wearing underpants.

ALA – All Letters Answered

ALWPA, ALAWP – All Letters, With Photo, Answered; All Letters Answered With Photo

Aromas – Poppers (nitrites)

AT – Animal training

Auto – Does to him/herself; sex involving cars

B

B – Alone, means bondage; in combination can mean balls.

B/D, B&D – Bondage and Discipline

Baldies – Bald men or women

BB – Body Builder; Body Building

Bi, Bi-Guy, Bi-Gal – Bisexual

Black – As a colour code: heavy SM or whipping; also used to indicate race

Blowjob, BJ – Cocksucking (fellatio)

BM – Black male

Bottom – Masochist, subservient, slave, etc.

BT – Ball torture

C

C/B/T, CBT – Cock and ball torture or other games

CC – Chubby chaser

Cheese – Smegma (sweaty substance under the foreskin)

Compliant – Bottom, slave, masochist, subservient

CP – Corporal punishment, beating, caning, flogging

Crisco – U.S. cooking fat, used as a lubricant (not to be used with latex items; also good for cooking quiche)

CT – Cock torture

Cut – Circumcised

D

DIY – Masturbation; making one's own equipment

DMs – Doc Marten boots

DOM, Dom – Dominant, Top, Master, sadist, etc.

F

Fats – Overweight

Fees – Expects payment, or is willing to pay for play

Fem – Effeminate man

FF – Fist fucking

Filthy – Mud, shit, piss, spit

501s – Jeans (after Levi jeans, model 501)

FR or French – Oral sex

G

G/S, GS, Golden Showers – Piss scenes

GBF, GBM – Gay Black Female or Male

Generous – Will pay for play

GOF, GOM – Gay Oriental Female or Male

GR, Greek – Anal sex

GWF, GWM – Gay White Female or Male

H

Hazing – U.S. college fraternity initiation ritual

Head – Cocksucking (fellatio), as in: "gives head" or "likes head"

Health conscious – Wants safer sex

Hirsute – Hairy

HIV+ – Has tested positive for HIV

HIV- – Has tested negative for HIV (note that this is *never* a guarantee that the person has not contracted the virus since the test)

Hum – Humiliation

Hung – Large penis (and possibly balls)

I

Infantilism – Likes dressing up as a baby; wears diapers/nappies

J

JO, J/O – Jerking/Jacking off, masturbation

Jocks, JS – Jock straps. Jocks alone can also refer to college football types, normally in uniform

K

KO – Knockout (in context of play usually means boxing)

KS – Kaposi's sarcoma (a skin cancer often associated with people living with AIDS)

L

LDU – Leather, denim, uniform

Lonsdale – Fighter/boxing gear

Lycra – (Pedal) cycling gear

M

M – Masochist (not used much nowadays due to the potential for confusion with M for Master)

Meat – Generally refers to penis, although it can refer to a muscular body (as in: Full Meat Dinner)

N

Negative – Has tested nega-tive for HIV (note that this is *never* a guarantee that the person has not contracted the virus since the test)

No Fees – Will not pay or charge for play

O

O – Oral sex

121, 1-2-1 – One-on-one, monogamous

ONO – Or Nearest Offer

P

PE – Physical education or exercise (also PT)

PH – Photography

PLWA – Person living with AIDS

Positive – Has tested positive for the Human Immuno-deficiency Virus

PT – Physical training

PWA – Person living with AIDS

S

S – Sadist (not used much nowadays due to the potential confusion with S for Slave)

SAE – Self-addressed envelope

Safe – Practices safer sex

SASE – Self-addressed stamped envelope

SBF, SBM – Straight Black Female or Male

Scat – Play involving fæces

Shaven – Generally means all over the body

69 – Mutual cock sucking

Skin – Skinhead, shaven headed

SM, S/M, S&M – Sado-masochism

Smokes – Marijuana; also often refers to cigar or cigarette smoking

Smooth – Naturally hairless body

SOF, SOM – Straight Oriental Female or Male

Speedos – Swimming gear

Strongminded – Top, Master, Sadist, dominant

SWF, SWM – Straight White Female or Male

T

T/W – Tit work

ToF – Tom of Finland

Toilet – Person who likes to be pissed or shat upon

Top – Master, sadist, dominant

Toys – Sexual equipment, e.g. dildos

TS – Transsexual

TT – Tit torture

TV – Transvestite

U

U/C, UC – Uncircumcised, Uncut

U/D – Undressed (usually associated with photos to be sent with reply)

W

W/E – Well endowed; large penis

W/H – Well hung; large penis

W/S – Watersports (play involving urine)

Watersports – Play involving urine (see also G/S)

Wax – Use of hot candle wax to stimulate skin; use of cold wax to remove hair

Weenie – Has or seeks small penis

WF, WM – White female or white male

BIBLIOGRAPHY

American Psychiatric Association, *Diagnostic and Statistical Manual of Mental Disorders (Third Edition, Revised).* © 1987 The American Psychiatric Association. Published by The American Psychiatric Association, 1400 K Street, North West, Washington, DC, 20005. ISBN 0-89042-018-1. LCCIP RC455.2.C4D54. 1987 616.89′075 87-1458.

Baldwin, Guy, M.S., *Ties That Bind.* © 1993 Guy Baldwin. Published by Dædalus Publishing Company, Suite 375, 4470-107 Sunset Boulevard, Los Angeles, California, 90027. ISBN 1-881943-09-7.

Bannon, Race, *Learning The Ropes.* © 1992 Race Bannon. Published by Dædalus Publishing Company, Suite 375, 4470-107 Sunset Boulevard, Los Angeles, California, 90027. ISBN 1-881943-07-0.

Bannon, Race, *The S/M Resources Guide.* © Race Bannon. Published by Dædalus Publishing Company, Suite 375, 4470-107 Sunset Boulevard, Los Angeles, California, 90027.

Bean, Joseph W., *Leathersex: A Guide for the Curious Outsider and the Serious Player.* © 1993 Joseph W. Bean. To be published in 1993 by Haworth Press/Harrington Park.

Berkow, Robert, M.D. (Editor-in-Chief), *The Merck Manual, Sixteenth Edition.* © 1992 Merck & Company, Inc.. Published by Merck Sharp & Dohme Research Laboratories, a Division of Merck & Company, Inc., Rahway, New Jersey. ISBN 0911910-16-6. ISSN 0076-6526. LCCCN 1-31760.

Califia, Pat, *Macho Sluts.* © 1988 Pat Califia. Published by Alyson Publications, Boston, Massachusetts.

Califia, Pat, (Editor), *The Lesbian S/M Safety Manual.* © 1988 Pat Califia. Published by Lace Publications, an imprint of Alyson Publications, Boston, Massachusetts. ISBN 1-55583-301-2.

Canadian Diabetes Association, *Diabetes First Aid Awareness for Emergency Personnel.* Publication number 03221059137, 1986, Canadian Diabetes Association, 78 Bond Street, Toronto, Ontario. M5B 2J8.

Cohen, Conant, Pappas, Judson, Graves, Rosenberg, Potts, Harvey, Liskin, & Solomon, *Condoms for Prevention of Sexually Transmitted Diseases.* From *MMWR,* 11th. March, 1988, Volume 37, Number 9, pp. 133-137.

Cyr, Gantz, Lytle, Kotilainen, & Truscott, *Ability of the 1000mL Water Leak Test for Surgical Gloves to Detect Potential for Virus Penetration.* 1990.

Friedman, Rodney M., Editor, University of California at Berkeley *Wellness Letter.* © 1992 December 1992 Health Letter Associates, P.O. Box 412, Prince Street Station, New York, New York, 10012-0007.

Green, Frances (Editor), *Gayellow Pages,* © 1992 Renaissance House. Published by Renaissance House, Box 292, Village Station, New York, New York 10014. ISSN 0363-826X.

Mains, Geoff, *Urban Aboriginal, A Celebration of Leathersexuality.* © 1984 Geoffrey Mains. Published by Gay Sunshine Press, P.O. Box 40379, San Francisco, California 94140. ISBN 0-917342-38-0.

Master Jackson, *Sir! More Sir! The Joy of S&M.* © 1992 Leyland Publications. Published by Leyland Publications, P.O. Box 410690, San Francisco, California 94141. ISBN 0-943595-39-8.

Miesen, Don, *A View of Sadomasochism,* Drummer, 1985.

SAMOIS, Members of (Editors), *Coming To Power.* © 1981, 1982, 1987 SAMOIS. 3rd. edition published by Alyson Publications, Boston, Massachusetts. ISBN 0-932870-28-7.

Stein, David, *Black Cross: A Handbook of Health and Safety Precautions and First Aid for S/M.* A work in progress, © David Stein.

Szarewski, Anne & Guillebaud, John, Contraception (a regular review), *The British Medical Journal*, Volume 302, 25 May, 1991. © 1991 The British Medical Journal. Published by the British Medical Association, Tavistock Square, London, WC1H 9JR. ISSN 0959-8146.

Talmead, *The Editor's Niche*, DungeonMaster 23.

Thompson, Mark (Editor), *Leatherfolk*. © 1991 Mark Thompson. Published by Alyson Publications, Boston, Massachusetts. ISBN 1-55583-186-9.

Townsend, Larry, *The Leatherman's Handbook II*. © 1983, 1989 Larry Townsend. Published by Carlysle Communications, Ltd., 462 Broadway, New York, New York 10013. ISBN 0-503-09999-6.

Weinberg, Thomas & Kamel, G. W. Levi (Editors), *S and M, Studies in Sadomasochism*. © 1983 Thomas S. Weinberg & G. W. Levi Kamel. Published by Prometheus Books, 700 East Amherst Street, Buffalo, New York 14215. ISBN 0-87975-230-0. LCCCN 83-610030.

Wiseman, Jay, *SM 101, A Realistic Introduction*. © 1992 Jay J. Wiseman. Published by Jay Wiseman, P.O. Box 1261, Berkeley, California 94701.

Vesalius, Andreas (1514-1564), Brussels. *De Humani Corporis Fabrica (1543)* and *Epitome (1543)*. © 1950 The World Publishing Company. Republished by Dover Publications, Inc., New York, 1973. ISBN 0-486-20968-7. LCCCN 72-94756.

Periodicals:

Bad Attitude. Published by Fantasia Publications, P.O. Box 390110, Cambridge, Massachusetts 02139.

Bear. Published by Brush Creek Media Inc., #148, 2215-R Market Street, San Francisco, California 94114.

Body Play and Modern Primitives Quarterly. Published by Insight Books, P.O. Box 2575, Menlo Park, California 94026-2575.

Bound & Gagged. Published by Bob Wingate, The Outbound Press Incorporated, Suite 803, 89 5th. Avenue, New York, New York 10003.

Checkmate. Published by Telecentral Electronics, P.O. Box 354, Wyoming, Pennsylvania 18644-0354.

Daddy. Published by The Ganymede Press, Inc., 1735 Maryland Avenue, Baltimore, Maryland 21201.

Drummer. Published by Desmodus Inc., 24 Shotwell Street, San Francisco, California 94103.

DungeonMaster. Published by Desmodus Inc., 24 Shotwell Street, San Francisco, California 94103.

The Leather Journal. Published by Cedar Publishing Corporation, P.O. Box 109-368, 7985 Santa Monica Boulevard, West Hollywood, California 90046.

Mach. Published by Desmodus Inc., 24 Shotwell Street, San Francisco, California 94103.

Manifest Reader. Published by Alternate Publishing Co., Box 1069, Forestville, California 95446.

On Our Backs. Published by Blush Entertainment, 526 Castro Street, San Francisco, California 94114.

Piercing Fans International Quarterly (PFIQ). Published by Gauntlet II, Santa Monica Boulevard, West Hollywood, California.

Powerplay. Published by Brush Creek Media Inc., #148, 2215-R Market Street, San Francisco, California 94114.

The Sandmutopia Guardian. Published by Desmodus, Inc., 24 Shotwell Street, San Francisco, California 94103.

Skin II. Published by Tim Woodward Publishing Ltd., BCM Box 2071, London WC1N 3XX.

A Taste of Latex. Published by Lily Burana, P.O. Box 460122, San Francisco, California 94146.

Further reading about whipping:

The Quartermaster, *Fundamentals of Flagellation*. An article in *Sandmutopia Guardian*, issue number 5.

Jim the Whip Maker & Carlson, Dick, *Bulls, Snakes, & Other Scary Critters*. An article in *DungeonMaster*, issue number 33.

For further reading about how to tie rope, see any good book on macramé or something like a sailing book. We have also found the following to be useful.

Scouts Canada, *Fun with Knots*, © 1991. Published by Scouts Canada, 1345 Baseline Road, P.O. Box 5151, Station F, Ottawa K2C 3G7. There is no ISBN for this book.

Cassidy, John, *The Klutz Book of Knots*, © 1985 John Cassidy. Published by Klutz Press, Palo Alto, California. ISBN 0-932592-10-4.

Cassidy, John, *The Scout Book of Knots*. Published by Scouts of America. This is a republication of *The Klutz Book of Knots* (see previous item) under the Scouts' own title. It is no longer sold in this manner, the Scouts now recommend and sell the Klutz book.

Further reading about drugs:

Cohen, Sidney, *Drugs of Hallucination*, © 1964. Fletcher and Son Ltd., Norwich. No ISBN available.

Leary, Metzner, & Alpert, *The Psychedelic Experience*, © 1964. Pitman Press, Bath. ISBN 0 902620.

Malcom, Andrew I., *The Pursuit of Intoxication*, © 1970. Simon and Schuster Inc., New York. Library of Congress number 70-142249.

de Ropp, Robert S., *Drugs and the Mind*. © 1957 H. Wolff, New York. Library of Congress number 57-11779.

Schultes, R. E. & Hoffman, A. , *Plants of the Gods: Their Sacred, Healing, and Hallucinogenic Powers*, © 1992. Published by Healing Arts Press, Vermont. ISBN 0-89281-406-3.

Tart, Charles T., Editor, *Altered States of Consciousness, Third Edition*, © 1990. Published by Harper Collins Publishers, New York, New York. ISBN 0-06-250857-1.

GLOSSARY

Abrasion – A term applied to any form of play that consists mainly of rubbing, stroking, pinching, or gently pricking the skin. Often referred to as an "abrasion scene."

Addiction – A style of living that is characterized by compulsive use and overwhelming involvement with a drug. It may occur without physical dependence. Addiction also implies the risk of harm and the need to stop using the drug, whether or not the addict understands or agrees to this.

Age Play – Play that involves taking on the rôle of someone of a different age from one's own.

Algolagnia – The dictionary definition of this is "the derivation of sexual pleasure from the giving or receipt of pain." Note that his is not necessarily SM, because SM does not necessarily include pain. It is a form of SM in its broadest sense.

Anal Receptive Intercourse – Ass fucking.

Bondage – The catch-all phrase for restraining someone during play. The restraints could range from closing one's eyes to handcuffs to leather suits to rope to metal restraints and anywhere in between.

Bottom – The Bottom is generally the person to whom things are done during play, i.e. the person more likely to be referred to as being controlled in one manner or another. The Bottom may be able to do little but receive the ministrations of the Top.

Brown Shower – Erotic play that involves one person defecating on another. Due to the high risk of disease transmission, this practice is considered unsafe.

Bulletin Boards – Short for Computer Bulletin Boards (BBS). These are electronic means of posting mail, having conversations, advertising, etc. by computer. There are many SM-related boards in North America and Europe. They are often listed in the SM publications.

Butt Plug – A device about the size of an erect penis, designed to be inserted into the anus. Normally, these are designed with a large flange to prevent the plug from entering completely into the rectum. Used for erotic physical stimulation and as a form of mind-play. A butt plug can be left in a suitably prepared rectum for extended periods of time, for instance during a day at the office.

Caning – Using a cane or thin rod as the main stimulus during a scene. Often during a corporal punishment scene.

Cat – A whip with many braided tails. Short for cat-o-nine tails.

Club – Club can have two meanings within the context of the SM world: it can be an organization designed for SM players, or a bar/nightclub for them.

Cock & Ball Torture – The erotic use of pain of the male genitalia. Methods include squeezing, pinching, pulling, electricity, mild flagellation, etc..

Coming out into SM – The process a person goes through as he/she admits, explores, and accepts his/her SM sexuality.

Consent – One of the three most important aspects of proper SM play. All players fully understand the potential risks of their intended play and have consented to the activities. This consent can be withdrawn or modified by any player at any time.

CPR – Cardio-Pulmonary Resuscitation. This is the method used by paramedics and ambulance staff to try to save the life of a person whose heart has stopped beating and/or who has stopped breathing. We strongly urge you to learn these techniques. They are simple, and you could save a life. Check for courses by the Saint John Ambulance brigade, Heart Association, or your local hospital.

Cross Dressing – As opposed to transvesticism (the use of clothes to be like to opposite sex), cross dressing is when someone gets pleasure from wearing the clothes only, not from wanting to be like the opposite sex.

Cutting – A term used to describe a form a play in which one person cuts the skin of the other. It appears to be somewhat more common among women.

Dependence – It is not possible to have a single definition for drug dependence, rather a dependence of a specific type will emphasize that different drugs have different effects: 1) Psychologic dependence (addiction) involves feelings of satisfaction and desire to repeat the administration of the drug to produce pleasure or to avoid discomfort; 2) Physical dependence is the state of adaptation of the body to a drug, accompanied by development of tolerance, and it is manifested by a withdrawal or abstinence syndrome.

Depilatory – The removal of hair from the body. Usually used in reference to cold wax removal of hair.

Discipline – Play involving one person training the other to obey and act in a manner that the first player wants. Also refers to the punishment given by the Top for a transgression by the Bottom.

Dominant – A person who takes the rôle of dominating another during play. It is one of many rôles one can take during a scene. The term may be somewhat more prevalent in the heterosexual community. A professional dominant will charge money for performing the rôle; reputable ones will not have sex with their clients, although they may do anything but that.

Dominatrix – A female dominant.

Drug Abuse – This is definable only in terms of societal disapproval and involves different types of behaviour: 1) experimental and recreational use of drugs; 2) unwarranted use of psychoactive drugs to relieve problems or symptoms; and 3) use of drugs at first for the above reasons, but development of dependence and continuation of the drug at least partially to prevent the discomfort of withdrawal.

Fantasy – Any imagined SM event that brings pleasure to the person who thought of it.

Fetishism – The use of objects as one of the preferred methods of producing sexual excitement.

Fisting – Inserting a hand carefully into the anus or the vagina.

Flagellation – The use of a device to strike another person, often with whips, paddles, canes, rods, etc..

Flogger – This is a fairly recent term for a hitting implement that has a short handle and many, flat tails. It is usually made of leather. The effect of a flogger is due to the weight of the many strands as they land, and the texture of the material used to make it.

Gender Play – Play in which one or more of the players takes on a rôle normally associated with the opposite sex.

Golden Shower – Play where one person urinates on another.

Humiliation – Play where one partner makes the other feel shame and/or embarrassment, such as making the other urinate in his/her pants in public.

Hurt – The sensation when any stimulus is very strong and the person being stimulated would rather not be experiencing it. Hurt does *not* necessarily involve injury (See also Injury.)

In Rôle – The assumption of a rôle during play, often while in public, such as in a bar. While in rôle, a Top or Bottom may temporarily appear modify responses to other people.

Injury – When more than slight damage (such as cuts and bruises) is done by any action or stimulus to the body. (See also Hurt.)

Key Word – Another word for *safeword*. Not as common as the latter.

Masochism – The act of enjoying, sexually or otherwise, being humiliated, beaten, bound, or otherwise made to suffer.

Master – A male dominant.

Mind Fuck – Playing a trick on someone within the context of SM play. (Maybe having someone believe one thing and then making another happen or putting a person in an embarrassing situation as part of a scene.)

Mistress – A female dominant.

Negotiation – The discussion and agreement, before a scene, about what the players would like to do and the limits of what they permit during the scene. Negotiation should also include discussion of any relevant medical or other physical condition that may affect play.

New Guard – The "new breed" of SM player, armed with knowledge of safe, sane, and consensual play. Far more likely to switch from Top to Bottom (and back) than players would have been two decades ago. Also, more likely to involve spirituality in their SM play.

Nipple Torture – Another term for tit torture.

Novice – Someone learning about SM play.

Old Guard – A term used to describe the way SM players used to define themselves. People would be Tops or Bottoms, but rarely changed or were seen to enjoy both.

Paddling – Play involving striking the other player with a rigid item, such as a paddle or hairbrush, usually on the buttocks.

Pain – The sensation when a stimulus is very strong and the person being stimulated would rather not be experiencing it. Hurt does *not* necessarily involve injury. (See also Injury.)

Panic Snap – A simple device used instead of a hook or eye to attach chain or rope to an anchor point or another chain or rope. It's great advantage is that it can be released without having to pull harder on the attachment. When used for suspension, it means that the suspended person does not have to be lifted further to be released. It can save time and lives. It should be used for all suspension play on each major weight bearing attachment.

Percussion Play – Any form of play involving one player striking the other, either with the hand (or other part of the body) or with an implement such as a paddle or whip. Spanking and flogging are examples of percussion play.

Phone Lines – Services, normally provided for a fee, for placing or responding to voice advertisements using a phone. Also, services to connect two or more people for the purposes of simple conversation or for sexual talk.

Physical Limits – The limitations of a person's body with respect to a scene. Some people have physical conditions (such as not being able to stand in one place for too long) that stop them from enduring the physical strain put upon them during a scene.

Play – Any activity between consenting adults that produces mental, physical, and/or sexual pleasure, as in "I played with her last night."

Playroom – A place where SM activities can be carried out. It will often be outfitted specifically for SM play. Also known as a "dungeon." The term playroom is preferred, since not all SM play requires a dungeon atmosphere as its setting.

Pleasure/Pain – The mix of pleasurable and painful sensations, or the point at which they meet, which produce an effect where one is indistinguishable from the other. Consequently, to have more pleasure, more of what used to be painful is desired.

Predilections – Whatever turns you on.

Privacy – In the situation of group play, the right of those involved in a scene not to be disturbed by others around them. This means not disturbing players with loud noises, talk, or other distractions.

Professional Dominant – A person who provides SM domination for a fee. They will not provide sexual services; the customer will have to masturbate, if required. People who provide sexual services with SM activities are prostitutes who also provide SM services.

Pushy Bottom – A term for a Bottom who deliberately, often humorously, tries to provoke his/her Top into action or further action. A term for an aggressive, dominant masochist.

Raunch – Any play that involves bodily secretions and odours as sexual turn-ons.

Reality – Cold hard fact that determines the extend to which your fantasies can be attempted safely during an SM scene.

Recreational Drug – Any prescription or non-prescription drug that is used for reasons other than its medical purpose.

Rimming – Analingus; licking of the anus.

Sadism – The act of enjoying, sexually or otherwise, causing someone to be humiliated, beaten, bound, or otherwise made to suffer.

Sadomasochism – A term coined be Richard von Krafft-Ebing to described both the activities of sadism and masochism.

Safe – All players have taken the necessary precautions to prevent psychological and physical damage to themselves, including the transmission of disease.

Safe, Sane, and Consensual – The reason for writing this book. If your play does not meet *all* of these criteria, you are not playing properly. This phrase has become the measure by which SM players judge themselves, their play, and other players. (Please see the Introduction for further information.)

Safeword – A word, preferably not the name of your partner, used to stop an SM scene *immediately*. Where a Bottom cannot speak, a motion of a part of the body may be substituted for the safeword. The word *safeword* is an excellent safeword.

Sane – All players are in full possession of their mental faculties and are fully aware of the risks involved in the play they intend.

Scat – Any play that involves fæces. Butyric acid can be used to simulate the smell of fæces, thereby making scat scenes safer.

Scene – A scene is any interaction between two players, be it a fleeting glance across a bar or a full weekend in the playroom.

Session – Another term for *scene*.

Slave – A rôle that may be taken up for a short scene or a prolonged relationship, where the submissive partner submits to one or more others.

SModdler & SMoldster – Humorous terms for *SM toddler* (novice) and *SM oldster* (experienced), respectively.

Spanking – Hitting the buttocks with a hand. When a flat, rigid implement is used, the term *paddling* is more appropriate.

Straight – A term used to describe heterosexual people or those who do not enjoy SM play, c.f. "kinky." It is used to distinguish them from homosexual or bisexual people; it is never used in this book as a pejorative term.

Submissive – A player who takes the rôle of submitting to another person. It is one of the possible rôles for a Bottom.

Suspension – Any activity in which the Bottom is suspended, upright, upside-down, or otherwise.

Switch – A person who enjoys being both the Top and the Bottom (generally at different times). In the last decade or so, switches have become more evident in the SM community.

Tit Torture – Play primarily involving stimulation of the nipples with clamps, toothbrushes, teeth, etc..

Top – A player who takes the more controlling, perhaps dominant, rôle during play.

Torture – The use of erotic pain (without injury) during a scene. Most likely not by whipping.

Toy – Any object used during play. Most often thought of as those that can be bought in a sex store, but spatulas, toothbrushes, rubber gloves, feathers, etc., etc. can also take be used as toys.

Vanilla – A term used to refer to non-SM play or players. It is never used in this book as a pejorative term.

Watersports – Any play that involves urine. Also used to refer to play involving enemas.

Whipping – The use of fairly flexible instruments, such as cat-o-nine tails and floggers, to produce erotic pain during a scene.

Withdrawal Syndrome – An untoward physical change that happens when a drug is discontinued or when its effect is counteracted by something else.

Wrapping – A term that refers to the unintended wrapping of the end of a whip around the body of the Bottom and land on the side or front of the body. Often leaves marks on the Bottom. In bondage play, can refer to using strips of material (bandage, rubber, etc.) to wrap the body of the Bottom, sometimes in the style of an Egyptian mummy.

INDEX

So, you thought SM was just about pain?
Ouch!

SM Play is set in 10-point Palatino, with sideheads in 9-point Palatino Bold. Section and subsection headings are set in 30-, 20-, 15-, and 10-point Helvetica Bold. Figure and table legends are set in 10-point Palatino Bold. Tables are set in 9-point Helvetica and Helvitica Bold; the index is set in 8-point Times. The original draft was produced on an Apple Macintosh PowerBook 100, using Microsoft Word at the editorial office of WholeSM Publishing Corporation, in Toronto, Ontario. The manuscript was typeset at the WholeSM Publishing Corporation office on a PowerBook 100, using Microsoft Word; camera ready copy was printed on an Apple LaserWriter Pro 630. The book was printed on 60-pound Phœnix paper on a Royal Zenith sheet-fed printer at Edwards Brothers Incorporated, Ann Arbor, Michigan, U.S.A..

Notes

Notes

Notes

Notes

Notes